W9-BFL-204

Southern Biography Series
William J. Cooper, Jr., Editor

W. J. Cash

W. J. CASH

A Life

Bruce Clayton

LOUISIANA STATE UNIVERSITY PRESS

Baton Rouge and London

Copyright © 1991 by Louisiana State University Press
All rights reserved
Manufactured in the United States of America
First printing
00 99 98 97 96 95 94 93 92 91   5 4 3 2 1

DESIGNER: PATRICIA DOUGLAS CROWDER
TYPEFACE: LINOTRON 202 GOUDY
TYPESETTER: G&S TYPESETTERS, INC.
PRINTER AND BINDER: THOMSON-SHORE, INC.

LIBRARY OF CONGRESS CATALOGING-IN-PUBLICATION DATA

Clayton, Bruce.
    W. J. Cash, a life / Bruce Clayton.
      p.   cm. — (Southern biography series)
    Includes bibliographical references and index.
    ISBN 0-8071-1647-5
      1. Cash, W. J. (Wilbur Joseph), 1900–1941.   2. Historians—United States—
Biography.   3. Southern States—Historiography.   I. Title.   II. Series.
E175.5.C27C57   1991
975'.007202—dc20
    [B]
                                                            90-43462
                                                            CIP

Letters between W. J. Cash and Alfred A. Knopf are quoted courtesy of the Harry Ransom
Humanities Research Center, the University of Texas at Austin. Excerpts from the Joseph L.
Morrison Papers and the Howard W. Odum Papers are quoted courtesy of the Southern
Historical Collection, Library of the University of North Carolina at Chapel Hill. Excerpts
from The Mind of the South by W. J. Cash, copyright 1941 by Alfred A. Knopf, Inc., and
renewed 1969 by Mary R. Maury are reprinted by permission of Alfred A. Knopf, Inc., and by
permission of Thames and Hudson Ltd.

The frontispiece is reproduced courtesy of the Harry Ransom Humanities Research Center, the
University of Texas at Austin.

The paper in this book meets the guidelines for permanence and durability of the Committee
on Production Guidelines for Book Longevity of the Council on Library Resources. ∞

For Carrah
and for Horace Stoessel and John Salmond

Contents

Illustrations

Acknowledgments

It is a pleasure to acknowledge the help so many people have given me. My mentors at Duke University, Robert F. Durden and Richard L. Watson, Jr., pointed the way years ago and have remained exemplars of friendship and scholarship. I remain indebted to my friends from our Duke days: Michael E. R. Bassett, W. J. Breen, Lawrence Curry, Robert A. Hohner, John Kirkland, Erik N. Olssen, and Anthony Wood. At moments when it counted, they offered more encouragement and helpful criticism than they know. Thanks also to Alfred Kern, Lyle W. Dorsett, Jeffrey J. Crow, Abel Alves, John David Smith, and Barry William Fisher, M.D., who read portions of the manuscript, as did my fellow historians at Allegheny College, Richard W. Turk, Paula Treckel, and Barry Shapiro, all of whom were of considerable help. I am particularly grateful to William J. Cooper, Jr., editor of the Southern Biography Series of Louisiana State University Press, for being buoyantly enthusiastic about this biography from the start, and to Margaret Fisher Dalrymple and John Easterly. Special thanks to my copy editor, Trudie Calvert. My colleagues Demerie Faitler, Jonathan Helmreich, and Stephen Lyons helped me maintain my own enthusiasm by listening patiently and asking good questions. Special thanks to colleagues Frederick S. Frank, friendly fount of knowledge about all things literary, and Nels G. Juleus, rhetorician, creative problem solver, and walking companion.

Each of the following deserves a warmer word of praise than these dry lines convey: Jackie Juleus, Judith Bassett, Carin and Michael Piraino, Beverly Jarrett, Adrienne Moffet, Katherine Meerse, Lyn Trace, Janet and Walt Berkov, Phyllis Stoessel, Sarah Clayton, John Clayton, Jennifer and Alexander Gelman, Elisabeth and Paul Visintainer, Anne Marie Beebe, Kristin Schiffhauer, and, of course, Frances Marie and Daniel Clayton Visintainer.

One of the joys of doing this book was the chance to meet and talk with W. J. Cash's brothers, Allen and Henry Cash, and their wives, and Cash's sister, Elizabeth (Bertie) Cash Elkins, and her husband and their son, Charles H. Elkins, Jr., who graciously allowed me to borrow family scrapbooks and to reproduce photographs, letters, and the original manuscript of *The Mind of the South*. Equally helpful were Lindsay Dail, Burke Davis, Harriet Doar, Reed Sarratt, and many others who generously gave of their time as they talked about W. J. Cash. From start to finish, my load was made lighter by Joe DePriest, columnist for the Shelby (N.C.) *Star*, who gave renewed meaning to southern friendliness.

I want also to express my gratitude to librarians, unsung heroes of scholarship: Alleghenians Dorothy Jeanne Smith and Don Vrabel; the late Mattie Russell of Duke University; John E. White and Richard Shrader of the Southern Historical Collection at the University of North Carolina, and Carolyn Wallace, former director of the Southern Historical Collection; and the reference librarians at the Public Library of Charlotte and Mecklenburg County.

For scholarly encouragement and financial assistance, I wish to acknowledge the support of the National Endowment for the Humanities and Provost Andrew T. Ford and President Daniel F. Sullivan of Allegheny College.

The dedication of this book only partially and feebly expresses the gratitude and affection I feel for my wife, Carrah, who was there during both the gray and sunny days of doing this book, and for John Salmond and Horace Stoessel, dear friends from way back. They read every sentence, sometimes the same ones over and over again, and cast an improving eye on every word. All errors, either of omission or commission, are mine alone.

W. J. CASH

Prologue / Of Men and Monuments

The remains of W. J. Cash lie buried in the Sunset Cemetery in Shelby, North Carolina. Just around the corner stands his parents' unpretentious red brick house, where Wilbur Joseph Cash lived in the 1930s as he struggled to write portions of *The Mind of the South*, a task that consumed his adult life. His grave is marked by a small, flat stone. His family wanted a monument, a symbol in granite of what their boy had accomplished. But the Depression still had its uncaring hand on Shelby and the Carolina piedmont, and the native son was laid to rest beneath a humble marker. In the summer, grass threatens to obscure his gravestone completely, and the ravages of time since his death in 1941 have begun to erase the simple inscription, which reads in part: "A great mind, a sweet nature, a scholar, author, and editor. He loved the South with intensity and was to all a friend. 'God's finger touched him and he slept.'"

No intimations of immortality here. If a visitor to the Sunset Cemetery knew nothing else about Wilbur Joseph Cash, if one had not read his book or learned that it was one of those sticks of dynamite that unsettle the mind and has continued to do so ever since it appeared just a few months before his death, Cash's grave could be easily missed.

Stand at Cash's simple marker and look South. There, across the road in a grove of maple trees rises a substantial monument directing attention to the grave of another native son, Thomas Dixon, Jr. Dixon had brought fame to Shelby and fortune to himself long before his death in 1946. By the turn of the century he had covered himself in glory, first as a lawyer and a minister and then as the author of bestselling novels about the South. They were sentimental works, even by the standards of the day. What is more, they were racist novels, depicting blacks as savages and brutes. But so great was their appeal that Hollywood's D. W. Griffith converted the scurrilously racist novel *The Clansman* into the huge cinematic triumph *The Birth of a Nation*. In time the nation outgrew his literary creations and forgot him, but Shelby and the piedmont honored him until his death. His frequent visits to the piedmont were much commented on by the press; his words, quoted or uttered by the honored guest, rang out from local pulpits. When Dixon died, his friends, distressed at his recent financial misfortunes, dug into their pockets to place six feet of granite above his grave. It is chiseled in stone that the Reverend Thomas Dixon was the "most distinguished son of his generation."

Men and women must have their monuments. In time, it would be clear that Cash had fashioned a lasting memorial in his monumental book, *The Mind of the South*. Unlike Dixon's now forgotten novels, Cash's book has grown in reputation and influence. It is, after all these years, still read and pondered. It continues to provoke and demand attention. Why? Because Cash, in his attempt to portray his people's past realistically and honestly, courageously faced up to the South's troubled history. If the past could be confronted on its own grounds by someone who had a vision of life beyond racism, beyond sentimentality, beyond fear, beyond men and women's worst instincts, then southerners could be brought out of the darkness of prejudice and into the light of a new day beyond history. If so, his countrymen might, just maybe, escape history and free themselves from endlessly and recklessly repeating the mistakes of the fathers and mothers.

Such was his enormous goal. No wonder it consumed his life. If he succeeded only in opening a window on the present and future by looking critically at the past, his achievement was truly remarkable. Perhaps even the breeze blowing among the cedars and maple trees in the Sunset Cemetery whispers that about men and monuments.

1 / *From Darkness into Light*

On the evening of May 3, 1900, the city fathers of Gaffney, South Carolina, switched on the town's first electric streetlights and, amid genial and general backslapping, said even more good things were sure to come to the piedmont town. "They are the very latest design and give a splendid light," the local newspaper hymned. "We have now been ushered from darkness into light." The day before, W. J. Cash was born in Gaffney and christened Joseph Wilbur Cash. His people were plain, strongly religious country folk, Scotch-Irish mainly, who named their first son for an admired Presbyterian preacher, J. Wilbur Chapman, and a grandfather and uncle named Joseph. Had he not later reversed the order of his names, Joseph Wilbur Cash would have had the same initials as his father, John William, a good man, hardworking and unpretentious.[1]

The Cashes were of the middling sort. They worked hard, occasionally succeeded, yet seemed perpetually to be starting over again in life. "In the Old South," W. J. Cash told his publisher, Alfred A. Knopf, "we were never rich or aristocratic, certainly, but good upcountry farmers with land and niggers in proportion to most of our neighbors." The Cashes, he reported to H. L. Mencken, editor of the *American Mercury*, "were considerable landowners, and most of them were slaveholders in the days of the cotton oligarchy." Cash repeatedly said that the rags-to-riches Old Irishman, celebrated in the opening pages of *The Mind of the South* as the archetype of the aspiring frontier planter, was modeled on his great-great-grandfather. Perhaps so. There were

1. Gaffney (S.C.) *Ledger*, May 4, 1900.

numerous Cashes in the Old South, some of them planters, including one Colonel E. B. C. Cash, who killed a man in a duel. But Cash's bragging words, in addition to being unsubstantiated, have the ring of the southerner, common in William Faulkner's novels, who knows that in the South to have "no past" is unforgivable.[2]

When the Civil War began, Cash's grandfather and great-grandfather, James Henry Cash and Sidney Cash of Cowpens, just south of Gaffney, were not planters, nor did they become officers in the Confederate army, as Cash planned for his Old Irishman to become in a proposed novel. They were not even foot soldiers. Rather, they were working at the large iron and steel mill at Hurricane Shoals on the Pacolet River, twenty miles away at Spartanburg. When the Rebels later converted the mill to a munitions plant, James Henry and Sidney stayed on until Yankee soldiers—some of General William T. Sherman's destroyers, according to family lore—burned the mill.[3]

After the war James Henry Cash worked a small farm, ran a sawmill in Clifton (formerly Hurricane Shoals), and fathered ten children, including John William Cash, born in 1872. Mainly, the family fought off hard times. But the Carolina piedmont was changing along with the rest of the South. Everywhere, entrepreneurs, caught up in the dream of profit making and "service," built textile mills, providing jobs for the impoverished whites and promising prosperity for the region. A Clifton attorney financed a cotton mill on the site of the old steelworks, and two more mills were built in due course. For the ambitious and able like John William's go-getting older brother Edward Rufus Cash, the mills stood as the door of opportunity. Uncle Ed started at Clifton Cotton Mill No. 1 as a boy, carrying bricks to build the new factory. He rose quickly to become superintendent. In 1893, when offered the management of a new mill in Gaffney, north of Spartanburg and just below the North Carolina line, Uncle Ed stepped lively. There was not much to Gaffney then—two or three stores, unpaved streets, a Baptist church, an eatery (restaurants would come

2. W. J. Cash to Alfred A. Knopf, author's form, April 29, 1936, in Joseph L. Morrison Papers, Southern Historical Collection, University of North Carolina, Chapel Hill; "Editorial Notes," *American Mercury*, XXIV (1931), xxviii; Joseph L. Morrison, *W. J. Cash, Southern Prophet: A Biography and a Reader* (New York, 1967), 10; W. J. Cash, *The Mind of the South* (1941; rpr. New York, 1969), 15; William Faulkner, *Absalom, Absalom!* (1936; rpr. New York, 1972), 52.

3. Elva Gheen, "John W. Cash," *Cleveland Times* (Shelby, N.C.), August 14, 1964. See also manuscript of Elva Gheen's interview with John W. Cash, in Charles H. Elkins Family Scrapbook, in possession of Charles H. Elkins, Jr., Winston-Salem, N.C.

later), and several big, old, solid houses. Still, an aroma of anticipated prosperity permeated the air; folks in Gaffney, as elsewhere in the piedmont, talked excitedly about a New South on the horizon. Uncle Ed bought a big house, large enough to accommodate lodgers, including his kid brother John William, just seventeen when he arrived in 1894 and found work as a clerk in the Gaffney Manufacturing Company Mill's company store.[4]

John William Cash was medium of height and spare of frame—an unprepossessing lad, but earnest and thankful to have escaped an unloving stepmother. Although work kept him busy, he managed to squeeze in some formal schooling at the Gaffney Male and Female Seminary—the public school was in its infancy, and no high school would be built for a decade. To the end of his days John William recalled proudly how he and Olan Macomson had argued the affirmative in a school debate on higher education for women. Meticulously John William spelled out his position in a schoolboy tablet which he treasured until his death in the 1960s, when he was in his nineties. A God-fearing man, John joined the Cherokee Avenue Baptist Church soon after arriving in Gaffney. From his vantage point in the church choir, he espied the pleasingly devout and attractive church organist, Nannie Mae Lutitia Hamrick. Nannie, recently arrived in town to teach music lessons at the graded school, was comely, almost plump, as constant in church attendance as he was. She was two years his junior; her folks lived in Boiling Springs, North Carolina, a crossroads village just across the state line. Her father was a stonemason there, a Baptist, and something of a town leader. He was Boiling Springs' first mayor and, that rarity in local politics, a Republican, who boasted of his party affiliation. "I had heard of Miss Nannie Hamrick," John recalled proudly, "and had even read her name in the society items in the newspapers, but when I met her I had no thoughts of getting married." Even so, John and Nannie were married at the Cherokee Avenue Baptist Church on December 30, 1896, with Pastor G. P. Hamrick officiating. The marriage occurred barely two months after John Cash's political hero, William Jennings Bryan, and the Democratic party had been vanquished by the Republican William McKinley. John was twenty-two; Nannie was twenty.[5]

4. Gheen, "John W. Cash."
5. *Ibid.*

By the turn of the century innumerable Hamricks dotted the Carolina piedmont and much of western Tennessee. They sprang from one Hans Georg Hamerick, a Rhineland Protestant fleeing Catholic persecution, who had arrived in America in the early eighteenth century. At least three Hamricks made their way to what is now Cleveland County—home of Boiling Springs and Shelby, the county seat— where they put down their roots as farmers, merchants, and tradesmen, multiplied abundantly, and melded into the South's great yeoman class.[6] They, too, as Cash loved to say, had their share of Scotch-Irish blood, thus assuring him a Celtic heritage he would treasure, and never more so than when excited or when arguing in *The Mind of the South* that the South's Celtic heritage shaped it indelibly. "In religion," Cash remembered, "they were mainly Calvinists—Baptists and Presbyterians—but I never heard of a Methodist among them or a minister. One of them, a waggish old fellow with a notable reputation as a connoisseur of the liquors to be had in the back country, was a militant atheist, much given to spouting Tom Paine and to dramatic expositions of his convictions." That nonconformist temperament in the innumerable Hamricks withered over the years and almost died out completely—until W. J. Cash boldly told about the South.[7]

Nannie Hamrick and John Cash were sturdy and serious, comfortably at one with each other and with their like-minded neighbors. Gaffney was a drab, sooty mill town, but the young couple had never known anything better. Besides, their world revolved around family, the Cherokee Avenue Baptist Church, and the prospering Gaffney Manufacturing Company Mill. John and Nannie, who called each other Daddy and Mama, lived at the end of Railroad Street—the tracks ran down the center of town—in a small wooden frame house "in a little stream-split valley," midway between the mill and the monotonous row houses provided for the factory hands. John Cash and his family were one step removed from the "mill people," the "wool hat boys," as they were uncharitably called. As clerk of the company store John dealt daily with the spendthrift, frequently transient mill hands. The Cashes' modest house suited their needs, and Wilbur's birth was received as a blessing; a few months earlier John and Nannie had lost a two-year-old daughter to Bright's disease. Wilbur, as his

---

6. Morrison, *W. J. Cash*, 11.
7. "Editorial Notes," *American Mercury*, xxviii–xxxii.

family called him, was born at home—Gaffney had no hospital then—as were his brothers, Henry (1902) and Allen (1904), and his sister, Elizabeth (Bertie), born in 1910, and two other babies who died in infancy.[8]

Wilbur had few companions during his early years. The mill children, even if they had not been toiling at their looms ten or twelve hours a day, were unsuitable playmates. Besides, Wilbur was shy, retiring, moody, scrawny, awkward, and unathletic. His companions were his younger brothers and "a little black nurse-maid," he remembered, "who filled me with preposterous notions, particularly in regard to sex." Once when one of the mill boys pushed him around, Wilbur ran home like a whipped pup, only to be admonished by his father to return and "act like a man." Wilbur obeyed, albeit halfheartedly. He much preferred reading to fighting or roughhousing with the town boys. From the day his mother taught him to read at age five, books were his passion. "Every time Wilbur got a nickel or a dime—and there were not many of them—he would go uptown and buy magazines and books," said his father. Local lore had it that the bespectacled Wilbur—he wore eyeglasses from an early age—"ruined" his eyes by too much reading. Townspeople, noticing his habitual squint, took to calling him "Sleepy" and repeating (and probably embellishing) the story of his arriving at school one Monday with a bruised face and the explanation that he had been reading on the front porch on Sunday afternoon, drifted off to sleep, and tumbled out of his chair and down the stairs, book and all.[9]

Wilbur's first encounter with formal reading and schooling came at the Gaffney Male and Female Seminary, run by a Baptist minister with a love for Latin. Wilbur was an indifferent student, even though (or maybe because) his teacher was his pastor's wife, Mrs. G. P. Hamrick. He whiled away many a day, sometimes when he should have been in school, hiding under the front porch with a book. "I used to play sick," he remembered of his youth, "so that I might devote myself to the pleasant business of building Indian tents out of cottonseed hull sacks." A dreamy boy, he liked to sneak away from everyone to sit on a tree limb with a book in hand, or listen to the wind and daydream in the fashion of southern boys of those years about charging with Gen-

8. *Ibid.*
9. Manuscript of Elva Gheen's interview with John W. Cash, in Elkins Family Scrapbook.

eral George Pickett at Gettysburg, or fancy himself gallantly rescuing beautiful women in distress. "I literally played with the wind and ran with Pan," he reported to Mencken, "spending whole days in the tops of maple trees, and sometimes leaping down to flee in incomprehensible terror before the rustling of the leaves and the rippling of the brook beneath." [10]

One of Wilbur's bittersweet childhood memories pertained to summer vacations spent visiting his maternal grandparents in Boiling Springs, thirteen miles away. Wilbur loved Grandpa D. J. Hamrick's comfortable two-story country house with its wraparound front porch and spacious yard. Years later, memories of the bountiful orchard and the sweet smell of the slowly rotting apples in the summer sun aroused waves of nostalgia in Cash. When he was old enough and strong enough to work, summers with the Hamricks also meant working the fields—which he heartily detested. Still, the memory of summers in tiny Boiling Springs (population four hundred) would remain in his mind as a bucolic interlude, never to be repeated. "Riding home from the fields in a wagon after dark and seeing the new ground burn red against the dark woods I was tired and often angry, for I resented farm work, and yet I am sure I was more quietly happy than I ever have been since or will be again. And do you remember how the sand followed the felloes [the rim of the wheel] around, hissing, and breathing in the pines when you awoke at night and the wind was about to rise but had not yet quite begun?" [11]

"Americans," Thornton Wilder once said, "are abstract. They are disconnected," their relation is "to everywhere, to everybody, and to always." They are eternally caught in the thrall of newness and sent reeling by freedom and mobility. But southerners, certainly of Cash's day, were different. There was nothing abstract or disconnected about them or about Gaffney or Boiling Springs. Life there was distinctly and specifically interrelated. There, Baptists, Methodists, a few Presbyterians, mills, mill houses, wool hat boys, blacks who "knew their place," big talking politicians, coronet bands blaring "Dixie," the Democratic party, Fourth of July potato sack races, baseball games with another town's team, pastures of plenty just a mile outside of town in any direction, arm-waving preachers, revivals, baptism down by the riversides, and above all family—these were specific, con-

10. Charlotte *News*, October 23, 1937; "Editorial Notes," *American Mercury*, xxviii.
11. W. J. Cash to R. P. Harriss, March 20, 1941, in Morrison Papers.

nected constants. The southerner's world was immediate, known to all, and embraced both the physical and emotional. It was real; it was palpable; it entered into the bone, into the soul. One grew up knowing everything about the place and the people; one had an identity. As David Minter writes of Faulkner's youth: "With the sense of place and family pressing on him from all sides, it was other perils that he learned. Deeply exposed to the play of associations with creatures living and dead, he became acutely aware of the force of human heredity and the flow of generations." The past is never completely over and done with—and few, in Cash's day, wanted it to be forgotten. The future flows as much, if not more, from the past as the present. Southerners, as C. Vann Woodward put it, feel an intimate relationship to a specific time, place, and group. In short, not having been "born free" and living intimately with defeat, southerners, unique among Americans, feel history as an ever-present reality, even a burden. [12]

All hustle and bustle by 1900, Gaffney joined in the New South's love of mills and growth with the reckless passion of a romantic starved for love. Gaffney and the New South embraced prosperity and the dollar—what genteel southerners had traditionally dismissed as "crass commercialism" and scorned as "hurry" and Yankee worship of the almighty dollar. Was Gaffney, with a population of six thousand, as boosters proclaimed in 1911, not growing? Never mind that the 1910 census put the figure at 4,767. "Utterly preposterous," the town paper fumed; the census count had taken place when "almost all the mill people had fled the city because of an epidemic of smallpox." In 1911 fourteen trains puffed into and out of town daily. That year Gaffney boasted five cotton mills, an equal number of Protestant churches, two hotels, one theater, a hospital and seven physicians, a high school—overwhelmingly approved by the voters in 1907—and an up-to-date drugstore where the halt and the lame could find the latest patent medicines, including "Dr. Wooley's Painless Opium and Whiskey Cure." Perhaps Dr. Wooley's was in brisk demand because Cherokee County, harassed by editorials and sermons, had in 1904 resoundingly rejected Benjamin Tillman's pet project to allow the state to sell liquor through local dispensaries. [13]

12. David Minter, *William Faulkner: His Life and Work* (Baltimore, 1980), 3; Thornton Wilder is quoted in C. Vann Woodward, *The Burden of Southern History* (Baton Rouge, 1960), 22–23.

13. Gaffney (S.C.) *Ledger*, April 11, December 19, 1911, November 11, 1904, November 26, 1907, July 4, 1902.

By 1910, horseless carriages, Ford Model T's, chugged along Gaffney streets, and more were on order. Three years later Gaffney's first
"automobile fire truck" excited "the interest and admiration of all the
curious." If these were not the best of times, the arrows of progress
were nevertheless everywhere in flight and on target. In 1913, Andrew Carnegie gave the city a new library, and a team from the State
Board of Health spent six weeks in the city treating the county's thousand or more who suffered from hookworm.[14]

To Gaffney's boosters, men like Uncle Ed, chairman of the Board of
Public Works in 1911, and Ed DeCamp, exuberant editor-publisher of
the town newspaper, the *Ledger*, progress had spread its golden wings
and promised to carry the town to even greater heights. Nothing made
DeCamp's eye glisten more than the mills. His editorials regularly sang
the same litany of praise: the mills provided jobs for the common
folks, earned money for owners and managers, and even benefited the
blacks, who held none but the most menial positions. Reporting in
1902 on the success of the new Limestone Mills, where Wilbur's father
now clerked in the company store and Uncle Ed was superintendent,
the *Ledger* found the mill working around the clock, operating with
the "latest" machinery and producing the "finest" cloth. "The houses
for the laborers . . . are models of convenience, comfort and neat-
ness. They contain four and six rooms each, and in most of them we
notice not more than one family." As a result, the incidence of fatal
sickness was far lower than in thickly populated towns—of that De-
Camp was sure. Springtime in "busy Gaffney" made DeCamp's heart
leap. The sixty-two thousand spindles at the Gaffney Manufacturing
Company Mill hummed "a requiem of peace and contentment to
thousands of industrial souls."[15]

The twelve-hour workday and the six-day workweek troubled the
city fathers, the *Ledger* confessed. Although "the work is not heavy
nor hard and is always comfortable," the workers were away from home
too long and had no time for household or parental duties. As for child
labor, endemic in southern mills and the object of bitter scorn—even
from such moderate southern critics as Alabama's Edgar Gardner Murphy and North Carolina's Alexander McKelway—the *Ledger* repeated
the familiar litany about jobs, prosperity, and the paternalism of the

14. *Ibid.*, February 4, August 29, November 18, 1913.
15. *Ibid.*, January 24, 1902, May 5, 1903.

owners, themes that Cash would later mercilessly deride as shallow faith in progress. DeCamp rationalized the use of child labor as a means of helping widowed mothers. In addition, he said, many mills had continued operating even when they lost money, so complete was their commitment to providing employment. Child labor was undoubtedly a "problem," but the blame, said the town fathers, repeating a refrain common throughout the piedmont, should be placed on those unscrupulous "trifling daddies" who refused to work, thus "forcing" the mills to rely on children and women, many of whom were glad to have their children in the mills with them and thus safe from drunken, abusive fathers.[16]

John Cash was never one of those "trifling daddies." He arose at five o'clock each morning, breakfasted on simple country fare, walked the half mile to the mill, and was ready to go to work when the starting whistle blew. His day was long, frequently twelve or thirteen hours. He returned home in the evening, usually around seven or eight o'clock, weary of bone and muscle. During the winter months he and the mill hands rarely saw daylight except through a window or on Sunday, their day of rest. But he did not grumble. He was a company man from head to toe and glad to say so, though he was a man of few words. He was pleased to have a "good job," proud to be known as one of those who "gave a day's work for a day's pay." No doubt, now and then, he allowed himself the luxury of dreaming that one day he would be able to provide a better life for his children. But for now he had to settle for the occasional congratulatory pat on the back from the owners or the glory of reading in the newspaper that he and the go-getting Uncle Ed "were two of the most polite and businesslike young men we've personally known about anywhere."[17]

Sunday was the Lord's Day. Scrubbed and inspected, the Cash children trooped off to church with Mama and Daddy to worship and hear the gospel rightly divided by Pastor Hamrick or a visiting Baptist dignitary or a saint on furlough from China or some other mission field. Nannie played the organ and taught Sunday School, John Cash sang in the choir, and Wilbur and his brothers sat where a family member such as Uncle Ed, who was a church deacon, or some ubiquitous Ham-

16. *Ibid.*, January 24, September 26, 1902.
17. Interview with Jay Jenkins, August 11, 1984; Gaffney (S.C.) *Ledger*, January 2, 1902. See also *ibid.*, January 24, 1904; interview with Allen Cash, August 7, 1984; interview with Henry Cash, August 9, 1984.

rick could keep an eye on them. The indefatigable Uncle Ed chaired the Board of Deacons and, in 1910, expertly guided the Building Committee when the church announced plans to build a new, bigger structure that could seat a thousand. Gaffney's big news in April, 1911, was the opening of the new $20,000 Cherokee Avenue Baptist Church with pews overflowing and a brace of preachers on hand to consecrate the building.[18]

Fear of and distaste for religion, not piety or faith, were festering in Sleepy's mind. There were no outward signs, no wayward behavior or rebellious actions—these would not have been tolerated in the Cash household. In fact, Wilbur at a very young age had surprised his folks by announcing that he was considering "coming forward" to be baptized. John and Nannie said no. He was too young. He had not yet reached the age of accountability, they reasoned, and should wait. In truth, Wilbur was different from the other children—more sensitive, moodier, more of a loner. After his aborted decision to join the church in Gaffney, Wilbur resolutely postponed baptism until late in his teenage years. When he recalled his earliest years for Mencken, unpleasant memories of a "drab" Gaffney, mills, and a terrifying religion fused. "The keening of the five-o'clock whistles in the morning drilled me in sorrow. And for years, under the influence of the Baptist preacher's too graphic account of the Second Coming, I watched the West take fire from the sunset with a sort of ecstatic dread."[19]

Violence, much of it intertwined with race and politics, was as much a part of life in Gaffney and the South as religion. Race riots and unspeakably brutal lynchings occurred regularly and disgraced the South at the turn of the century. The standard defense was that lynchings, many of them sadistic, ritualized public mutilations and burnings, were understandable reactions to rape, even though any literate person had ample opportunity to learn the truth—that rape was rarely the cause of lynchings. The racial nightmare, which one noted historian has compared to South Africa's, was exacerbated by a generation of ruthless race-baiting politicians, none worse than South Carolina's coarse extremist, Pitchfork Ben Tillman. He and the others—Charles B. Aycock, the racist "education governor" in North Carolina, James K. Vardaman in Mississippi, Hoke Smith in Georgia—had learned, in

18. Gaffney (S.C.) *Ledger*, May 7, 1910, April 25, 1911.
19. "Editorial Notes," *American Mercury*, xxviii–xxxii.

the crucible of the Populist challenge to white supremacy in the 1890s, the effectiveness of racism as a weapon for beating back all challengers and keeping the Democratic party in power.[20]

In the process of destroying Populism, Democrats altered the laws to disfranchise and segregate blacks. Mississippi led the way in 1890, then South Carolina in 1895 following Tillman's leadership, and Louisiana in 1898. North Carolina, with Red Shirts intimidating and harassing blacks (and recalcitrant whites), made Jim Crow the order of the day in 1900, the year Cash was born. For sensitive Carolinians, the traumatizing and searing event was the Wilmington, North Carolina, race riot of 1898 that left at least eleven blacks dead and many more wounded. The city completed the job by electing as mayor the leader of the mob, a former Confederate officer and congressman. That same year an election race riot near Tillman's home claimed the lives of twelve blacks and wounded many others.[21]

Gaffney and the region shared fully in the violence and racism. Stories of blacks being burned alive or mutilated by savage crowds, sometimes swelled by the presence of schoolchildren, made the front pages of the *Ledger*, usually accompanied by strong disclaimers that the "better sort" of whites were not involved and charges that the mob was "composed of illiterate white trash." Black crime was reported with a thoroughness bordering on the compulsive—as was common in southern white newspapers—ostensibly as a warning to blacks and as a way of putting southern violence in "perspective." Even so, town fathers worried that Cherokee County's record of twenty murders—with only one conviction—during its first ten years (1897–1907) was shockingly high and shamed the county.[22]

Most shameful of all during Cash's early years was a bestial lynching in neighboring Greenwood County in 1906. A mob of more than a thousand whites took an accused Negro rapist from jail, tied him to a tree, and riddled his body with bullets. "The negro's head was literally shot into pulp," the *Ledger* reported, "his brains covering his hat and face." The crowd would have burned the poor wretch alive had not Governor Duncan Clinch Heyward been there. Heeding Heyward's

20. William H. Gleason, "The Statistics of Lynching," *South Atlantic Quarterly*, V (1906), 342–48; C. Vann Woodward, *The Strange Career of Jim Crow* (1955; 3d rev. ed. New York, 1974), 77–109; Francis B. Simkins, *Pitchfork Ben Tillman, South Carolinian* (Baton Rouge, 1944), 224–25, 397–400.

21. C. Vann Woodward, *Origins of the New South, 1877–1913* (Baton Rouge, 1951), 351.

22. Gaffney (S.C.) *Ledger*, August 26, 1904, April 5, 1907.

plea for decency, "a humane man pulled the doomed negro's hat over his face before the crowd started shooting." A month later, news of race rioting in Atlanta, Georgia, shocked the entire nation. For four days white mobs, inflamed by the Democratic party's successful white supremacy election, "looted, plundered, lynched, and murdered."[23]

Did young Wilbur Cash hear of these and countless other racial atrocities? How could he not hear? Racial talk, crude racial slurs, were on every tongue. And everyone knew who the lynchers were. As Cash would one day write, young lads in the country were quick "to see that the man who was pointed out as having slain five or eight or thirteen Negroes (I take the figures from actual cases) still walked about free," a villain to some, a hero to many others. "One day, sometime during your childhood or adolescence," Lillian Smith, Cash's contemporary, would write of her growing up days in the Deep South, "a Negro was lynched in your county or the one next to yours." Everyone knew what had happened, "but no one publicly condemned it and always the murderers went free. And afterward, maybe weeks or months or years afterward, you sat casually in the drugstore with one of the murderers and drank the Coke he casually paid for." Impressionable lads, Cash remembered, "inevitably tended to see such a scoundrel very much as he saw himself: as a gorgeous *beau sabreur*, hardly less splendid than the most magnificent cavalry captain."[24]

The ranting, racist politicians made sure the populace remained aware of the proper attitude toward blacks. Coleman Blease, at least as racist as Tillman, succeeded to political power in South Carolina during Cash's youth. A hero of the wool hat boys—the man who proudly "planted" a black victim's cut-off finger in his garden—"Coley" Blease visited Gaffney and the region frequently. He triumphantly toured the town in 1911 after capturing the governorship from the moderate forces behind Heyward, the incumbent. Coley came as a special guest of the Local Order of Red Men, a nativist group open only to "men of pure white blood and under the tongue of good repute." Other fraternal groups admitted "niggers" to segregated orders, Blease reminded the trailing throng that cheered and clapped as the Gaffney Coronet Band strutted down the main street, filling the air with choruses of "Dixie," but not the Red Men or their ladies' auxiliary, the Order of

23. *Ibid.*, August 21, 1906; Woodward, *Origins of the New South*, 350.
24. Cash, *Mind of the South*, 126; Lillian Smith, *Killers of the Dream* (1949; rev. ed. New York, 1978), 97.

Pocahontas. The *Ledger*, though usually critical of Tillman's and Blease's coarse rantings while agreeing with them in substance, approved Blease's refusal to comment on a local lynching because "there were ladies in the crowd." But Coley shouted that "when a nigger laid his hand upon a white woman the quicker he was placed under six feet of dirt, the better." Such language and such events permeated the world of Wilbur Joseph Cash in his formative years.[25]

So also did the imposing popularity of the Reverend Thomas Dixon, Jr., the celebrated author of best-selling racist novels. The favorite son of Shelby, North Carolina, Dixon had shed his clerical collar to become the South's premier racist novelist, outdistancing the polite Virginian Thomas Nelson Page. First came *The Leopard's Spots*, a saga of Reconstruction, in 1902, followed in 1905 by the runaway best-seller, *The Clansman*, a crude but stirring celebration of the Ku Klux Klan. The book blossomed into a Broadway play and then into the hugely successful film *The Birth of a Nation*. Onstage with its troop of horses and white-robed paladins of racial purity, *The Clansman* was a gaudy spectacular. When it appeared in Gaffney in 1907 as part of a ballyhooed southern tour, Dixon himself—with flowing mane and wearing a cutaway coat—was on hand to introduce the play and vouch for its historical authenticity. The packed house at the Star Theater roared its approval. Here, as President Woodrow Wilson would say ecstatically when he saw the film, "was history written with lightning."[26]

Equally melodramatic was Dixon's novel *The Sins of the Fathers*, staged in Gaffney in 1911, again with Dixon onstage bowing to overflow crowds and thunderous applause. The preachy play revolved around a racist politician who had illegitimately fathered a light-skinned mulatto daughter. His secret is safe, he thinks, but to his horror he learns that his son has fallen in love with the ill-begotten girl. To the taboo of incest Dixon added the even greater sin of miscegenation. Tragedy followed, just as it would in Faulkner's later powerful novel of incest and miscegenation, *Absalom, Absalom!* So strong was Dixon's devotion to racial purity that he intended his play to call the

25. Gaffney (S.C.) *Ledger*, November 21, 1911.

26. John Inscoe, "*The Clansman* on Stage and Screen: North Carolina Reacts," *North Carolina Historical Review*, LXIV (1987), 131–61. For more on Dixon see Joel Williamson, *The Crucible of Race: Black-White Relations in the American South Since Emancipation* (New York, 1984), 140–79.

South "to be true to her best traditions and save American civilization." Two years after the staging of *The Sins of the Fathers*, a dramatized version of *The Leopard's Spots* played to full houses in Gaffney.[27]

"Sleepy" Cash probably never saw these plays. His parents, as he would later say, were "foot washin' Baptists," not the sort to hold with theatergoing. But no one, least of all an impressionable, bookish lad, who even as an adult instinctively thrilled to any rousing version of "Dixie," could have missed the hoopla or the penetrating emotional significance of the play. The name of Dixon, pride of the piedmont, was on everyone's lips. Cash read Dixon's novels and saw the acclaimed *The Birth of a Nation* soon after it appeared in 1916, "alternately bawling hysterically and shouting my fool head off"—an adolescent reaction he shared with many of his generation. In Chattanooga, Ralph McGill's boyhood hometown, the film caused a sensation, playing "night after night to a packed house." Nine-year-old Hodding Carter sat trembling in a jam-packed New Orleans theater with his father and Confederate veterans who screamed the Rebel Yell from the opening scene on. His father, caught up in the crowd's emotion, started hollering too and flung his hat into the air, "never to see it again." The film's appearance in Shelby made such an impression on one of Wilbur's young friends that she could not sleep that night. Even in her seventies, after a lifetime of yearning to shake free of prejudice, pangs of fear unsettled her whenever an unknown black man walked up behind her.[28]

However mechanical Dixon's plots, however sentimental and obvious his message or neurotic his obsession with sex, his novels embodied a reality in the white psyche in which race, sex, violence, and death are intertwined—just as *Absalom, Absalom!*, *The Sound and the Fury*, and other Faulkner novels would later elevate the same themes to art and profound social commentary. In *The Leopard's Spots* a black gang, brandishing guns, invades a white wedding party and abducts the bride-to-be. "Shoot men! My God shoot!" screams the distraught father to the rescue party. "There are things worse than death." Following the accidental killing of the young virgin, her father consoles the aggrieved rescuers: "It's all right boys, you've been my friend

27. Gaffney (S.C.) *Ledger*, January 10, 13, 1911. See also *ibid.*, October 28, November 1, 1913.

28. Charlotte *News*, February 9, 1936; Ralph McGill, *The South and the Southerner* (Boston, 1963), 129; Hodding Carter, "Furl That Banner?" *New York Times Magazine*, June 25, 1965, pp. 13–15; John Kneebone, *Southern Liberal Journalists and the Issue of Race, 1920–1944* (Chapel Hill, 1985), 9; interview with Bea Morris, September 15, 1984.

tonight. You've saved my little gal. . . . If you hadn't been here—my God, I can't think of what would 'a' happened. Now it's all right. She's safe in God's hands."[29]

There is an interesting parallel between Dixon's overheated, racist dialogue and one of Tillman's characteristic bellowings (it was Tillman, by the way, who told Dixon the story that became the plot of *The Clansman*): "I have three daughters," Tillman shouted once from the hustings, "but, so help me God, I had rather find either one of them killed by a tiger or a bear and gather up her bones and bury them, conscious that she had died in the purity of her maidenhood, than to have her crawl to me and tell me the horrid story that she had been robbed of the jewel of her womanhood by a black fiend." Anyone wondering why Cash would later in *The Mind of the South* link sex and race so provocatively as integral to the southern psyche need look no further than his growing-up years, when life and "art," the art treasured in the Cash household and in millions of others across the South, mirrored each other.[30]

Dixon's reverence for sexual purity and racism represented far more than the outpouring of a popular novelist's tortured psyche. Of all the southern racists from Tillman to Vardaman, Dixon best summed up the dogma of southern white supremacy. The white supremacy movement was far more than politics or the revolt of the rednecks, as New South liberals fretted. It was a riveting, destructive myth with proscribed rules governing everyone's behavior. "So we learned step by step by step, the dance that cripples the human spirit," Lillian Smith remembered, "we who were white and we who were colored, day by day, hour by hour, year by year until the movements were reflexes and made for the rest of our life without thinking." White supremacy expressed a corrosive romanticism that could be exploited at will by the strutting Tillmans, Bleases, and Vardamans or the scribbling Dixons and Pages. Tillman's biographer has written that except for his justification of lynching, his words "were merely emphatic repetitions of words heard wherever Southerners foregathered." In Dixon's hands the myths of the past intertwined with deep-seated hopes and fears to produce a literature of shallow realism and sentimental romance—all enshrined in an ideal of racial purity and a grandiose patriotism that

29. Thomas Dixon, *The Leopard's Spots* (New York, 1903), 126–27.
30. Quoted in Simkins, *Pitchfork Ben Tillman*, 397.

would "save American civilization." Dixon's writings were popular everywhere in the nation, even where blacks were a rarity, and his racism was a retelling of the late nineteenth-century fascination with portraying the threatened defilement of white women by "savage" Indians. In the South, however, Dixon's words spoke to an immediate, concrete present.[31]

Dixon's cheap, sentimental racism bred a distorted and regressive romanticism that left its mark on young, imaginative southerners. "All of us," Cash recalled, "who grew up in the south in the first decades of the 1900's—in that south with its heroic rhetoric, its gyneolatry, its continual flourishing of the word noble, and its constant glorification of the past—were foreordained to the thing." Thomas Nelson Page's "Two Little Confederates" was Cash's generation's primer, the Civil War and its doleful aftermath their great historical myth. Lolling under a tree on a sultry summer afternoon, a dreamy young boy could lose himself in fantasy. If only he had marched with Pickett, been there to assist James Longstreet and Stonewall Jackson at Gettysburg on that far-off day in July, 1863. This time Pickett's rear guard would move faster and Cemetery Ridge would be taken. "Ten thousand times [we] stepped into the breach at that critical moment on that reeking slope at Gettysburg, and with our tremendous swords, and in defiance of chronology, then and there won the Civil War." That would make the world right for Mama and Daddy, for everyone, indeed, for the South.[32]

Wilbur's musings went to the heart of his generation's fascination with southern history and, in C. Vann Woodward's words, its "quite un-American experience with defeat." Listen to Faulkner, writing in *Intruder in the Dust*: "For every Southern boy fourteen years old, not once but whenever he wants it, there is the instant when it's still not yet two o'clock on that July afternoon in 1863 . . . it hasn't happened yet, it hasn't even begun yet, it not only hasn't begun yet but there is still time for it not to begin. . . . *This time. Maybe this time* with all this much to lose and all this much to gain."[33]

31. Smith, *Killers of the Dream*, 96; Williamson, *Crucible of Race*, 140; Simkins, *Pitchfork Ben Tillman*, 404. See Thomas Beer, *The Mauve Decade* (New York, 1926), 37, for a popular melodrama in Chicago in which a bullet is reserved for a white woman's heart should she ever be in danger of being raped by red men.

32. Charlotte *News*, November 17, 1935.

33. William Faulkner, *Intruder in the Dust* (New York, 1948), 194–95.

In late 1912 John Cash made a decision. He would swallow his pride, move his family to Boiling Springs, and accept his father-in-law's offer to help him manage a general store. Old D. J. Hamrick could be overbearing, and John loathed his cocksure Republicanism, but the move would allow him to build a big house (which his growing family now needed) and perhaps move up in the world. Talk had it that a new mill would be opening soon in Boiling Springs. Men of his experience would be in demand, he hoped. Nannie would be near her parents, and Boiling Springs was a country town with a good Baptist church and sound values—the town charter even prohibited traveling carnivals and the sale of cigarettes. By fall of 1913 the house was completed and John Cash and his family said farewell to Gaffney.[34]

The town was home to the Boiling Springs High School, a first-rate private Baptist school that was superior to the fledgling public school in Gaffney. To the Cashes, it promised to provide moral training as well as scholastic rigor. Each school day began with required chapel and prayers. "The Bible," the students were reminded, was "the only safe text-book in moral training." The curriculum was traditional with no frills; the emphasis was on Latin, English, history, and the sciences, mainly mathematics. The teachers were God-fearing "scholars," several of them Hamricks. Euzelia Hamrick taught Latin and history, O. P. Hamrick was the English master, and all the teachers were of the old school, convinced that they were molding character and responsible for the recognition and obeying of conscience and, the catalog announced, "the cultivation of honor." Most of the students boarded, and not a few of the male students were older than the usual high school age, having recently heard the call to the Baptist ministry.[35]

Sleepy, a day student, was indifferent to his studies at Boiling Springs High School and its unrelenting commitment to religion. But he found other, more challenging diversions. "The principal business at hand was the making of love," Cash later reported with Menckenian bravado. Sleepy apparently approved—having just discovered girls—but he was still shy, still skinny, a bit puny, and an amateur at the principal business. The older boys "laughed at me as an infant, and so,

34. Gheen, "John W. Cash"; interview with Henry Cash, August 9, 1984; interview with Allen Cash, August 7, 1984; Morrison, W. J. Cash, 18.

35. Boiling Springs High School catalog, 1917–18, pp. 22–23, in Gardner-Webb College Library, Boiling Springs, N.C.

for two years, I suffered horribly. A bit later, after I had shot up to my growth, and had developed a deep voice and some capacity as a debater, I had better luck." After discovering girls, he boasted to his publisher, Knopf, he abruptly "abandoned the Harvard Classics somewhere in the middle and spent the next fifteen years contemplating them—the girls, not the Classics—often painfully."[36]

Whatever his luck with the girls, Sleepy became a pretty good student or "scholar" as "Professor" J. D. Huggins, the principal, would say. Like other southern boys of his time—Asheville's Thomas Wolfe comes to mind—Sleepy excelled as a debater and served as an officer in one of the two literary societies. A serious young man in a high stiff collar, dark tie, and stylish pompadour stares out somberly from a picture of the officers of the Kalagathian and Kalliergeonian literary societies in 1917. Again like Wolfe, whose appetite for reading would become legendary, Cash was a voracious reader. Reading was now an ingrained habit, and Sleepy turned naturally to the classics as well as "tons of trash." He read Shakespeare, Dickens, Bunyan, Sir Walter Scott, Hawthorne, and Edmund Burke. Twenty years later he marveled in disbelief at how earnest and "mistaken" he had been in his reverence for Burke's reactionary *Reflections on the French Revolution*. In his senior year Sleepy wrote what his teachers considered perceptive themes on *Julius Caesar*, George Eliot's *Adam Bede*, Jane Austen's *Pride and Prejudice*, and Scott's *The Talisman*, among others.[37]

Taken all in all, W. J. Cash, class of 1917, had received a sound education. He and his fifteen classmates were, by virtue of their awards and diplomas dispensed at various ceremonies in April, among the South's and the nation's elite, and present to hand out the gold medal for the best student oration was the Honorable Clyde R. Hoey, a rising star in the Democratic party. Wilbur was chosen as the historian of his class, and, standing before a packed auditorium on a stage decorated with red, white, and blue bunting, American flags, and a large picture of President Woodrow Wilson, Cash delivered one of the student addresses. One proud orator patriotically lauded "the call of our country," while another youngster pointed out "the perils of Catholicism." Did Cash, as class historian, look backward? Or did he try his hand at foretelling the future or even the meaning of the present? Alas, his

36. W. J. Cash to Alfred A. Knopf, author's form, April 8, 1940, in Morrison Papers.
37. Boiling Springs High School catalog, 1916–17, p. 29; Charlotte *News*, September 20, 1936; David Herbert Donald, *Look Homeward: A Life of Thomas Wolfe* (Boston, 1987) 17.

speech on "Columbia and her people" has not survived. Graduation day was April 18, 1917. Two weeks earlier, the nation, following the lead of President Wilson, a southern Democrat, had declared war on Germany and ushered the United States into the Great War.[38]

The Boiling Springs High School class of 1917 was prepared to meet the world. That much the commencement speaker, the Reverend Walter Nathan Johnson, a Baptist clergyman of local repute, knew for sure. They had, so Johnson and the proud parents assumed, put on the whole armor of God and absorbed knowledge that was timeless and therefore efficient. The Reverend Johnson had recently written *The Southern Baptist Crisis: A Readjustment for Efficiency* and was therefore aligned, at least in North Carolina, with one of his generation's most cherished values, "efficiency."[39]

Sleepy's generation would need all the efficiency it could muster. With America at war and business booming everywhere as a result of a war-stimulated economy, John Cash, having experienced a modest measure of success, branched out. He purchased several automobiles and operated a company to ferry soldiers to and from Spartanburg's army cantonment, Camp Wadsworth. John and hired hands drove the cars and Wilbur helped out in a variety of ways, even volunteering to drive—a request John Cash wisely refused.[40]

After the navy turned him down, Wilbur, despite his bad eyes, managed, after "fudging" his age, to pass the physical and join the Students' Army Training Corp (SATC). Mainly, he helped out around the cantonment, performing a variety of unexciting odd jobs from clerical duties to carpenter's helper. He made his way up and down the East Coast working at shipyards and cantonments but spent most of the winter of 1917–1918 at Spartanburg, where he suffered his own war wound, frostbite, that left his eyelids slightly but permanently narrowed. Now everyone could call him "Sleepy." By the time of the Armistice in November, 1918, Wilbur had risen to the rank of corporal in the SATC, doubtless to the pleasure and surprise of his father.[41]

With the end of the war in sight in September, 1918, John Cash decided that Wilbur should enroll in Spartanburg's Wofford College, a

38. *Cleveland Star* (Shelby, N.C.), April 17, 1917.

39. *Ibid.*, April 24, 1917.

40. Interview with Allen Cash, August 7, 1984.

41. Cash to Knopf, author's form, April 8, 1940, in Morrison Papers; Morrison, *W. J. Cash*, 21–22; interview with Allen Cash, August 7, 1984; interview with Henry Cash, August 9, 1984.

small Methodist school. Wilbur objected. He did not want to go to a "preacher's school"; he wanted to go away somewhere to a real college. But as his father pointed out, if he enrolled in the school's SATC program, the army would pay the tuition, leaving only the cost of room and board. For John Cash, with two younger sons attending Boiling Springs High School and a daughter enrolled in the preparatory primary school, the financial arrangements available at Wofford made college affordable.

Wilbur lost the argument. For a time he lived on campus, then moved in with his father, whose business was doing well. We know little about Cash's year at Wofford. He tried his hand at creative writing, including poetry—none of which has survived—joined the Pipe Dreamers Club, and smoked a pipe and tried to look wise. One member of their Cicero class recalled him fondly but remembered that "he didn't have much to say." A young woman inscribed his yearbook with the tantalizingly cryptic: "'Sleepy hum,' 'member the night at the——. Well, you know!" But mainly Cash endured the place. It was a provincial preacher's school, he grumbled, asking if he couldn't please go somewhere else. He had a friend who was going to Valparaiso University in Indiana, and Wilbur pleaded with his parents to let him go there too. John and Nannie Cash reluctantly assented, and Cash entered Valparaiso in the fall of 1919.[42]

Valparaiso was a growing "people's university" in those days, with low tuition and a populist philosophy of education—no entrance exams, no graduation exams. It was to be a quality school for poor boys and girls who needed and wanted an education, and it attracted ambitious, poor kids from all over the country. Had young, poor Gerald L. K. Smith not sped through in two and half years, graduating in January, 1918, Cash and the future right-wing zealot would have been classmates. Cash took on a full schedule: American literature, two courses in Latin, French, physics, and a semester course devoted to Emerson. The southern boy shivered through the fall and part of a cold winter, but he gave out by Christmas. He could not go back, he told his parents. "He about froze to death" up there near Lake Michigan, John Cash recalled.[43]

42. Quoted in Morrison, W. J. Cash, 22.
43. Gheen, "John W. Cash."

Wilbur agreed to go to Wake Forest College, mecca to many Baptists around Boiling Springs but just another "preacher's school" to Sleepy. Still, it was away, up by Raleigh. What about the University of North Carolina? Did Sleepy ever beseech his father to allow him to go to Chapel Hill? It would have been slightly cheaper than Wake Forest. It appears that John Cash set his foot down with Wilbur and insisted on a religious campus, although he apparently agreed without a word of protest when his next two boys, Allen and Henry, said they wanted to go to Chapel Hill. Their understanding, they recalled years later, was that Wilbur could have gone anywhere he wanted and that their father had not forced him to go to Wake Forest. Nevertheless, Wilbur certainly felt his father had been unyielding.

Wilbur and his father had never been close. Was it because Wilbur was the first son, the first child, who often is forced to follow stricter rules than his younger siblings? Or was it because during Wilbur's earliest years John Cash was usually away at work, and the two had never really gotten to know each other? Or was it because John Cash, a taciturn, reserved, emotionally aloof man, was not given to demonstrating love in direct, physical ways? For love, for affection, whether in moments of anguish or joy, Wilbur turned to his mother. Nannie Cash understood, at least better than her husband did, that Wilbur was sensitive, emotional, tender in his feelings, not strong and assertive and loud as southern men are supposed to be.

John Cash was a simple, proud man whose horizons were limited by his rural, small-town background, a good man who would, like many well-meaning but fearful fathers, protect his firstborn from falling too far in life by convincing him never to reach too far. "I didn't want him to think he was extra smart," John Cash recalled meekly years later. "His mother realized that he was an extra bright boy long before I did. I never did teach Wilbur that he was smart. I never did want him to think that he was smarter than most other people. I never taught him that he was extra smart. But he was."[44]

44. *Ibid.*

2 / Light over a Darkling Land

Wake Forest College, nestled in rural Wake Forest, North Carolina, was not, as it turned out, just another "preacher's school." There were some clergymen on the faculty, to be sure, and the student body of five hundred included one hundred young men whose hearts were set on a Baptist pulpit. And, too, the college was sectarianly Baptist, with required chapel services four days a week and a vigorous, godly president who taught Sunday School at the stately campus Baptist church and, word was, attended more religious services than anyone for miles around. But President William Louis Poteat was a biologist, a true scientist, trained in Germany, not an ordained man. More than that, Poteat was an evolutionist, a Christian evolutionist but a Darwinian all the same, as his tireless critics never stopped proclaiming. Boundlessly energetic and brimming with good cheer, "Dr. Billy" hired the best faculty he could lure to Wake Forest. Their influence permeated the campus, creating a distinctive tone of excitement that Cash and many others would never forget. "Truly, Wake Forest was a rare phenomenon—a small Baptist college with the liberality and the integrity of a university," one of Cash's closest friends remembered. "Light streamed from its windows," said Gerald W. Johnson, class of 1911, "over a darkling land."[1]

1. Edwin Holman to Joseph L. Morrison, September 20, 1965, in Joseph L. Morrison Papers, Southern Historical Collection, University of North Carolina, Chapel Hill; Suzanne Cameron Linder, *William Louis Poteat* (Chapel Hill, 1966), 85; Johnson quoted in Fred Hobson, ed., *South-Watching: Selected Essays by Gerald W. Johnson* (Chapel Hill, 1983), x; Gerald W. Johnson, "Billy with the Red Necktie," *Virginia Quarterly Review*, XIX (1943), 551–61.

Gracing the faculty in Cash's day were Benjamin Sledd, a veritable Renaissance man, who seemed to know everything remotely connected with English literature; C. Chilton Pearson, a Virginian, who taught history and political science; and the president's son, Hubert M. Poteat, who succeeded the highly popular John Bethune Carlyle as professor of Latin in 1912. Except for occasional one-year appointments, Poteat, Pearson, and Sledd *were* their departments, teaching all the courses in their fields and doing administrative work as well, as they would continue to do for years thereafter. (When classicist William Bailey Royall died in harness at age eighty-four in 1928, he had led Wake Forest lads through the mysteries of Greek for sixty-two years. Campus rumor had it that Professor Royall died of overwork.) By all accounts, they were fine teachers, possessed of a dedication "completely new to me then," remembered Gerald W. Johnson, another son of the Carolina piedmont, "and which I have seldom encountered since."[2]

Spurred on by Dr. Billy, the campus became a lively marketplace of ideas. William James, Josiah Royce, George Santayana, and George Lyman Kittridge "were all ours for the asking on some drowsy afternoon beneath a magnolia tree," remembered Laurence Stallings, class of 1915, who would one day write the antiwar play *What Price Glory?* "And if you didn't find 'Sleepy' Cash expounding under one tree," said one classmate, "you would certainly find him going full blast under another not far away—so long as the company was congenial." Sleepy and his loquacious friends loved to argue about ideas and literature— and whether the South had either—and poke cynical fun at the "skys," the earnest men and boys preparing to be pastors.[3]

Sledd, Pearson, the Poteats—each was a Mr. Chips, content to be who he was and where he was. (Word was that Dr. Billy had thrown away the likelihood of a distinguished career in science by returning to Wake Forest in 1883.) Sledd, bald of pate, with a wispy red beard and pale blue watery eyes magnified by thick glasses, was "Old Slick," who seldom spied any reportable unruliness in his assigned tours of the dormitories. In class he won over fellows like Cash, Stallings, Johnson,

2. Quoted in Hobson, *South-Watching*, x.

3. Stallings is quoted in Sylvia Cheek, "Three Alumni Writers: Laurence Stallings," *Wake Forest Alumni Magazine*, 8, clipping in Morrison Papers; Edwin Holman to Joseph L. Morrison, September 20, 1965, *ibid.*

and many others by extolling a well-turned phrase and the beauties of English literature, not its minutiae. "If we turn out an occasional scholar, that will do no harm," he would say in his soft Virginia drawl, "but the real business of this place is to turn out men. If we fail in that, an army of Doctors of Philosophy will not save us." As a graduate student at Johns Hopkins University in the early 1880s he had dreamed of scholarly glory, but failing eyes had ended that. In his thirties he had published two slender volumes of verse, and he retained a fine poetic nature to the end.[4]

Like most professors of English of his time, Sledd worked confidently in the genteel tradition, extolling masterpieces—meaning the best of English and European literature—and merely nodding at American writers. And like many young moderns of his generation, Cash, in time, complained mildly that his education failed to give him an appreciation of American literature, particularly the vibrant voices of his own generation. Studying contemporary drama, Cash read the Americans Augustus Thomas and William Vaughn Moody and found them distinctly inferior to the likes of Oscar Wilde, William Butler Yeats, John Millington Synge, August Strindberg, and Anton Chekhov. One recalls Malcolm Cowley's complaint that theirs was a collegiate generation constantly reminded of the glories of other people's literature with little said about the American national genius.[5]

Soon after arriving at Wake Forest in 1916, "Skinny" Pearson, lean, balding, and armed with a Yale doctorate, had formed the Political Science Club to foster discussion of the historical and contemporary issues a college man ought to be up on. The club, open by invitation only and usually numbering about a dozen, met monthly at the professor's bachelor apartment to debate an issue. That perennial problem the "Negro question" was the topic the evening Cash was taken into the club midway through his first year. That night a student read a paper on Hinton Rowan Helper, the Tar Heel who had combined abolitionism and racism in his disturbing, prophetic book of 1857, *The Impending Crisis*. To round out the evening, "a gentleman from Alabama gave his opinion as to the proper attitude that should be shown the colored man." Such informal discussion clubs were common on southern campuses. At Chapel Hill the venerable Horace

4. Johnson, "Billy with the Red Necktie," 553; Gerald W. Johnson, "Old Slick," *Virginia Quarterly Review*, XXIV (1950), 206–207.
5. Charlotte *News*, February 7, 1937.

Williams, professor of English, had "his boys" to his house regularly to pursue philosophical and social issues. Like Cash at Wake Forest, Thomas Wolfe prized his invitation to join Williams' evening sessions.[6]

Wilbur continued his nonchalant attitude toward formal study. He was the sort of introspective, book-reading, intellectual-in-the-making Pearson hoped to challenge. The two liked each other from the start, which helped create a lively, congenial atmosphere in class and at the monthly meetings. Pearson was sure to get a rise out of Sleepy by suggesting that the "mind of a Virginian" was a tad more enlightened and aristocratic than that of a Tar Heel. The older boys, attuned to notice the twinkle in Pearson's eye, enjoyed watching Sleepy take the bait and begin arguing. Usually quiet and shy, Sleepy got excited in discussions and was voluble, even eloquent, in his pronounced piedmont drawl. His words were borne along on the wings of half-understood experiences, wide-eyed reading, and a passionate, if embryonic, desire to stand outside the mind he and Pearson hoped to probe. In truth, Sleepy was, however haltingly, beginning to go beyond his professor's understanding and talk about something grander that he called "the mind of the South."[7]

In President Poteat Wake Forest had a courageous exemplar of New South liberalism—that idealistic, perhaps even sentimental notion that social change could be effected by moderate middle-class reformers (college professors and the like) who embraced the basic assumptions of industrial capitalism, education, and white supremacy. A humane man, a man of good cheer, a product of a North Carolina tidewater plantation, Poteat was at the height of his influence as a tireless champion of social causes and what his generation called racial decency when Cash arrived in 1920. The year before, Poteat, Will Alexander, a leader in the Young Men's Christian Association (YMCA), and others, including M. Ashby Jones, had received a grant from the YMCA to found the Commission on Interracial Cooperation (CIC). Together Poteat and the others persuaded various college presidents, professors (Pearson was a member), and liberal newspaper editors to meet with them for calm consideration of the race situation. The CIC

6. *Old Gold and Black*, February 25, 1921; Edwin Holman to Joseph L. Morrison, September 20, 1965, in Morrison Papers; David Herbert Donald, *Look Homeward: A Life of Thomas Wolfe* (Boston, 1987), 54.

7. Edwin Holman to Joseph L. Morrison, September 20, 1965, in Morrison Papers; Joseph L. Morrison, *W. J. Cash, Southern Prophet: A Biography and Reader* (New York, 1967), 27–28.

issued periodic calls for racial harmony and denounced lynchings and other forms of racial violence. They hoped to undermine the "extremists"—the Bleases and Vardamans on the right and the W. E. B. DuBoises and leaders of the National Association for the Advancement of Colored People on the left. In addition, Poteat, a short, bald, portly, but robust man who frequently sported a bright red necktie, was president of the North Carolina Anti-Saloon League from 1919 to 1923 and a leader in the state's branch of the Mental Hygiene Society, an organization that worried about the reproduction of the retarded, the insane, and other socially troublesome groups. The society advocated sterilization of the feeble-minded, the insane, epileptics, the inebriate, victims of chronic contagious diseases, and the congenitally defective of any type. "It is right to save them," said Poteat the Christian evolutionist, "but it is perilous to allow them parenthood."[8]

The sea changes in manners and morals that swept across American colleges in the 1920s lapped gently along the shores of Baptist Wake Forest during Cash's stay. "Young Moderns" slipped away to strictly forbidden off-campus dances—Sleepy was known to be light on his feet, particularly after a forbidden beer or two—sported hip flasks when away from the constabulary eye of the college authorities, read Michael Arlen's naughty novels (intellectuals like Cash also savored James Branch Cabell), and heard now and then about Sigmund Freud and Karl Marx. Occasionally a genuine radical like Emmeline Pankhurst showed up via the college lecture circuit. At Wake Forest during Cash's first year, she gave a speech titled "The Woman Voter vs. Bolshevism" and impressed her listeners not as a wild-eyed suffragette, as many had warned, but "a refined, cultured little English woman with a charming personality which endears her to all who meet her."[9]

To his friends, the owlish, bookish Sleepy Cash was a lovable oddball, usually disheveled and distracted, known for his chaw of tobacco and prodigious spitting—traits and skills that impressed his male friends but severely limited his love life, which was all but nonexistent during his Wake Forest days. For fun, Sleepy and pals hitchhiked to

8. Quoted in Linder, *Poteat*, 92, 100–101; Johnson, "Billy with the Red Necktie," 551. See also Wilma Dykeman and James Stokeley, *Seeds of Southern Change: The Life of Will Alexander* (Chicago, 1962), 59–68, 102–109, 131–37. For an expression of liberal opinion by one of Cash's Wake Forest professors see C. Chilton Pearson, "Race Relations in North Carolina: A Field Study of Moderate Opinion," *South Atlantic Quarterly*, XXIII (1924), 109.

9. *Old Gold and Black*, December 10, 1920.

Raleigh to swill beer or something stronger, ogle the girls at the traveling burlesque shows, or, more properly, court the Meredith College women. Nearer campus, a meandering stream conveniently cooled many a keg of beer for Wake Forest rulebreakers like Sleepy, who liked to loll about and sip beer and philosophize about heady matters. Feeling mischievous, Cash and his buddies formed a secret fraternity during his senior year—only to be caught and expelled. But the indulgent authorities promptly readmitted them and even exempted them from final examinations. Considering Wilbur's innocence in 1920 and the limited social freedom he experienced in college, his biographer Joseph L. Morrison was surely right in concluding that "Don Juans like Wilbur Cash were fortunate in having chosen Wake Forest to help cushion the shock." [10]

Sleepy even tried out for the football team. Astonishingly, he made it, only to turn in his helmet and cleats immediately and be ridiculed playfully by the college newspaper: "The gentleman states he is a poet by birth, a dreamer by nature, and a loafer by force of habit. He feared that the rough and tumble game and the violent contact with other members of his race would darken his bright, cheerful view of life. In this case, the poet claims that he would no longer be able to write, with beautiful simplicity, his touching verses on love, maidens and pastures green. Thus a good man was lost to the cause." [11]

Indeed, Sleepy's first ventures into print were as a poet. He debuted in the college's literary magazine, *Wake Forest Student*, in the spring of his first year with a celebration of spring, which, romantic lad that he was, he equated with love and kisses. Then came "The Spirit," "Vanished Days," and "Dream Winds," each poem revealing more intense emotion than poetry, more refined feeling than evocation of feeling. He displayed the normal sensitive undergraduate's infatuation with emotive expression, but his poetic flowering released only the faintest aroma of literary talent and revealed little indication of intellectual precocity. There are, however, a few hints of unsettled feelings. The opening stanzas of "The Spirit" sound like nothing more than a young boy's warm tribute to his mother. But the concluding lines point to darker, more troubled emotions: "And then she bends to kiss me /

10. Charlotte *News*, March 23, 1937; Morrison, *W. J. Cash*, 25.
11 "Round About Town," *Old Gold and Black*, October 1, 1920.

With a smile all glad and gay / And I read the love in my mother's eyes— / But the vision fades away / Leaving me alone with shadows / And the ashes, cold and gray."[12]

"The Buddha," the last of Wilbur's seven poems, would have baffled every Cash, Hamrick, Baptist, and Methodist back in Gaffney and Cleveland County. And doubtless its last four lines would have raised an eyebrow or two down at the barber shop or on the "deacons' bench" outside the Boiling Springs Baptist Church, where Sleepy and friends used to sit after Sunday evening services. "Yes—old Sakyamuni—I can understand / Why you should care to believe / That Heaven could but be / In ceaselessly forgetting." But what was young Wilbur J. Cash, as he signed his poems and short stories, so eager to forget?[13]

Although his seven poems and three short stories were well received, Cash never became a frequent contributor or an insider at the literary magazine. He wrote no critical or historical essays or book reviews as did several of his contemporaries. Yet he was closely identified with the "literary fellows," both on campus and at nearby schools. Student editors regularly exchanged issues with other schools and noted and quoted what other student writers were saying. The Wake Forest editors exchanged issues with a few New England schools but mainly with small southern colleges. An intellectual camaraderie and an unofficial network prevailed among southerners with literary or intellectual aspirations. In nearby Meredith College Cash's critical reputation was well known. "I just hate to send our quarterly over to Wake Forest," one coed complained. "Old Sleepy Cash will tear our article to pieces."[14]

His stories, like his poetry, are slight, gloomy, more melodramatic than sad or tragic, and devoid of social comment. All three are ghost stories. "The Curse" and "The House of Hate" are tales of haunted houses with cobwebs, creaky floors, blood-stained carpets, apparitions with "hawk-like" features and sunken eyes, and the like. In these and in "The Derelict," his characters talk of revenge and death, and murders occur. Such themes might be meaningful for understanding young

12. Wilbur J. Cash, "Spring," Wake Forest Student, XL (1921), 275; "The Spirit," ibid., 310; "Vanished Days," ibid., XLI (1921), 23–24; "Dream Winds," ibid., 146; "Autumn Night," ibid., 157; "The Unanswered," ibid., XLII (1922), 1; "The Buddha," ibid., XLII (1923), 175–76.

13. Wake Forest Student, XLII (1923), 176.

14. Interview with Bea Morris, September 15, 1984.

Cash's mind had they been more developed or crafted in any original way—and if they were not the standard fare of youthful writers of meager talent. Even so, "The Curse" and "The Spirit" waltzed away with faculty prizes for the best story and the best poem of the year. The *Old Gold and Black*, the student newspaper, introduced the "new literary celebrity—one Sleepy Cash"—and pronounced "The Curse" an "exceptionally good" yarn, containing "originality and thought," rare items in the student literary magazine, the editors sniffed.[15]

In "The Derelict," a tale of a young innocent in the Congo who catches a ride aboard the ill-fated sailing vessel the "Mollie B," Cash edges closer to literary achievement. But "The Derelict," too, is a haunted house story, this time set aboard ship. In style, locale, and subject matter, the story makes clear that Cash had begun reading Joseph Conrad in earnest, a practice that would remain with him the rest of his life, shaping his style and subtly influencing his thought. The impress of Conrad's *Victory* and *Heart of Darkness* on "The Derelict" is unmistakable. Cash sets his tale in the Congo, the locale of *Heart of Darkness*, and his innocent narrator bears some imitative resemblance to the innocent but damned protagonist of *Lord Jim*. From the opening sentences of "The Derelict" on, Conrad's influence is evident: "Just a black rudderless hulk—all that is left of the once proud vessel. The plaything of the waters, it drifts along seemingly driven on and ever onward by the inexorable decree of Fate until presently it lies in the path of a sister ship, hidden by the blackness of the night or the thickness of a fog, and brings disaster to, perhaps, those very souls to whom it once meant happiness."[16]

Despite his admiration for Conrad, Cash was not yet mature enough as a writer or a thinker to create anything more than a surface imitation. Unlike Conrad, whose sea tales probe and expose white racism and the interlocking of race and power, Cash's stories were only that, stories. Indeed, they reveal little literary talent and suggest that Cash's oft-stated dream of being a writer would remain only a dream and that the power of his writing would never attain the level of Conrad's masterful, subtle peeling back of layer upon layer of prejudice and violence.

15. Wilbur J. Cash, "The Curse," *Wake Forest Student*, XL (1921), 282–88; "The House of Hate," *ibid.*, XL (1921), 388–99; "The Derelict," *ibid.*, XLI (1922), 403–15; *Old Gold and Black*, March 18, 1921.

16. Cash, "The Derelict," 403.

In any case, during his Wake Forest days Cash's heart was in the *Old Gold and Black*. And it was as a journalist, not a poet or short story writer, that Cash first shone. Initially he functioned as one of four associate editors and spent most of his time learning about making up the pages and doing odd jobs. His one signed piece, a letter to the editor written during his junior year, criticized the college's commitment to intercollegiate athletics at the expense of intramural sports, a perennial undergraduate cause he and the editors would return to again and again. Sleepy opposed the college's plan to build a new, longer field for intercollegiate sports when the old field "is exactly five feet longer than the distance covered by the longest ball 'Babe' Ruth ever slammed out."[17]

In his senior year, Cash was the sole associate editor and became actively involved in the paper, writing editorials and working closely with fellow senior Edwin Holman, the knowledgeable editor, who went on to a long career in southern journalism. Their highly literate, unsigned editorials pumped for school spirit, bemoaned the low level of culture in the South, touched on the race issue, and, occasionally, landed the young editors in hot water.[18] They were fortunate in having Professor Hubert Poteat as faculty adviser. Poteat the Younger, as he was known to several generations of students, lavished his attention on Latin and bestowed benign neglect on the young editors. While the boys got the paper out, Poteat marked papers or refreshed himself reading aloud and chuckling over some barb from W. C. Brann, the Texas iconoclast whose complete works had appeared in 1919. When a sticky editorial question arose, Poteat put down his Brann, smiled, patted the boys on the back, and pointed to the "rule of reason."[19] Poteat the Younger was a kindly, humane man. He had organized discussion groups among the students to foster an enlightened view of the Negro and introduced them to the writings of fellow New South liberals such as W. D. Weatherford and Edgar Gardner Murphy. Their writings summoned the South's "better sort" of whites to tame the roiling masses and lead the way to racial harmony. In a sense, these were safe authors; no one was recommending W. E. B. DuBois to the

17. *Old Gold and Black*, October 21, 1921; Morrison incorrectly dates this piece to Cash's first year, 1920–21 (*W. J. Cash*, 31).

18. See, for example, "The Negro Question," *Old Gold and Black*, February 3, 1922, and "The New Athletic Status," *ibid.*, March 3, 1922.

19. Edwin Holman to Joseph L. Morrison, September 20, 1965, in Morrison Papers.

young men. In *Negro Life in the South: Present Conditions and Needs*, Weatherford, as well-intentioned as any white liberal, assured whites that if treated fairly the Negro would never demand social equality.[20]

The high point in Cash's senior year came in early 1922, when he and Holman blithely chided the *Biblical Recorder*, the state's leading Baptist journal, for wringing its hands over "Jazz dancing" in the White House. The White House had heatedly denied the accusation that the Hardings had practiced or allowed any "indecent" dancing. The sharp, irreverent style and tone of the *Old Gold and Black's* editorial tut-tutting convey the fun Holman and Sleepy had composing their rejoinder to the silliness. The editor of the *Biblical Recorder* "has impressed upon all comers that he is not a follower—not even an admirer—of Terpsichore and her host of gauze clad muses, who danced and skipped upon the balmy zephyr and downy green, while Apollo, king of all dandies, performed quite creditably upon the lyre." Baptists looked on dancing as a sin, but surely, the editors declaimed, even the *Biblical Recorder* knew that it was also an art. "As we see it, Mr. Harding has not committed one of the cardinal sins . . . but, at the worst, only perpetrated a doctrinal error."[21]

"Does this represent Wake Forest?" the *Biblical Recorder* snapped. Various state newspapers commented on the teakettle tempest, sometimes gravely, usually with tongue in cheek. All the while, Sleepy and Holman moseyed around campus, chuckled at the imbecility of Baptist zealots, continued hurling quotations from Robert Ingersoll at the unamused "skys," and winked knowingly when rumor spread that the faculty was silently cheering them on. President Poteat, himself battling fundamentalists who were after his scalp, calmly invited the boys to his home for refreshments and good-naturedly reminded them that good, gentle humor rather than a bludgeon was their best weapon. From Washington, D.C., Stallings cheered the editors on.[22]

In the spring of 1922, just as Dr. Billy was defending his wayward seniors, the fundamentalists stepped up their attack. The immediate object of their scorn was Poteat's recent utterances in the *Biblical Recorder* that Christians could certainly be evolutionists. St. Paul himself

20. W. D. Weatherford, *Negro Life in the South: Present Conditions and Needs* (New York, 1915), 174.
21. Editorial, "Our Dancing President," *Biblical Recorder* (Raleigh), LXXXVII (November 16, 1921), 6; Editorial, "Dr. Johnson and the President," *Old Gold and Black*, January 27, 1922.
22. Morrison, *W. J. Cash*, 32.

had been one.[23] Poteat's critics screamed. For several years fundamentalists as far away as London, Texas, and Chicago, home of Dwight L.
Moody's evangelical-fundamentalist Moody Bible Institute, had fumed
over Poteat's championing of evolution. It was one thing for confessed
agnostics and atheists, who were beyond hope, to talk up Darwin, said
Poteat's critics, and good people knew to pay them no heed. The dangerous foes of true faith were admired religious leaders like Poteat who
had been duped by evolutionists.[24]

Leading the attack on Poteat in 1922 was the Reverend Thomas T.
Martin, a Baptist from Blue Mountain, Mississippi. This was "Hell in
the High Schools" Martin, known far and wide for his thunderous rantings denouncing the teaching of evolution and "Godlessness" in the
schools. Then J. Frank Norris, a pugnacious preacher from Texas—
who once had been accused of shooting a man and burning his own
church—and a leader of the growing World Christian Fundamentals
Association, denounced Poteat. (Not to be outdone, one Charles F.
Bluske, an antievolution zealot, challenged Poteat and any other
three scientists to meet him in a boxing ring. He would knock out all
four in less than two minutes, "proving to the Public that Scientists
are weak in mind and body.")[25]

Sensing the danger and the fun of smiting Dr. Billy's foes, the editors of the Old Gold and Black defended Poteat heartily, with Sleepy
writing a lengthy, brilliant tour de force editorial on intolerance. By
turns sarcastic, idealistic, cynical, hopeful, and irreverent, Cash pum-
meled William Jennings Bryan as the real culprit and thwacked Poteat's enemies at every turn. "The forces of intolerance are never
asleep," Cash began. He cited the Spanish Inquisition, the persecution of John Wycliffe, even the crucifixion of Christ. He invoked Darwin, Huxley, Haeckel, Emerson, and Roger Williams, the founder of
the Baptist church in America. Poteat was no more an atheist, said
Cash, than was Williams, who had been driven out of Massachusetts.
"It is a pity that the Baptist denomination, with a history made
glorious by championing, almost without exception, the cause of free-

23. William Louis Poteat, "Was Paul an Evolutionist?" *Biblical Recorder* (Raleigh), LXXXVII
(March 8, 1922), 1–2; William Louis Poteat, "May a Christian Be an Evolutionist?" *ibid.*,
LXXXVII (April 26, 1922), 3–4.

24. Linder, *Poteat*, 106–108; Ray Ginger, *Six Days or Forever? Tennessee v. John Thomas
Scopes* (New York, 1958), 39.

25. Linder, *Poteat*, 107–11; Bluske quoted, *ibid.*, 107.

dom of conscience and thought, should be so prominently identified with this pernicious effort."[26]

The real culprits were "a few self-anointed bigots" who had been emboldened by "Willie J." Bryan, who "gets hot over the question of evolution on the ground that he knows quite positively that no one ever fed peanuts through the bars of a cage to his great-great-great grandpa." Bryan knew nothing about science or the great proponents of evolution, Cash wrote, but fosters "the spirit of intolerance toward all who believe in evolution in any form, and the effort to crush liberty of thinking in the colleges." Sleepy concluded with a sledgehammer blow at the fundamentalist movement. "Conceived in the primitive slime of ignorance, it seeks to thwart and retard the march of truth and knowledge by playing upon the fears and superstitions of the credulous and the willful blindness of the prejudiced. What strange instruments does his Satanic Majesty sometimes choose to carry out his work." Such words, written three years before Bryan's appearance as the chief prosecutor at the "Monkey Trial" in Dayton, Tennessee, where John T. Scopes, a high school biology teacher, was put on trial for violating Tennessee's law banning the teaching of evolution, brought praise from several newspapers, including the Durham *Morning Herald* and the Raleigh *Times*.[27]

Two weeks later Cash editorialized that should Poteat be fired "Willie J." be named his successsor. "His brain is untainted by any of the newfangled kinds of education," and "he has steadfastly refused to find out anything about the theory of evolution lest he place his immortal soul in jeopardy." And if not Bryan, why not consider that fellow who ran a theocracy in Zion City, Illinois, Glenn Voliva, who preached, among other things, that the earth was flat.[28]

At the height of the controversy Poteat graciously and courageously invited the Reverend Amzi Clarence Dixon to campus to give the commencement address. Brother of Thomas Dixon, a graduate of Wake Forest, a powerful orator, and a renowned holy man with a lofty pulpit in London, A. C. Dixon was the scourge of evolutionists everywhere. He used the occasion of Sleepy's Commencement to blast away

26. "Intolerance," *Old Gold and Black*, April 21, 1922.
27. *Ibid.*; Linder, *Poteat*, 121.
28. "Possibilities," *Old Gold and Black*, May 5, 1922.

at "the menace of evolution."[29] John and Nannie Cash listened attentively. To them, Dixon spoke the truth, though they greatly admired
Dr. Poteat. But the great man, for all his oratorical skills, was a hollow
wind that day and "made everybody a better friend of Dr. Poteat, and
gave the institution its opportunity to show its catholicity." Wilbur J.
Cash, robed and solemn for his graduation, paid the Cleveland County
native no mind and left with an even greater contempt for puffed-up
parsons.[30]

For all their bluster, Dr. Billy's adversaries failed, at least for the
moment. A *Biblical Recorder* poll revealed widespread support for Poteat among alumni. A special investigative committee appointed by
the college trustees reaffirmed that Poteat—the man Mencken called
"the liaison officer between Baptist revelation and human progress"—
was sound in the faith.[31]

At Wake Forest Cash came under the sway of H. L. Mencken,
whose lashing strictures against the South influenced, or infuriated,
Cash's generation of southerners. Cash read Mencken's monthly, the
Smart Set, and then, from 1924 on, the more sophisticated and classier
American Mercury. From the moment he read the debunking masterpiece "The Sahara of the Bozart" in Mencken's *Prejudices* (1920) Cash
was an unabashed Menckenite. What many others in Dixie took as
South-baiting in Mencken's many tirades about the low state of "Kul-
ture" in the South, Sleepy took as bracing realism. Mencken's diatribes against fundamentalism, Ku Kluxery, bigotry, and southern
narrowness pushed Cash toward intellectual liberation. In place of
Thomas Dixon and Thomas Nelson Page, Mencken touted Conrad
and Cabell and was probably responsible for turning Cash to these authors. Doubtless, given the appeal Conrad and Cabell had for many
aspiring southern writers, Cash (like Faulkner and Wolfe) would have
found his way to them in time, but Cash's enthusiasms were so close to
Mencken's and Cash's prose style so Menckenian at this time that
Cash sounded like a cotton-patch Mencken.[32]

29. *Biblical Recorder* (Raleigh), LXXXV (June 16, 1920), 4–5; Willard Gatewood, *Preachers, Pedagogues and Politicians: The Evolution Controversy in North Carolina, 1920–1927* (Chapel Hill, 1966), 38.
30. Quoted in Linder, *Poteat*, 120.
31. Quoted in Gatewood, *Preachers, Pedagogues*, 30–31; Linder, *Poteat*, 118.
32. Fred Hobson, *Serpent in Eden: H. L. Mencken and the South* (1974; rpr. Baton Rouge, 1978), 111–20.

Intoxicated by Mencken's wonderfully extravagant style and his diatribes against the low state of southern culture, Cash in his senior year let loose with a roar of his own against the shallowness of "North Carolina culture." The truth of Mencken's charges against the South could not be denied, Cash began. "It is a desert—a barren waste, so far as the development of culture and the nature of the beaux arts are concerned, and North Carolina comes near being the dreariest spot in the whole blank stretch. In all the long years of its history the State hasn't produced a half dozen writers who might, by any sort of standard, be called worthwhile. Worse—it hasn't even raised up readers for books that others have written." The South talked up its mills and material progress, but what about its mental and spiritual barrenness? And nowhere was the region's narrowness and superficiality greater, said Cash, than among college students, who contented themselves with a quick skim of important books and read trashy novels and junk magazines. "Babbitt calls up memories of the crankshaft bearings on paw's old Ford." Evelyn Scott's new novel, *If Winter Comes* (one of Cash's favorites), was thought to be about the coal shortage, and Carl Sandburg's poetry was "plain Greek." The following week, responding to a flurry of dissenting letters, Cash hit back at the philistines, noting that many listed *Tarzan* and *Wild West Magazine* as their favorite reading.[33]

How emancipated was Sleepy Cash? Joseph L. Morrison repeats a story that when Cash went to Valparaiso University in 1919, a Negro sat down beside him only to be turned away rudely. W. J. Cash was not "about to sit with a nigger." Nor would he as long as he lived, says Morrison. Cash's friends, however, including some who knew him well in 1919, find the story difficult if not impossible to square with the young man they remember. But suppose it is true. It was another era, when racism honeycombed his culture and ingrained the etiquette of racial segregation in everyone. Cash would have been a truly extraordinary person in those times had he been completely emancipated from racist behavior and language. He was a teenager in 1919, far from home, where blacks did not sit down beside whites in a public place. Perhaps Wilbur Cash acted rudely out of some instinctive fear or out of bravado, needing to impress someone (even himself) in an alien en-

33. *Old Gold and Black*, February 13, 20, 1922.

vironment. Probably every white southerner of his generation had a racial experience and a horrified response similar to Cash's. At Wellesley College in 1921, eighteen-year-old Virginia Durr, a freshman from Alabama, was seated at dinner next to a Negro girl. "My God, I nearly fell over dead," Durr remembered. "I couldn't believe it. I just absolutely couldn't believe it. . . . I promptly got up, marched out of the room, went upstairs, and waited for the head of the house to come. . . . I told her that I couldn't possibly eat at the table with a Negro girl." Durr, later a civil rights activist, grudgingly relented when the college officials stood firm, but she never befriended the black girl. But Durr's reaction was nothing compared to young Thomas Wolfe's outrage in 1923 when he was arrested in Greenville, South Carolina, and, according to one version of the story, placed in a jail cell with a Negro. Wolfe, who would never outgrow his racism, was so infuriated that he physically assaulted the officer in charge. The shock Wolfe, Durr, and Cash experienced was so common that Gerald W. Johnson explored it in 1924 in Mencken's *American Mercury*, saying, that "the Southerner will not permit the Negro to sit beside him in a theatre or a public conveyance" because "most white Southerners have attained a standard of civilization at which a bath is a matter of routine, or reasonably frequent occurrence, and most Negroes have not."[34]

Under Poteat, a liberal who never challenged segregation, Wake Forest College was an island of racial paternalism. Thomas Dixon was a frequent visitor. Poteat kept a fine bird dog, and Dixon's visits were usually the occasion for some good quail hunting. Poteat's participation in the Commission on Interracial Cooperation was well known, as was Professor Pearson's work with the North Carolina branch.[35] At the all-white college in Cash's day everyone loved Tom Jeffries, its "old-timey" black janitor. Everyone from Dr. Billy to the most stoop-shouldered old grad to the newest freshman knew and loved "Dr." Tom. He had been born in slavery days and had been at Wake Forest for over

34. Morrison, *W. J. Cash*, 21; interviews with Harriet Doar, September 7, 1984, Erma Drum, August 30, 1984, and Charles A. McKnight, September 15, 1984; Virginia Durr, *Outside the Magic Circle: The Autobiography of Virginia Foster Durr*, ed. Hollinger F. Barnard with a Foreword by Studs Terkel (Tuscaloosa, 1985), 56–58. In Germany Virginia Durr's future husband, Clifford Durr, another future civil rights advocate, felt "outraged" at the sight of black soldiers who seemed to him to be acting in an uppity manner. See John A. Salmond, *The Conscience of a Lawyer: Clifford J. Durr and American Civil Liberties, 1899–1975* (Tuscaloosa, 1990), 29–30; Donald, *Look Homeward*, 106; Gerald W. Johnson, "The South Takes the Offensive," *American Mercury*, II (1924), 76.

35. Linder, *Poteat*, 55.

forty years when Cash arrived. "Dr." Tom worked continuously—and never seemed to tire. He loved everyone. At college functions, he showed up in a cutaway coat and was often given a part in the formal program. Folks loved hearing installments of "Dr." Tom's philosophy; it put them in mind of Uncle Remus. Old grads remembered his words of wisdom, like the time at a watermelon cutting when he expounded on the fine qualities of the Wake Forest men to a group of young ladies: "'I just wan to admin' de young ladies here dat any of you dat gets a Wake Fores' boy sho' will get a prolific enterprise.'"[36]

In 1922 Cash was probably a racial paternalist. Under his editorship the *Old Gold and Black* praised Poteat's work with the CIC and, in praising his paternalism, reiterated the main points of New South liberalism. A long editorial on the "Negro question," lauded Poteat's view "as a true solution of a vital question" and warned blacks—never mind that few blacks ever read the Wake Forest student newspaper—not to listen to those like DuBois, "whose policy is to wage bitter and aggressive war against the White race and their principles." The editorial repeated the familiar "we-know-the-Negro-best" litany and expressed the comfortable assumption that Negroes should (and would) be given the vote "in time" by whites, who would know when the Negro had proved himself capable of exercising the ballot intelligently. In the meantime, blacks should keep in mind that the white man "does not intend for political equality to pave the way for social equality."[37]

Did Cash write this editorial? Could these threatening, smug, even mean-spirited words have been written by W. J. Cash, who would one day deeply criticize as shallow and self-serving the creed of New South liberalism and reject the assumptions of white superiority? The language, the diction, and the style do not sound like Cash: "The average Negro still retains the instincts and characteristics of the savage stage, from which he is barely three hundred years removed. Of course, these instincts of the jungle are covered over somewhat by the contact with White civilization." Yet Holman was confident in his memory that Cash wrote this editorial. Cash worked closely with Holman and practically worshiped Poteat, who symbolized a benign, humane con-

36. Quoted, *ibid.*, 86–87. For a contemporary view see "'Dr.' Tom," *Old Gold and Black*, April 21, 1921.
37. "The Negro Question," *Old Gold and Black*, February 3, 1922.

science in an era of savagery. The thoughts expressed in the editorial were reiterations of what Poteat and the paternalists said—and they were considered benign men by moderates and radicals by reactionary racists. For young Cash to have turned his back on Poteat's brand of decency, to have called it into question, would have required an extraordinary intellectual and psychological emancipation from his own time. That is probably asking too much of a twenty-two-year-old from the racist culture of Gaffney, South Carolina, even if he was the young man who would one day write *The Mind of the South*, a cri de coeur from someone who did as much as anyone ever has to shed "light over a darkling land."

Sleepy learned a great deal while at Wake Forest, probably more from his classes than he let on or his marks indicated. It was not so much what Dr. Billy or his professors said as how they said it. They were rational, idealistic, moral. They were unpretentious embodiments of Emerson's notion of the American Scholar as "man thinking." Their way of looking at things was critical, but not in an angry, denunciatory way—an ever-present, irrepressible twinkle in Dr. Billy's eyes "usually defeated his best efforts to look solemn," said Gerald W. Johnson. Poteat and his hand-picked professors embodied the Victorian notion that thinking was an ethical act, at one with the Bible and with the white South. Although Cash in time deliberately moved away from the optimistic social and racial assumptions of his mentors, he never rejected their tacit position that thinking was an ethical act of moral courage. And to the end, Dr. Billy and the rest symbolized humane, critical intelligence for Cash, as they did for generations of Wake Forest graduates. "Wake Forest was a lush, green pasture for him because of the stimulating, liberal atmosphere—ready and waiting to be inhaled by the students. A few of them merely sniffed it, but most of them gulped it. And nobody gulped more abundantly than 'Sleepy' Cash."[38]

38. Edwin Holman to Joseph L. Morrison, September 20, 1965, in Morrison Papers.

3 / Years Shrouded in Shadows

The postcollege years in Cash's life are shrouded in shadows. The outlines of his life are discernible—what he did, when, and where—but seldom reveal why. Little else from his graduation in 1922 through most of the decade can be known, particularly the thoughts and feelings he would later pour into his great book. He kept no diary then or ever. He hated to write letters and seldom did; none survive from the mid-1920s, when he lived away from home. The stray bits and pieces of evidence available suggest that he suffered through aimless years, characterized by nervousness and depression and stalled attempts to write something important. His stern self-consciousness of his limitations haunted him. While many of his generation—according to the received wisdom—indulged themselves happily in the revolution in manners and morals, Wilbur Joseph Cash searched desperately for himself and found instead recurring melancholia.

After a summer working the night shift at his father's hosiery mill in Boiling Springs for the going wage of twenty cents an hour, Cash returned to Wake Forest and enrolled in the college's law school. The decision was probably his father's. Wilbur had never evinced the slightest interest in being a lawyer—just the opposite. "I don't want to be a lawyer," he told his father, "you have to lie too much." Wilbur had one interest in life and that was writing, but in the summer of 1922 he had difficulty convincing his father (or himself, one suspects) that he knew how to go about "becoming a writer." At least at Wake Forest he could drift around to meetings of Doc Pearson's Political Science Club and, better, continue working on the *Old Gold and Black*. So he went to law school. He treated his classes with his customary polite nonchalance, though he seems to have enjoyed the lectures on Blackstone by one of the school's revered teachers, Professor N. Y. Gulley. He attended several evening sessions at Pearson's home and was listed as editor of the newspaper, though there is little indication that he did much writing or editorial work. But it does seem certain that torts and contracts did not engage his energy or attention. At the end of the year he returned Blackstone to the shelf, convinced more than ever that practicing law would be the "dullest of professions," and applied for and got a job for the fall teaching English at Georgetown College in Kentucky.[1]

But first, that summer the Charlotte *Observer* had an opening for a reporter. The job was temporary, just what he needed, and would give him an opportunity to write. It was certainly preferable to living in Boiling Springs and working for his father. He had seen enough of mill people, anyway. He was, as he later confessed, "a thorough Bourbon in my attitude toward all these people—and flatly in favor of putting down strikes with the bayonet." But the callow young man's views regarding workers' rights, based on his father's paternalistic treatment of his workers, were soon tested. In late August, when he was preparing to leave for Kentucky, a strike erupted at the Highland Park Mill in north Charlotte, one of four owned by the large C. W. Johnston chain.[2]

In late July, Y. A. Young, a forty-three-year-old employee who had started to work at the mill at age nine, was fired without an explanation. In his thirty-four years with the company he had earned a reputation as a good worker, as evidenced by several promotions. But he had also become active in the Charlotte Central Labor Union and had talked up the union at the Highland Park Mill. He had recently been quoted in a union publication as saying that the mill's newly hired "social workers" had been brought in to "distract" workers from joining the union, which the managers angrily refused to recognize. Soon several other workers were summarily fired, including a mother and daughter and two women in their early twenties who had worked at the mill since they were young children. All, including Young, his wife and six children, and one young woman who was the sole support

1. Elva Gheen, "John W. Cash," *Cleveland Times* (Shelby, N.C.), August 14, 1964; "Editorial Notes," *American Mercury*, XXIV (1931), xxxii; Joseph L. Morrison, *W. J. Cash, Southern Prophet: A Biography and Reader* (New York, 1967), 34.

2. W. J. Cash to Alfred A. Knopf, author's form, April 29, 1936, in Joseph L. Morrison Papers, Southern Historical Collection, University of North Carolina, Chapel Hill.

of her aged, infirm mother, were told to move out of their mill houses within a week, an edict which a local judge upheld. With rumors swirling of an impending sympathy strike, a citizens group, including the president of the Chamber of Commerce, formed to act as an intermediary. But management refused to meet with any group or to explain its actions. When pressed in early August by the Charlotte *News*, the superintendent "flatly refused" to offer any explanation. He would speak "when he was ready" and "without solicitation."[3]

After several additional firings, on August 21 a majority of the workers walked out. The company refused to make any concessions to the workers, hired new hands, and welcomed back all nonunion workers. Strike leaders denounced the mill for "hiring only old men, women and children" but had to admit that some of their members were crossing the picket lines. Two days later, the strike was broken. All of those originally fired were banned from the plant, the eviction notices were carried out, and business returned to normal. Union leaders tried to put a brave face on their defeat, saying they had shown management that the workers were far from content and fully capable of striking.[4]

The unrest of August, 1923, an event of little moment in the South's labor history, left its mark on young Wilbur Cash. He had been assigned to cover the strike by a crusty, cynical editor who embodied the Charlotte *Observer*'s hearty dislike of unions and hostility to all strikes. As a result, while the livelier evening paper, the Charlotte *News*, gave the strike daily coverage, including bold front-page headlines, and displayed considerable sympathy for the workers, the *Observer* provided scant coverage, reporting little of the union's point of view, and relegating the strike to the inside pages. The strike made the front page only after it had failed, a failure the *Observer* editorially attributed to lack of support from the workers and dissatisfaction in the union ranks.[5]

It is unlikely that Cash, a rookie summer reporter, wrote any of the *Observer*'s accounts of the strike. But in the process of seeking the facts, Cash attended the strikers' meeting at which the workers voted overwhelmingly to refuse to remain on the job. When management

3. Charlotte *News*, August 12, 1923.
4. *Ibid.*, August 25, 1923.
5. *Ibid.*, August 12, 14, 17, 18, 21, 22, 24, 25, 1923; Charlotte *Observer*, August 14, 18, 25, 1923.

agreed to meet the press, Cash went to the mill with the other reporters to interview the superintendent. To Cash, the mill manager appeared to be a hard-hearted man who made it clear that because management provided jobs and a place to live, it was completely free to
dictate terms. If Wilbur was not quite a full-blown Bourbon reactionary when the summer began, in Charlotte in 1923 he detected the
iron fist in that velvet glove of paternalism the owners always presented to the world and to themselves. The conduct of the mill owners
shocked him. He also came to a new awareness of and a deeply felt
sympathy for the lot of common workers. Never again would he talk of
putting down strikes with bayonets. He saw, too, as his later writings
indicate, that the common mill worker, usually one step removed
from his mountain or country individualism, had little sense of worker
solidarity and held few, if any, of the values necessary for strong unionism. He saw little during that summer of 1923 to alter his perception
of the incorrigible individualism of mill hands or to convince him that
for them class consciousness was anything more than a frail reed in a
storm.

Another grim reminder of a harsh fact of southern life occurred in
the summer of 1923. On August 17, two blacks were brutally lynched
on the same day in Georgia, a record, even for the South, the *Observer* noted, expressing chagrin and shame. The *News*, willing to sen-
sationalize the death of one of the victims, headlined the ghastly
events on the front page: "Georgians String up Negro Fiend." There
followed a graphic account of how the "fiend" had been taken by a
mob of nearly a hundred to the front yard of the woman he had al-
legedly attacked. There the poor wretch's body was riddled with bullets while children and the avenged woman looked on approvingly.
The number of lynchings had declined dramatically from the prewar
years, but there were enough ghastly reminders of the rule of rope and
shotgun that Cash could not escape knowing that the South might
resort to barbarism at any time.[6]

In September Cash packed his bags and set out for Georgetown,
Kentucky, to instruct collegians in the rules of English usage and the
beauties of English prose masterpieces. Such, at least, was his charge
when he took up his duties at Georgetown College, a small Baptist
school. Apparently the old hands on the faculty, bored to death after

6. Charlotte *Observer*, August 18, 1923; Charlotte *News*, August 17, 1923.

years of browbeating sophomores into reading and writing, delighted in telling the greenhorn professor what a mistake he had made to choose teaching. "I remember with terror to this day the warnings issuing from the elder members of the faculty when I once upon a time briefly and ingloriously set up for a college instructor," he recalled some years later. Cash's experiences as a professor were apparently thoroughly unpleasant from the start. Few of his students cared about literature or, if they cared, had the ability to master it. Imagine the terror the shy, moody Cash felt as he stood before such students and labored to explain the meaning of a given piece of literature or why nouns and verbs should agree. Or imagine Cash, himself an avid learner but never a conventional student, sitting quietly marking English A themes or enduring faculty meetings or teas where the dean of students held forth on good manners. Cash shuddered to think he had to force someone to read his favorites, Conrad or Shakespeare. Anyway, his heart was in writing, and forcing a youngster to write was not for W. J. Cash. He remembered the experience as a year in purgatory at a "jerkwater" college. "There I lost such illusions as had survived college," he told Mencken, "suffered an incipient nervous breakdown, and discovered that I had no business in a sectarian institution."[7]

One bright spot in that purgatory year was Peggy Ann, a freshman. She was petite, pretty, and demure. She had, she told him breezily, set her heart on a career as an actress. Always a romantic in his thoughts about women, Cash idolized her and could not stop thinking about her. His moonstruck looks whenever she entered the room betrayed his feelings immediately. Soon they were ignoring the traditional college code prohibiting professors and students from undue fraternizing and familiarity. Wilbur was in love. And he loved the feeling. To his naive mind, he was the pursuer: that had to be true, he assumed, because she was beautiful and purity itself, and he was so stammeringly awkward. They held long, earnest conversations. At first they talked about his likes in books and her reading—she was precociously aware of social issues and strongly convinced that the arms merchants had helped bring on the late war. They talked about her other college courses and his dreams of becoming a writer. Later, slyly holding hands, they talked about more personal matters.

7. *Charlotte News*, October 23, 1937; Morrison, *W. J. Cash*, 37, 38; "Editorial Notes," *American Mercury*, xxxii.

At the end of the year, just before they were to leave for the summer, a balmy late afternoon was too perfect for the repressed young lovers to resist. With a blanket under one arm, a picnic basket in hand, and a bottle of wine neatly hidden from sight, they strolled to nearby secluded woods away from the knowing eyes of students and the disapproving frowns of the college authorities. By evening the weather had turned chilly, but romance and wine had worked their magic. Inhibitions melted. Freshman and young instructor gave way to their pent-up passions. Almost. The young instructor could not perform the manly deed. Mortification overcame him, and he apologized profusely. Pretty Peggy repeatedly assured him that everything was fine, but nothing she could say nullified his chagrin. They packed up and went back to school, said their embarrassed good-byes, and parted a few days later.[8]

The failed Don Juan would never be the same again. That disastrous evening haunted him for years; he never completely recovered his confidence with women or in himself. For years he was plagued by the terrifying fear that his "nervous condition" was far more serious than anybody knew, that he was sexually impotent. One could hardly imagine a more crushing blow to Cash's sensitive, romantic psyche. Moreover, in the South, impotence was not just a problem, it was an utter disgrace. Someone who was impotent was not a man. Once the word got out, his impotence might even be talked about in polite circles. And in those places where menfolk gathered, sexual prowess (admittedly always exaggerated) was the mark of a true man. Every southern boy, even Baptist boys, had heard crude jokes and stories about men who could not satisfy their women. A disappointed newlywed could count on everyone's sympathy, including that of the divorce court judge, should her husband prove incapable of performing sexually. So great was Cash's shame that he suffered an "incipient nervous breakdown."[9]

Nothing went right for W. J. Cash that year. He plunged into writing a novel, piling up pages daily between meeting classes and dreaming about Peggy Ann. He was serious; he wanted to produce a real

8. Katherine Grantham Rogers to Joseph L. Morrison, in Morrison Papers; Charlotte *News*, May 2, 1937.

9. "Editorial Notes," *American Mercury*, xxxii. For a discussion of the roots of the southern attitude toward impotence, see Bertram Wyatt-Brown, *Southern Honor: Ethics and Behavior in the Old South* (New York, 1982), 289–91.

novel, not mere puffs of sentimentality of the Thomas Nelson Page–
Thomas Dixon variety. Nor did he, apparently, wish to imitate the
naughty tales of fantasy James Branch Cabell spun out in such novels
as *Jurgen* and *The Rivet in Grandfather's Neck*, two of Cash's favorites.
In short, the southern literary tradition, as it stood in 1923, offered
little to commend itself or to nourish someone of Cash's temperament
and seriousness. As a result, he tried to model himself on his first and
great love, Joseph Conrad, specifically the masterpiece *Lord Jim*. He
labored mightily, but to no avail. Halfway through he concluded "dis-
mally" that "Conrad knew more of life and the English language than
I knew." His second-rate strivings were fit only for the fireplace. If he
showed it to anyone, even Peggy Ann, there is no record of it, and so
we have only Cash's despairing appraisal.[10]

Cash did not return to Georgetown College for a second year. He
never explained why, beyond saying that he and sectarianism did not
mix. The college archives say nothing of his year there. Later he said
he left the college with a bleak view of students and the conviction
"that only a handful have any genuine interest in the ideas that begin
to circulate in some of them, and the great mass is satisfied with football, rah-rah, and Commerce A." The students were not totally, or
even primarily, to blame, Cash observed some years later. The real
culprits were the professors of literature, who had "no spontaneous lik-
ing" of books and ideas and did not have the minds to understand
what they read. He was a gentle man, he said rhetorically some years
later when reminded of his stint as a college instructor, but there were
days when he favored hanging most literary academics for what they
had done to literature and students' minds.[11]

Still, he had to make a living, and the fall of 1924 found him back
home again in North Carolina, teaching at the Hendersonville School
for Boys in tiny Hendersonville, just west of Boiling Springs. That
must have been torture for Cash, given his intellect, sensibilities, and
passions. His sojourn as a high school teacher convinced him "that
the average Southern high school graduate is about as well informed as
an inferior grammar school product should be, that he can't think,

10. Application for a John Simon Guggenheim Memorial Fellowship, October, 1936, in
Morrison Papers.
11. W. J. Cash to Howard Odum, November 13, 1929, in Howard Odum Papers, Southern
Historical Collection, University of North Carolina, Chapel Hill; Charlotte *News*, March 8,
1936.

and that, worse, incompetent teachers have made it pretty certain that he will never think." His experiences led him to believe that fully "90% of our high school graduates emerge to graduation with a total and permanent immunity to William Shakespeare and John Milton, an intense persuasion that all poetry is a terrific pain in the neck, and, in brief, an aversion to everything so unfortunate as to be listed in the manuals of literary history." The remaining 10 percent, having been forced to study "literature" in college, graduate asking only "that they may never hear of it again." [12]

The dullness of his colleagues and students, combined with the tedium of life in tiny Hendersonville (where he found no Peggy Ann), left him ample time to read. He kept a sharp eye on Mencken's stunning magazine, the American Mercury, brand new in 1924, and dreamed of what he could write that would interest Mencken. Cash's literary companions, to whom he turned throughout his life, included his enduring favorites—Voltaire, Shakespeare, Pepys, and Cervantes, whose Don Quixote he especially treasured, as did his contemporary William Faulkner in Mississippi. Cash valued the essayist William Hazlitt, Homer, Chaucer, Rabelais, Verlaine, the romantic poets Heine and Keats, the historian Gibbon, and a host of classical writers. Among the moderns his favorites were, after Conrad, Dreiser, Dostoevsky, Hardy, Willa Cather, and Cabell. At some point in the 1920s Cash patiently worked his way through Oswald Spengler's massive, bleak Decline of the West, Henry Adams' Mont Saint Michel and Chartres and The Education of Henry Adams, and Nietzsche's Thus Spake Zarathustra. Except for Cabell, no southern writer, past or present, seems to have gained his favor at this time. [13]

When he was not reading he was writing. (His fine disdain for schoolmastering left him time to follow his muse.) Once again, he tried to write fiction. This time his models were Dostoevsky, Dreiser, and Hardy, and sometime during his two years of teaching Cash attempted novels in the style of each. Again he judged his productions to be a disastrous failure. Again, he consigned them to the flames. What intense agony Cash felt staring point-blank at his own deficiencies before hurling months of work into the fire. He could not remem-

12. Charlotte News, March 8, 1936.
13. Ibid., December 22, 1935, June 28, 1936, September 5, 1937, March 27, April 3, 1938.

ber a time, he would say over and over, when he did not intend "to be a writer" and "above everything to be a novelist."[14]

But such was not to be, not in May, 1925, when he bade a final farewell to teaching and embarked on what he hoped would be a career in journalism. He moved to Chicago, worked as a free-lance journalist, then joined the Chicago *Post*. He lived in Chicago about a year, shivering through the winter but leaving no footprints in the snow for his biographer. Then in mid-1926 he returned to Charlotte, where he signed on with the Charlotte *News* in a capacity that appears not to have been very rewarding or memorable. In a later recounting of his career, he said only that he worked for the paper in 1926. During these years he apparently received several offers of better positions with newspapers in Cleveland and New York, but "increasing ill-health" disabled him for strenuous journalism. He had experienced a problem with hyperthyroidism in the early part of the decade and even during his college years had been plagued with a discomforting and slightly protruding goiter that forced him to keep his shirt collars unbuttoned. The condition subsided in the mid-1920s, along with the choking coughing spasms that had plagued him as early as his high school days. The glandular swelling had almost disappeared by 1925, but "it had left behind it a marked nervous erethism," he later explained. Always a moody, "sensitive" boy, he was now a frequently irritable adult, battling physical problems and psychological demons and unable to concentrate on such a serious task as writing a novel in the manner of the masters.[15]

"In the four years in which I was connected with newspapers," Cash recalled of the period from 1925 through 1928, "I attempted no creative writing, save for a subjective novel which I destroyed without submitting to any publisher, a blood-and-thunder romance which I disposed of in the same fashion, and two short stories," which he submitted to *Harper's* and the *American Mercury*. The latter, under Mencken's bold editorship, regularly published stories by promising southerners from Faulkner to Julia Peterkin and incisive, hard-hitting essays by Gerald W. Johnson and others, including the Raleigh jour-

14. Application for a John Simon Guggenheim Memorial Fellowship, October, 1936; W. J. Cash to Alfred A. Knopf, author's form, April 29, 1936, both in Morrison Papers.

15. W. J. Cash to Alfred A. Knopf, author's form, April 8, 1940; application for a John Simon Guggenheim Memorial Fellowship, October 20, 1932, in Morrison Papers.

nalist Nell Battle Lewis. But Cash had no luck placing any of his stories. He admired Johnson, who was almost a regular in Mencken's magazine, but Cash was so enthralled with the goal of becoming a "creative writer" that he was not yet ready to consider other forms of writing.[16]

There was enough going on in North Carolina alone to elicit essays from Cash and fill the pages of Mencken's magazine and several others besides. The state, awash with religious revivals in the 1920s, was the home of activist fundamentalists, a point Gerald W. Johnson had made in "Saving Souls" with telling effect in the very first issue of the American Mercury. Stomping, arm-waving, soul-saving "fishers of men" such as Baxter F. McLendon, affectionately known as "Cyclone Mack," the sensational Mordecai F. Ham, and the even greater ex-horter Billy Sunday found Tar Heels eager to rebuke the devil and his crowd, notably the modernists and the evolutionists. Ham was so wildly popular in North Carolina that he was invited back time and again to thunder at the evolutionists. Braced by such preaching and their own convictions, Tar Heel antievolutionists remained on the attack. Having suffered setbacks in their assaults on Wake Forest and the denominational colleges, the opponents of Darwinism had by 1923 trained their guns on the publicly supported schools. Governor Cameron Morrison, an orthodox Presbyterian and prominent in attendance at Mordecai Ham's tent-meeting revivals, attacked several biology textbooks used in the schools, singled out the University of North Carolina as a hotbed of godlessness, and continued to revile evolutionists after leaving the governor's office in 1925.[17]

In early 1925, Representative Davis Scott Poole, an antievolutionist member of the state legislature, introduced a bill similar to Tennessee's infamous "Monkey Law" making it illegal to teach anything in the public schools contrary to the orthodox Christian view of creation. Poole, who said he had read the infamous Origin of Species and had won his seat the previous year by denouncing Darwin, immediately introduced the appropriate restrictive bill. What had previously been a sectarian battle, mainly among the Baptists, thus moved

16. Fred C. Hobson, Jr., Serpent in Eden: H. L. Mencken and the South (1974; rpr. Baton Rouge, 1978), 80–120, 223–31.

17. Gerald W. Johnson, "Saving Souls," American Mercury, I (1924), 364–68; Willard B. Gatewood, Jr., Preachers, Pedagogues and Politicians: The Evolution Controversy in North Carolina, 1920–1927 (Chapel Hill, 1966), 40–46.

to the public arena. The debate over the Poole Bill galvanized the liberal forces in the state to take a stand. Unlike Tennessee's timid critics of antievolutionists, Tar Heel defenders of academic freedom rallied to their cause. Cash's hero, William Louis Poteat, spoke out forcefully. But because the issue was public education, Harry W. Chase, president of the University of North Carolina at Chapel Hill, became the field marshal in the war against the Poole Bill. The embattled Chase walked bravely into the state legislature and delivered a stunning defense of freedom of speech to the assembled solons. The major newspapers in the state closed ranks behind him. Only the Charlotte *Observer* took the other side and blamed the controversy on those "high brow professors" who preferred "to stick by the monkey" rather than the Good Book. In Raleigh, Nell Battle Lewis did Mencken one better in her caustic attacks on the antievolutionists in the *News and Observer*. During the hottest moments of the debate, Lewis published a weekly quiz on evolution, awarding to each week's winner a copy of Hendrik van Loon's *Tolerance*. The Poole Bill went down to defeat, 67 to 46.[18]

None of this debate was lost on young Wilbur Cash, sitting in Hendersonville trying to fend off depression and vainly trying to write Dostoevskian and Dreiserian novels. In just a few years, when he broke into print in Mencken's magazine, Cash heaped abuse on Cameron Morrison, the antievolutionists, and the reactionary attitudes of the Charlotte *Observer*. Later, in *The Mind of the South*, he praised Poteat, Gerald W. Johnson, Nell Battle Lewis, Chase, and his successor, Frank Porter Graham. They were men and women "of native good sense and good will," who spoke for, and touched, the best part of the southern mind.[19]

Cash was far from sanguine about the defeat of the Poole Bill. Immediately on the heels of the vote in Raleigh, the Mecklenburg County Board of Education authorized administrators to remove all "questionable books" from local libraries and banned the teaching of evolution or "'anything that brings into question . . . the inspiration of the Bible.'" In Charlotte and Durham, superintendents and school principals, faithful to their own religious feelings and alert to public opinion, introduced voluntary school courses in Bible study. In Ten-

18. Gatewood, *Preachers, Pedagogues*, 125–46; Charlotte *Observer* quoted, *ibid.*, 140, 160–61; Ray Ginger, *Six Days or Forever? Tennessee v. John Thomas Scopes* (New York, 1958), 1–7.

19. W. J. Cash, *The Mind of the South* (1941; rpr. New York 1969), 348–50.

nessee several communities vied with each other to be the first to fer-
ret out and indict a miscreant teacher. Dayton, a sleepy hamlet, won
and indicted, tried, and convicted John T. Scopes, a high school biology teacher, for teaching evolution. The Dayton "Monkey Trial," fea-
turing Clarence Darrow for the defense and William Jennings Bryan as
special prosecuting attorney, attracted national attention, most of it
ridicule, and made Dayton and Bryan synonymous with stupidity.[20]

The events of 1925 confirmed for Cash that the South was a backward-looking, narrowly religious, antimodern folk culture that could
tolerate no questioning of its basic ideas. When he wrote *The Mind of
the South* and coined the phrase "savage ideal" to explain the South's
fundamental intolerance, he pointed not only to the infamous Scopes
trial but also to the intensity of the antievolution sentiment. "Having
observed it at close range," he said, "I have no doubt at all that it had
the active support and sympathy of the overwhelming majority of the
people." And remembering the movement generated in Charlotte to
deny library appropriations to schools that refused to buckle under to
the fundamentalists, Cash wrote that "the anti-evolutionist organizations were everywhere closely associated with those others which quite
explicitly were engaged in attempting to wipe out all the new knowledge in the schools, to clear all modern books out of the libraries."[21]

His summers in Boiling Springs and his year with the Charlotte
News in 1926 brought daily reminders that religion permeated his
world. When he was home, Wilbur was expected to attend services
with his parents at the Boiling Springs Baptist Church. And to show
that he was sociable and not uppity, he was to join the "young folks"
after evening services and sit with them on the nearby "young deacons'" bench, situated under the sprawling oak trees. There, young
men and women (in groups, of course) were to have polite conversation and review the main points of the sermon, particularly if the
preacher had delivered a real "soul-saving" message, the sort, say, that
Billy Sunday or Mordecai Ham or other traveling evangelists delivered
in their periodic visits to the piedmont. Billy Sunday's last-minute decision in January, 1925, to squeeze in one day of preaching in Shelby
galvanized the community. Because he would preach on Monday
morning, the public schools were closed. The great preacher had con-

20. Quoted in Gatewood, *Preachers, Pedagogues*, 149; Ginger, *Six Days or Forever?* 92–189.
21. Cash, *Mind of the South*, 346, 347.

cluded his highly publicized revival in Charlotte, where he had promised to go to New York City and "skin that modernist crowd." Shelby and contingents from Boiling Springs were not about to let the great man and his entourage down. Plain folk and city fathers crowded the steps of Shelby's First Baptist Church hours before the doors opened, and three thousand people filled the auditorium to overflowing.[22]

Articles on religion regularly dotted the pages of the local newspapers, reminding folks that church membership or attendance was up or down (it was usually up) or that the Sunday School classes conducted by the town's leading citizens were always packed. Local ministers conducted their own annual tent-meeting revivals, attracting several thousand each evening, as did the Reverend Zeno Wall of Shelby's First Baptist Church in May, 1926. When the *Cleveland Star* ran an essay contest in late 1926 on Cleveland County's biggest needs, "better county roads" narrowly edged out a desire for "more old-time religion," followed by a hope for manufacturing and "more religious citizens" and "better Sunday Schools."[23]

In the piedmont good folks knew what was decent, and they luxuriated in the knowledge that public opinion (and police power) was on their side. No one, apparently, was upset when Tony Porcellini, a Shelby "ice cream salesman," according to the *Star*, was set straight on how to raise his daughter. The story had gotten around town that the youngster had been mistreated and ordered to burn the Bible she had been given in school. That it was a King James Version and therefore not recognized in the Porcellini family meant only that Porcellini, who was a Roman Catholic and a newcomer to town, deserved the threatening admonitions he received when a group, rumored to be Klansmen, called on him unexpectedly. The vigilantes denied being Klansmen, but the Klan had offered to form a group to bring the little girl up properly. When Porcellini complained to the chief of police, one of the ubiquitous Hamricks, he was told to "join a Christian church." Porcellini dropped from the news, but not before promising to mend his ways and allow his daughter to attend a proper church.[24]

"Train up a child in the way he should go, and when he is old he will not depart from it." That the folks of Cleveland County knew;

---

22. Interview with Jay Jenkins, August 11, 1984; interview with Henry Cash, August 9, 1984; *Cleveland Star* (Shelby, N.C.), January 15, 25, 29, 1924.
23. *Cleveland Star* (Shelby N.C.), May 21, December 31, 1926.
24. *Ibid.*, February 15, March 19, 22, 26, 1926.

and that Wilbur Cash's parents knew. But he did depart from it. His emancipation from religious orthodoxy had begun at least as early as his college days, and it may have begun much earlier. "Since child-hood," Cash told Knopf, "I have had an unconquerable aversion to parsons because of their cocksure certainty in a world in which noth-ing is certain but that nothing is certain; because their professions have always seemed mawkish; and because their inquiries have always struck me as indecent: a man's soul, if he has one, ought obviously to be his own private concern." In the 1920s he saw increasing evidence that confident parsons were even more intent on telling others how to live and think. When Cash wrote *The Mind of the South*, he main-tained a consistently critical attitude toward preachers and religion, particularly their role in fostering a spirit of fanatical intolerance dur-ing the 1920s.[25]

Alongside the imposing religious fundamentalism during Cash's era, dramatically present during his period of uncertainty in the 1920s, was the continuing centrality of race and racism. The men who put the fear of God into Tony Porcellini may not have been Klansmen, but Cleveland County and the entire piedmont was a hotbed of Ku Klux Klan activity. In June, 1925, the summer Cash returned to Boiling Springs from Hendersonville, thousands lined the streets of Shelby to cheer a throng of robed Klansmen who paraded to the courthouse steps to listen to Klan exhorters. The *Star* denied that it had any ties to the group, but the newspaper's coverage was consistently positive or apologetic at a time when various southern newspaper editors, as Ger-ald W. Johnson pointed out in the *American Mercury*, were winning awards, including the Pulitzer Prize, for attacking lynchings and the Klan. The *Star* frankly praised Klan activities such as the occasion in July, 1925, when Klan members invaded a traveling circus and laid a rough hand on the shoulders of some frolicking white men, in black-face, who were dancing with black women. The Klan's action was per-fectly justifiable in the face of such a "disgusting performance," the *Star* editorialized. The following year, when Klansmen announced that they would memorialize Flag Day, June 14, with a rally in Shelby, replete with rousing speeches and the showing of a propaganda film, the *Star* greeted the news warmly, predicting that the celebration

25. W. J. Cash to Alfred A. Knopf, author's form, April 29, 1936, in Morrison Papers; Cash, *Mind of the South*, 297–99.

would "bring back colorful memories of the old South." One Sunday morning later that fall, Klansmen trooped en masse to the Second Baptist Church, walked down the aisle, and presented the minister with a Bible and a statement of Klan principles. "Any organization that makes such gifts," intoned the minister in words the *Star* quoted approvingly, "must believe in the message of the Scriptures." According to the *Star*, the head of the local chapter was "one of the best known men in town, who is a mixer and has the reputation of being a good fellow."[26]

The violent racism of lynchings and race riots declined in the piedmont as it did everywhere in the South in the 1920s, perhaps because racial segregation and discrimination were now firmly in place and blacks had had seared into their psyches the lethal price for violating the racial codes. But savage acts of racism document a culture of racism. In July, 1927, one Commodore Burleson, a mountaineer and former policeman, tracked a black man, wanted for killing a young girl, through the Appalachian Mountains. After capturing and killing him, Burleson brought the body back to Morganton, north of Shelby, where the self-appointed executioner posed for photographs with his victim. When the news reached Shelby, Boiling Springs, and environs, carloads of people, many with cameras, hurried to Morganton to admire Burleson and his ghastly trophy. Many people returned to Shelby with pictures that they showed off "to admiring groups of people at the courthouse square." A curious crowd milled around the *Star*'s outside bulletin board to look at the large picture of Burleson and the slain black man. On another occasion, a young black man, facing electrocution for murder, asked to be baptized and forgiven for his sins. "With a quavering cry," the *Star* reported, the doomed man cried out, "'I wanna be ready for Gawd.'" A local doctor examined him for evidence of insanity, found none, and announced that he was the mental age of a "normal person" between the ages of nine and ten, "the mental age," the doctor explained, "of a large number of normal negroes."[27]

26. *Cleveland Star* (Shelby, N.C.), June 23, July 14, 1925, September 8, 1926, February 23, 1927; John Kneebone, *Southern Liberal Journalists and the Issue of Race, 1920–1944* (Chapel Hill, 1985), 76; Fred C. Hobson, Jr., *Serpent in Eden: H. L. Mencken and the South* (1974; rpr. Baton Rouge, 1978), 83–86; Gerald W. Johnson, "Journalism Below the Potomac," *American Mercury*, IX (1926), 77–82.
27. *Cleveland Star* (Shelby, N.C.), July 4, 1927, June 12, 1931.

How excruciatingly slowly the world must have turned in sleepy hamlets like Hendersonville and Boiling Springs and even Charlotte for a person of W. J. Cash's active mind. It was always "big doings," one refugee from Boiling Springs remembers of those days back in the 1920s, to go over to Shelby on Saturday night and mill about on the town square, go to a picture show, maybe sneak a beer, or wander as nonchalantly as possible into the "girlie" shows of the traveling circuses, or leer at one of those "loose women" the pastors and the *Star* warned against, or stand around on the street corner drinking a bottle of soda pop and maybe smoke a cigarette. There was always a crowd milling outside the drugstore listening to "Amos 'n' Andy" on the radio. They admired how well those two white fellows played Amos, the Kingfish, and Calhoon. One would swear they were southern Negroes.[28]

It was enough to make someone like W. J. Cash sick. In any event, something did. In early 1927 Wilbur returned home to Boiling Springs and told his parents he was too nervous, too depressed, and too "neurasthenic" to do sustained work. He consulted a urologist in Charlotte, Dr. Claude B. Squires, whose examination of Cash revealed a chemical "imbalance"—apparently a lack of adequate thiamine—which frequently was accompanied by nervousness and despondency. Not a great deal was known then about the relationship between thiamine deficiency and psychological states, and usually the neurasthenic's symptoms were treated. Cash appeared to be exhausted and on the verge of a nervous breakdown, so Dr. Squires, adhering to the traditional view, prescribed rest and travel, preferably somewhere far away where Cash could recuperate by "forgetting" about his problems. Cash told his parents he wanted to go to Europe. Continually worried about him, they agreed, with fear and trembling, to help him with expenses for the trip to New York City and abroad.[29]

Before sailing, he looked up Peggy Ann. Still beautiful, she still had her heart set on the stage, a passion her well-to-do parents were financing. She showed her former tutor some of the city's sights, from Broadway shows to expensive restaurants, and slyly handed him wads of dollars so he might gallantly pay all the bills. Her extravagance embarrassed him. Their entertainment expenses alone, he calculated and

28. Interview with Jay Jenkins, August 11, 1984.
29. Application for a John Simon Guggenheim Memorial Fellowship, October 20, 1932, in Morrison Papers; Morrison, *W. J. Cash*, 42.

later told a friend, matched the cost of his economy-class ticket to Europe. Still, not even her embarrassingly high standard of living could completely tarnish her image, he mused, as he set sail for Europe. Cash would never see her again.[30]

Being low in pocket, he did Europe on the cheap, walking and bicycling whenever he could. Exercise, and plenty of it, was what he needed, he told himself. He bicycled from Paris to Brest via Tours and then back to Granville in Normandy and from Lyons to Nîmes. He tramped the Riviera, the Pyrenees, and the French and Swiss Alps. There, far from the tight little island known as the Carolina piedmont, Cash walked long hours, sipped French wine, drank German beer, and lived a carefree, bohemian life of the sort he had read about in books. The French capital with its cafés and boulevards, its old churches and parks, and its bracing night life was irresistible and brought out the wistful romantic in him: "Paris is a wench, a charming, kissable wench," he wrote soon after returning home, "a dear, mad, naughty, wine-bibbing, happy, gallant city." Standing in front of the great cathedral at Strasbourg, Cash suddenly felt "a nearly irresistible impulse to burst out bawling," just why, he did not know, for "all my diligent searching of Freud." At Chartres he had the same experience, only this time his emotions overcame him and tears streamed down his face. He stood awestruck, gazing at the great cathedral, the same one that had moved Henry Adams to liken the majestic power of the Virgin to the dynamo of the modern steam engine. "As I stood looking at the magnificent blue lancets," he recalled to a friend soon after returning home, "and then at the rose window, I found myself crying. I didn't believe a God-damned word of the notions that inspired such a masterpiece, but I kept on weeping and damned near dropped to my knees. At last I blew my nose hard and went out and walked around that massive structure and started crying again."[31]

By November, 1927, he was back in North Carolina, sufficiently refreshed to rejoin the Charlotte *News* as an editorial writer and occasional book critic. On March 4, 1928, he initiated a weekly signed column called "The Moving Row." His inspiration, taken from the

30. Katherine Grantham Rogers to Joseph L. Morrison, September 30, 1964, in Morrison Papers; Morrison, *W. J. Cash*, 42.

31. W. J. Cash to Alfred A. Knopf, author's form, April 29, 1936, in Morrison Papers; Charlotte *News*, January 1, 1928, March 14, 1937; Katherine Grantham Rogers to Joseph L. Morrison, September 30, 1964, in Morrison Papers.

Rubaiyat, was "We are no more than a moving row of fantastic shapes that come and go." [32] Earlier he wrote three minor book reviews, each signed WJC. One took a gentle swipe at the mint julep view of southern history and another did the same for the opponents of evolution. Each of the reviews revealed an easygoing ambivalence toward modernist assumptions, the very ones he had taken on, that dismissed all the old certainties. He would, he said, return to the mint julep school of southern historians "when I am weary to tears of the smuggery and stupidity of modernity which jabs its elbows in my ribs and seizes my lapels." And in his Menckenian jabs at the antievolutionists as "Neanderthal hosts yelping for the blood of the professors," Cash chided the new Kultur for its arrogance and the failure of "naturalism" to remember that mankind is inherently romantic and insists on finding beauty and love. "I prefer to believe," Cash confessed, "that in 'flowers and stars and tears' there is more than the rearranging of molecules, the stirrings of Mr. Dreiser's 'chemisms.'" Several factors contributed to Cash's ambivalence: his own romantic nature, his reading in classic writers such as Hazlitt, Voltaire, Shakespeare, and John Stuart Mill, and a certain lingering regard for religion as poetry, as evidenced by his lifelong love of Ecclesiastes. [33]

Cash never spelled out a definition of modernism—newspaper columns were hardly the place for deep philosophical discussions or explications. But even by 1928 Cash's modernism was a compound of Freud, Darwin, Dreiser, Mencken, Hardy, and a host of novelists, including Conrad, who rejected the older certainties of traditional religion and middle-class virtues. Even in his ambivalence, Cash was very much a man of his times; he typified the young moderns' ambivalence toward the "revolution in manners and morals" that Frederick Lewis Allen felt and described in *Only Yesterday*. [34]

In five "Moving Row" columns for the *News* Cash wandered leisurely and good-naturedly through the true definition of Americanism, companionate marriage (which he opposed on the grounds that love was too gloriously irrational to be managed by trial marriages), writers' tendency to romanticize war, art and censorship, and

32. Cash had altered the original line from Edward FitzGerald's version to read "fantastic shapes," rather than "Magic shadow-shapes" (Joseph L. Morrison, "Found: The Missing Editorship of W. J. Cash," *North Carolina Historical Review*, XLVII [1970], 42).

33. W. J. Cash, review of Peter Mitchell Wilson, *Southern Exposure*, Charlotte *News*, January 15, 1928.

34. Frederick Lewis Allen, *Only Yesterday* (New York, 1931), 73–102.

the languid joys of Parisian life. The last had a dreamy quality about it as Cash experimented with one strain of modernism, a stream-of-consciousness style of writing. Despite its stylistic deficiencies, his reverie conveys how Paris had beguiled him. The other columns point up Mencken's continued influence and provide hints about Cash's reading and thinking. To get at a liberating sense of Americanism and to be done with the intolerance of the Klan and other such groups, Cash proposed a lodge, open to everyone who would read Mill's *On Liberty* and swear with Voltaire: "I do not agree with a word you say, but I will defend to the death your right to say it." Hoping that gentle humor would expose the cruelties of racism and ethnic prejudice embedded in most Americanist groups, Cash promised that in his lodge members could "yammer" about anything at all. "The Kluckers are granted full right to believe and proclaim that the Pope is a cannibal with dark designs on Baptist babies."[35]

In another column, Cash argued that even John Dos Passos in *Three Soldiers* and Laurence Stallings in his play *What Price Glory?* had succumbed to the tendency to glorify the brutality of war. There are characters in each book Cash mentions who might support his view, but one suspects that Cash had in mind Dos Passos' earlier novel, *One Man's Initiation*. Cash slipped into his Menckenian mode to say that the average man, lacking courage and imagination, "must resign himself to the monotony of business, a fat wife, and insatiate children." As to why one generation trains up another to equate adventure with war, Cash relied on his Freudian view: "Ego clearly lends countenance to any version of the problem which tends to make the veteran a hero."[36]

Cash also drew on Freudian notions about sex and repression to criticize recent attacks on nudity in art in Greenville, South Carolina, where the locals had objected to the unveiling of the statue of the Apollo Belvedere. Human beings, Cash explained, particularly highly repressed people, can see sex in many things or be sexually aroused even by a sermon on "the wages of sin is death." It is also true, "as every good Freudian knows, that these same people may so react to the sight of a shoe, an umbrella, a pail, a dagger." In America, the chief culprit was the Puritan heritage, said Cash, echoing Mencken and the popu-

35. Charlotte *News*, March 4, 1928.
36. *Ibid.*, March 18, 1928.

lar sentiment of the day. The Puritan looks at a nude statue and reacts to its obvious physical reality, while healthier people become absorbed in ideas. For the Puritan, "repression of his own desires has created a perverted attitude." [37]

His "diligent searching of Freud," his love of Voltaire and Mill, Conrad and Dreiser, Shakespeare and Cervantes, imparted to his thinking and newspaper writing a sharp angle of vision. But not even his deeply existential reading of Freud could cure his neurasthenia, his chronic, predictable tendency to fall apart emotionally from time to time. His "nervous symptoms" reappeared with a vengeance in the spring of 1928, just after he penned his panegyric to Paris. Once again, his neurasthenia left him feeling listless and despondent. He could not continue working, he explained to his long-suffering parents. Again, they understood. Wilbur resigned from the newspaper, left Charlotte, and moved back home to Boiling Springs.

Cash consulted his urologist in Charlotte, Dr. Squires, who concluded once again that Cash's depression resulted from his chronic hyperthyroidism. In addition to thiamine, the physician prescribed lots of fresh air and exercise. Cash was to heal his mind by letting it rest. Any reading or writing that troubled his thoughts or unsettled his digestion was off limits. Wilbur filled the hot, steamy days of summer by walking vigorously, sometimes ten or twenty miles a day. He got to know the countryside around Boiling Springs as never before, though he tended, as usual, to drift off into reveries that gave him a distracted expression and shuffling gait his countrymen recognized at a glance. Although, as he liked to say, he was "the laziest man alive," he chopped wood until the sweat burned his eyes and soaked his shirt. Even the sight of an unattended ax resting beside an unsplit log was loathsome. The regimen worked. By fall, the neurasthenic Cash pronounced himself fit to work.

37. *Ibid.*, March 25, 1928.

4 / Editing a Country Newspaper

In early September, 1928, C. J. Mabry made a business proposition to W. J. Cash, the recovered neurasthenic. Mabry, a Shelby printer and businessman, invited Cash to become managing editor of a new county newspaper. He had bought new printing equipment, enlarged his building in Shelby, and rounded up the necessary subscribers and advertisers. One of Mabry's journeyman printers, J. Nelson Callahan, a college boy from Chapel Hill, had crisscrossed Cleveland County that summer in a Model T persuading folks to part with two dollars for a year's subscription. For getting out the *Cleveland Press* every Tuesday and Friday Cash would receive fifty dollars a week, a modest salary for a college graduate who could write, but not bad for an unemployed fellow in a time when many people earned less.[1]

And anyway, Cash mused, it would be fun to provide an alternative to the conservative Shelby paper, the *Cleveland Star*, unofficial organ of the local demigods Clyde R. Hoey and O. Max Gardner. Hoey, in a cutaway coat, with his flowing mane and stentorian voice, was a successful attorney and rising Democratic star. He and his brother-in-law Gardner—"Mr. Max," to admiring locals—were on the threshold of forming the Shelby dynasty and ruling North Carolina politics for the next decade or so. In June, Gardner had won the Democratic party's gubernatorial nomination by acclamation. Thus in a one-party state, he was guaranteed victory in November, prompting Cash and others

1. Joseph L. Morrison, "Found: The Missing Editorship of W. J. Cash," *North Carolina Historical Review*, XLVII (January, 1970), 44. Morrison discovered the files of the *Cleveland Press* after the publication of his biography, *W. J. Cash, Southern Prophet: A Biography and Reader* (New York, 1967). Morrison was also able to locate and interview J. Nelson Callahan.

to call him "governor elect," a designation that made people smile, oblivious to Cash's cynicism and love of irony.[2]

When Mabry guaranteed Cash complete editorial freedom and control of the new paper, the two shook hands on the deal and Cash rolled up his sleeves to go to work. He knew a couple of local women who would love to do the personal column. Young Callahan would help him get out the first few issues. Cash could work at home and come to Shelby two or three days a week to get out the paper and pick up local political gossip, perhaps even getting a glimpse now and then of Mr. Max or Mr. Hoey. The twenty-five-mile walk from Boiling Springs and back would be good for him, he told Callahan. That fall, Cash became a familiar figure on the red clay county road as he slouched toward Shelby, hat pushed back on his head and rumpled suit coat slung over his shoulder. Neighbors recognizing Sleepy's sauntering gait offered him a lift in their Model T's and asked whether he thought that New York fellow Al Smith—"he's a Catholic, you know"—had a chance against Herbert Hoover in the presidential race. Most people around Cleveland County were lifelong Democrats, but Smith's religion was hard to swallow and folks remembered what Hoover had done after the war when he directed the American relief effort in Europe. Even though he was a Republican, he was the "Great Humanitarian." Hoover was for Prohibition, too. Could Sleepy say as much for Al?[3]

The Democratic nomination of Alfred E. Smith, a Yankee, a papist, and a wet, drove a sharp wedge between southern Democrats everywhere. The convention's choice of the popular Arkansas senator Joseph T. Robinson for vice-president calmed the storm only partially in North Carolina, and the campaign began under the cloudy, gray skies of party acrimony. At the convention in Houston the North Carolina delegation had vigorously opposed Smith, and no one now was enthusiastic about him or his chances of winning. Hoey, Gardner, Governor Angus W. McLean, Josephus Daniels, powerful editor of the Raleigh News and Observer, and Josiah W. Bailey, longtime Prohibitionist, returned from Houston voicing support for Smith. But each had to take a long breath before saying so, and the Raleigh News and Observer did not mention Smith for several days after the convention.

2. Joseph L. Morrison, Governor O. Max Gardner: A Power in North Carolina and New Deal Washington (Chapel Hill, 1971), 49.
3. Morrison, "Found," 44–45.

All of them had opposed Smith's nomination, and all looked with horror on Smith's choice of John J. Raskob as the party's national chairman. Raskob was a Roman Catholic, a wet, and a Republican refugee from the General Motors Corporation. But they were loyal Democrats to a man, and they would stand by their captain, Al Smith.[4]

But what would "The Senator" say? Furnifold M. Simmons, reigning Democratic party chieftain, usually got his way. "The Senator says" was usually enough to settle questions among the party faithful. Simmons had masterminded North Carolina's white supremacy campaign of 1900, and a grateful, admiring electorate had sent him to the Senate that year and returned him again and again. The senator had helped block Smith's nomination in 1924 and in July, 1928, had commanded his loyal troops in Houston to fight for Tennessee's Cordell Hull to the bitter end. Simmons was old, ailing—too sick to go to Houston—and not without opponents in his own party, but the delegation in Houston got him elected state national committeeman, and thousands of Tar Heels waited to follow him. Soon after the convention ended, Simmons dramatically resigned from the national committee, saying he could not stomach either Smith or Raskob. The Senator would not vote for either candidate, he announced, but his followers should vote for Hoover.[5]

By fall Simmons (now "the bolter") was working actively with the newly created, well-organized, well-subsidized "Anti-Smith Democrats" headquartered in Charlotte. At their head stood Frank Mc-Ninch, former mayor of Charlotte, ably aided by Simmons' secretary and strategist and by leading churchmen, conservative educators, and prominent businessmen and industrialists. Smith's Catholicism was the reason most disgruntled Tar Heel Democrats gave to explain their support of Hoover, but many from North Carolina's business community were alienated by Smith's progressive, liberal record on economic and social issues. The son of immigrants, Smith was lambasted as one who would recklessly reopen the gates to the flood of immigration—a point politicians and Klansmen pounced on in a not-so-subtle attempt

4. S. C. Deskins, "The Presidential Election of 1928 in North Carolina" (Ph.D. dissertation, University of North Carolina, 1944), 30–46; Morrison, *Governor O. Max Gardner*, 48–51; George B. Tindall, *The Emergence of the New South, 1913–1945* (Baton Rouge, 1967), 245–46.

5. Richard L. Watson, Jr., "A Political Leader Bolts—F. M. Simmons in the Presidential Election of 1928," *North Carolina Historical Review*, XXXVII (1960), 518–27.

to use the race issue against Smith. McNinch's organization could also count on unofficial but vigorous help from the Ku Klux Klan, Baptist, Methodist, and Presbyterian preachers, and organized Protestant groups.[6]

Such was the state of affairs when Cash and the eight-page *Cleveland Press* debuted on September 20, under the masthead "Independent of Political Bias or Prejudice." W. J. Cash was a disciple of Voltaire, he announced in his lead editorial: "I do not agree with a word you are saying, but I will defend to the death your right to say it." To make good his boast, he urged readers to let him know what was on their minds: "If you've got it in your system and simply must get it out, we'll even allow you to tell Cleveland [County] about the Pope and his vast hunger for fresh-roasted Baptist babies." A follow-up editorial congratulated Shelby for its "new factories, new buildings," and all the other signs of growth but chided the town for having no library.[7]

Cash's sheet may have been "independent of political bias or prejudice" in a region where most newspapers were traditionally openly partisan in their attachment to the Democratic party, but the *Cleveland Press* reflected a strong, unswerving liberal Democratic point of view and was partisanly pro-Smith from the first issue, and Cash himself took to the hustings on at least two occasions in October to speak for Smith.[8] Cash was unrelentingly critical of Hoover and Republican policies and aggressively critical of the vitriolic anti-Smith campaign under way in North Carolina and the rest of the South. Cash understood that nationally the contest was a clash between rural and urban America, with Al Smith's Lower East Side accent all too apparent over the radio airways and all too unpleasant to many outside New York City. Cash also knew that Prohibition (which the somber, serious Hoover personified) and immigration (which Smith's Catholic immigrant background seemed to typify) were fundamental issues to many people. But the Klan's scurrilous attacks on Smith and the outraged utterances of Baptist and Methodist clergymen convinced him that the real issue in Cleveland County and North Carolina was religious intolerance and bigotry and that Prohibition, in particular, was a smoke screen that allowed the "best people" to mask a bigotry the Klan openly espoused.

6. *Ibid.*, 527–37; Deskins, "The Presidential Election," 52–62.
7. *Cleveland Press*, September 20, 1928.
8. *Cleveland Star*, October 1, 10, 1928.

In the first issue of the *Cleveland Press* Cash revived his signed column "The Moving Row" to attack intolerance. Decent people should support Smith if only to rebuke the conduct of bigots such as Mabel Willebrandt, the United States assistant attorney general, who had publicly vilified Smith for his Catholicism. Closer to home, said Cash, the bigotry was uglier. The Klan, surreptitiously aided by Furnifold Simmons' office, had mailed and distributed "tons" of anti-Catholic literature. Postmen and night riders hand delivered scurrilous hate literature like *The Broad Axe*, the *New Menace*, and the *Fellowship Forum*, which one scholar has called "perhaps the most repulsive, reprehensible publication ever permitted circulation in the state."[9] To the contention, which Cash had heard many times (and would hear again) that Cleveland County was Klan country and people knew James Vance, editor of the *Fellowship Forum*, to be "honest," Cash fumed: "So also was Luther honest when he penned his 'Smite, strike, slay and burn' to send a hundred thousand helpless German serfs to their doom." Two weeks later, in a slashing editorial, Cash accused the editors and distributors of the *New Menace* and "the crawling sheet called the *Fellowship Forum*" of deliberately distorting the truth and playing on the fears and emotions of the masses.[10]

Cash was convinced that McNinch, Methodist Bishop Edwin Mouzon, an outspoken anti-Smith man, and Klan exhorters and fellow-traveling nativist groups like the Loyal Order of United Protestants, headquartered in Charlotte, were using Prohibition and immigration to hide their reactionary religious objections to Smith. It was true, said Cash in his first editorial, that Smith opposed the nation's restrictive immigration laws, but so had a good southerner, President Woodrow Wilson, when he vetoed similarly discriminatory legislation. Cash knew that few of his readers understood the intricacies of the nativist law of 1924—the legislation that slammed the door shut to millions of immigrants—and how, in picking 1890 as the base year for establishing quotas for each country, the lawmakers had severely restricted the "new immigrants" from southern and eastern Europe. Cash defended Smith, calling the restriction act "an absurd bill" framed "largely by anti-Catholics and Anglomaniacs." McNinch and Klan leaders shouted that America must remain "Nordic" and "Anglo-Saxon" and

---

9. Deskins, "The Presidential Election," 159.
10. *Cleveland Press*, September 20, October 5, 1928.

keep foreigners out, but they were wrong, said Cash, as well as deliberately racist. The laws restricted the flow of true "Nordics" into America by discriminating against southern Ireland, the Scandinavian countries, Poland, and Germany.

Cash continued telling his readers that Smith deserved their support because he was right on the immigration question, as he was on the other issues. Let there be restriction, Cash conceded, but let it be done fairly and humanely. "Let the fit of whatever race come," said Cash. "Let England's sweepings be rejected as completely as Italy's sweepings." [11] In this attitude Cash was very much a man of his generation of intellectuals but not the piedmont generation of 1928. By traveling abroad and reading Conrad, Mencken, Freud, Nietzsche, and the gods of modernism, Cash had internalized the view, held passionately in advanced intellectual circles in the North, that veneration of England was just so much misguided Victorianism, that the Continent was the true center of culture. [12]

For months Vance and others had saturated the state with thousands of copies of a bogus anti-Catholic "oath" attributed to the Knights of Columbus. The oath, dating back to the days of the Inquisition, was a forgery designed to smear Catholics with militant, blind loyalty to the pope and undying hostility to all Protestants. The oath was a fraud. Its authenticity had been denied by the Knights of Columbus, condemned by the Masons, and officially censured at a congressional hearing in 1913. Still, hate groups flooded the state with copies of the oath, marking the envelope "From the *Congressional Quarterly*." Politicians knew at once how dangerous to Smith the oath was. Hoey, in his first major address of the campaign, had denounced it as a fraud. [13]

The Klan's manipulation of the fraudulent oath infuriated Cash. In "Moving Row" columns, editorials, and news articles in October he rebuked the Klan and James Vance and urged decent people to join him. Revealingly, though, Cash made no mention of Hoey and the regular Smith Democrats who had attacked the oath. Instead, Cash praised one Horace Kennedy for having publicly exposed the forgery

11. Editorials, "Immigration," *Cleveland Press*, September 20, 1928, and "McNinch and Immigration," *ibid.*, September 28, 1928.

12. Henry May, *The End of American Innocence: A Study of the First Years of Our Time* (New York, 1959), 122–23, 236–44, 282–83.

13. Deskins, "The Presidential Election," 76, 86.

and confronted Vance with the truth. "Vance admits that he has no proof for the oath," Cash charged, "no proof for his claims. He asserts that he could not possibly have proof. And in a breath he hastens to tell Mr. Kennedy where copies of the oath may be secured for distribution. What kind of man is this who is eager to spread what he doesn't know to be true, can't—by his own confession—know to be true?"[14]

Hatemongers like Vance and religious zealots like Methodist Bishop James Cannon, Jr., of Virginia and North Carolina's Bishop Mouzon insulted Cash's sense of decency and fair play. After Mouzon slandered the Knights of Columbus, Cash replied: "There is the fact that thousands of members of the order have died under the flag. There is the fact that the order's membership constitutes, as a matter of record, one of the best bodies of citizenship to be found in the nation." And against that group, said Cash, singling out Vance, "there is nothing save an admitted falsehood and a creeping coward who couldn't stand by his guns."[15]

A week later, on October 12, the *Cleveland Press* carried news articles reporting that the Klan had "investigated" the oath and found that it was indeed a forgery. This information Cash and the public had on the authority of Dr. Amos C. Duncan, Grand Dragon for the state of North Carolina, from his headquarters in Forest City, outside Charlotte. Duncan denied that the Klan had had anything to do with its circulation but confirmed recent reports that he had urged Klansmen to contribute heavily to a war chest to defeat Smith because of "'the sinister, unAmerican and unholy special interests which he impersonates.'"[16]

Cash was convinced that the opposition to Smith flowed mainly from the great springs of anti-Catholicism and had little to do with immigration or Smith's much discussed "wetness." Smith probably played into his critics' hands when he stressed the liquor question, Cash admitted, but Cash could not believe that Prohibition was a legitimate issue. Nor would he give the topic much space in his newspaper. From the beginning of the campaign Cash underestimated the emotional depths of Prohibition's popularity, and he disagreed with the religious feelings of his countrymen. Throughout he would main-

14. "Kennedy and the Oath," *Cleveland Press*, October 5, 1928.
15. *Ibid.*
16. *Cleveland Press*, October 12, 1928.

tain a Menckenian notion that no sensible person could possibly be a Prohibitionist.

Cash editorialized in mid-October following one of The Senator's public pronouncements to the "moral forces" of the state that Simmons' embrace of Prohibition was certainly a fraudulent, last-minute conversion calculated to divert attention away from his favoritism of the Duke Power Company and to save his political hide in North Carolina. But it would not work, Cash charged. Simmons' gallant last stand for Prohibition was just so much tilting at windmills, as "The Little Man from New Bern" well understood. The people see that "The Little Man is an actor, a medicine-man," betting he can hoodwink the voters, but he is a "hypocrite," a "coward."[17] Cash's words, however heated, were the common stuff of partisan journalism in the Tar Heel state. One country editor in the northwestern part of the state said of Simmons' speech: "'that doddering, senile, mentally bankrupt old man of New Bern . . . belched up some gas.'"[18]

To Cash the issue was freedom. People had a right to prefer Protestantism to Catholicism or any other religion. But they had no constitutional or ethical right to insist that government be one religion or another. And that the anti-Smith forces were doing, said Cash, when they objected to Smith's or Raskob's Catholicism. To make that objection in the political arena—as Bishop Cannon did at an anti-Smith rally in Raleigh, where he called Raskob a "chamberlain of the Pope"—was a denial, said Cash, of freedom of religion and an attack on the very foundations of freedom that Thomas Jefferson and the founding fathers had designed. Cash's colleague in arms, the Raleigh journalist Nell Battle Lewis, had made the same point earlier in a campaign speech. Freedom of conscience, she said, was the chief issue in the campaign, and Smith's religion was the main reason for the opposition to him in North Carolina. She branded such opposition "unworthy of any Democrat who believes in the principles of his party and the Constitution of the United States. It is undemocratic, and worse, it is unChristian."[19]

The religious question was by no means theoretical in North Carolina and the South in 1928. In early August, soon after Smith's nomi-

17. Editorial, "Simmons," *Cleveland Press*, October 16, 1928.
18. A. W. Kinnard, editor of the *Hertford News*, quoted in Watson, "A Political Leader Bolts," 533.
19. Cannon and Lewis quoted in Deskins, "The Presidential Election," 58, 70.

nation, Bishop Mouzon had said at a meeting Bishop Cannon had called to organize anti-Smith pastors and leaders that Smith's candidacy "is no mere threat to prohibition. It is the impulse of the lawless elements in the great cities against American civilization." The bishop had tipped his hand when he published a hysterical attack on Catholic persecution of Protestants—deliberately neglecting to mention that the transgressions had occurred centuries earlier. Mouzon had issued a Protestant manifesto calling on all Methodist clergymen within his jurisdiction to take to their pulpits and declare the inherent, absolute differences between Protestantism and Catholicism. Mouzon had even prepared a list of sermon topics that would expose Catholicism's evil intentions. The bishop's flock of sheep loyally followed orders. Throughout the campaign Bishop Cannon roamed the South blasting Smith and Catholicism, all the while charging Smith with injecting the religious issue into the campaign. Cannon funneled thousands of dollars to anti-Smith forces in North Carolina and flooded the region with hundreds of thousands of copies of a polemical pamphlet, *Is Southern Protestantism More Intolerant Than Romanism?*[20]

In late October, just a week before the election, various prelates, including Mouzon and Professors Paul Neff Garber and Gilbert T. Rowe of Duke University's Divinity School, publicly rebuked Smith in Charlotte at the annual meeting of the Methodist Episcopal Church, South. After lavishing praise on his bishop, Garber lashed out at the "wet, subsidized partisan newspapers." "The eminent doctor," Cash stormed, "furnishes an excellent example of the kind of dunderplate a member of the learned faculty can be when he decides to talk about those things concerning which he knows nothing." Why did Garber refuse to name names or offer proof? Cash asked angrily. "The people of North Carolina will, in fairness, take note of the entry of Duke University into politics. It will not be difficult to account for that."[21]

It was not difficult for Cash to account for Garber's charges. In Democratic circles and in and around the Charlotte *News* offices it was taken

20. Edwin D. Mouzon, "The Roman Catholic Question," *North Carolina Christian Advocate,* LXXIII (August 2, 1928), 8–9; Deskins, "The Presidential Election," 55; Morrison, "Found," 45. For a more sympathetic view of Cannon's activities see Robert A. Hohner, "Dry Messiah Revisited: Bishop James Cannon, Jr.," in Bruce Clayton and John A. Salmond, eds., *The South Is Another Land: Essays on the Twentieth-Century South* (Greenwood, Conn., 1987), 151–68.

21. Editorial, "In Glass Houses," *Cleveland Press,* October 26, 1928. For Few and Garber, see Deskins, "The Presidential Election," 61, 113.

for granted that an interlocking power elite existed, consisting of the Duke Power Company, the Duke Endowment, Duke University—whose president, William P. Few, was a prominent anti-Smith man—key Methodist leaders like Mouzon, powerful piedmont industrialists and businessmen like Charles H. Iredell, and "the textile barons and their organ, the Charlotte *Observer*."[22]

Just days before the election, Cash savaged Mouzon in a "Moving Row" column. The bishop had retaliated against the charge that "political parsons" should stick to religion by telling the assembled Methodists that "we get our call from God, not from men." "If through your influence," the bishop warned the clergymen, "you permit evil institutions to come back to this country, you will be individually responsible for every girl deflowered, for every boy that is ruined." Cash countered with a little sermon of his own on the separation of church and state and the notion that the laity was as capable of interpreting the Bible as the "priests" in bishops' robes. If "as the Bishop suggests, preachers, and bishops, in particular, are vouchsafed extraordinary information from God, if the Words of Jesus are constantly being supplemented with new dispensations concerning Prohibition and Al Smith and the canonizing of Buck Duke or Lord Hoover . . . the doctrine of the separation of Church and State becomes ridiculous. The only sensible form of government, if the bishop be right, is a Theocracy, controlled, say, by the bishops."[23] If government could be turned into a theocracy controlled by Methodist bishops today, what about tomorrow? Could a Roman Catholic bishop decide who the rulers should be or what laws were good and acceptable? What if various Protestant divines, each having heard a special word from God, should have conflicting views?

That would never happen, religious folks around Shelby knew. But it had already happened, said Cash, pointing to Protestant leaders who disagreed on fundamental political and social issues. "How am I to steer my frail Homeric craft between the position of Dr. John Moore Walker, rector of St. Peter's Episcopal in Charlotte, who says that the 18th Amendment is 'a great mistake' and that of Bishop Mouzon, who is convinced that the law has become a lesser deity?" To clinch his argument, with its overtones of radical Baptist theology, Cash concluded: "And, if my private opinion is worth anything, I don't believe

22. Morrison, *W. J. Cash*, 45.
23. *Cleveland Press*, October 30, 1928.

God has anything to do with the opinions of Bishop Mouzon save insofar as he has to do with the opinions of the muddiest of us all. I think, if a cat may presume to look at a bishop, that Mouzon is merely propounding the medieval dogma of Papal infallibility."[24]

Folks around Boiling Springs wondered what on earth could have gotten into John and Nannie's boy. He surely did not get those ideas at home or from Reverend James L. Jenkins of the Boiling Springs Baptist Church or Reverend Zeno Wall, pastor of Shelby's growing First Baptist Church. Sleepy was an odd one, and that was the God's truth. But if one overlooks some of Cash's rhetorical flourishes, many of his ideas sound like traditional Baptist doctrines, as Cash pointed out in admiring references to William Louis Poteat's recent and continued advocacy of keeping church and state separate. Dr. Billy was still a shining example of intellectual integrity in Cash's eyes. "Dr. Poteat has an almost uncanny way of being right," Cash concluded. "And I believe no man in America more clearly understands what Jesus, the most misunderstood figure of all times, teaches."[25]

From the first, Cash spilled more ink criticizing Hoover than praising Smith. Cash did repeatedly call attention to Smith's political experience, his record of achievement as governor of New York for eight years—"while the other candidate was busy with a mere bureau"—his capacity for work, his unassuming manner, and his liberal values. But mostly Cash hammered against Hoover's reputation as a humanitarian. "Mr. Hoover is a noted engineer. He is an excellent business man. He is an organizer. As such he may be eminently qualified for being President. Certainly, it was because of these things that he was chosen to direct relief work in Belgium. The humanitarian credit properly belongs to those millions who contributed the vast sums which Mr. Hoover directed. The man's personality, his private acts, do not bear out the claim that he is a humanitarian." "Lord Hoover," said Cash, was a "reactionary"; his heart was reserved exclusively for big business and tycoons, as Hoover had made cynically clear on many occasions. Hoover's approach to government was "predicated on the doctrine that the common man is a dolt, a great booby congenitally incapable of seeing beyond the tinselled platitudes." Nor had Hoover created the prosperity that Republicans praised exuberantly. The

24. *Ibid.*
25. *Cleveland Press*, October 23, 1928.

credit, Cash editorialized in mid-October, should go to Calvin Coolidge—if it should be given to anyone—and he inherited it from the great demand created by the war. Besides, prosperity was a myth. American prosperity was mortgaged to excessive spending and flagging production. Look around, Cash argued, and try to "explain away idle factories and the millions of unemployed."[26]

Let anyone speak the truth about Republican policies, Cash editorialized on October 26, and "Lord Hoover" will "trot out the pet bogey of Reactionaries for the past hundred years—the bones of Karl Marx, of Socialism," as indeed Hoover had done in New York a few nights earlier before a throng at Madison Square Garden. Such charges were "red herrings," as Hoover well knew, said Cash. And Hoover knew, cynic that he was, that such scare tactics worked. Did one have to be a socialist, Cash asked angrily, "to recognize that, when one third of the people are chronically unable to meet their obligations, the nation already suffers from the greatest of economic ills?" Thus spake the Shelby Zarathustra one year before the stock market crash.[27]

In building his case against Hoover, Cash dismissed as baseless, unfair, or "silly" the slanders that Hoover was a drunk, or that southerners should reject him because he favored evolution, or that his Quaker religion disqualified him for the presidency. But in his zeal to persuade local voters that a Hoover victory was not in their interests Cash occasionally manifested a mild racism. When anti-Smith forces charged that the governor had appointed blacks to office in New York, Cash echoed the Democratic denial (which happened to be true), charging that Hoover had appointed far more blacks to the federal bureaucracy than his predecessors. In mid-October Cash reprinted an editorial from a Virginia newspaper warning that Hoover's camp included Congressman L. C. Dyer of Missouri, a well-known Republican advocate of federal antilynching laws and bills to "force" the South to allow blacks to vote. Dyer reportedly was rubbing his hands with glee at the prospect of Hoover's victory, which would allow Republicans to restore black suffrage in the South.[28]

---

26. Editorial, "The Man and the Myth," *Cleveland Press*, October 12, 1928; *Cleveland Press*, October 23, 26, 19, 1928.

27. *Cleveland Press*, October 23, 26, 1928.

28. *Ibid.*, September 28, November 26, 1928; editorial, "If the Solid South Breaks," reprinted from the Virginia *Times Dispatch*, *ibid.*, October 16, 1928.

Now and again Cash's semiweekly paper lapsed into the prevailing racial insensitivity. Cash ran no "darkey" cartoons and in general refrained from sensationalizing black crime, but Negroes were always identified as such and offhandedly and routinely referred to by their first names, as was customary in southern newspapers. In the *Cleveland Press* news of blacks mainly told of their minor crimes or buffoonish behavior. And on at least one occasion Cash's style degenerated into colloquial racism. He reported on a black woman who had been arrested and charged with setting fire to the house where her husband slept after they had quarreled violently.. "Minnie Morrow, black, is kind of unfriendly if you get her real roiled," Cash wrote. "Elegant funerals are all right, provided—well, it depends on whose funeral it is. No. Minnie ain't got none of the jazz black in her. She ain't no Harlem nigger, either." When her Tom got her "roiled" by throwing some furniture at her, she waited until he went to sleep and set fire to the house. "At least, that's what Tom says. And that's how Minnie got in jail." [29]

Cash's writings about race usually reflected a humane attitude and style. Nor did his mild racism even approach the bigotry expressed during the campaign. Much of the hubbub over immigration and religion was thinly disguised racism with each side accusing the other of coddling blacks and plotting to bring back "nigger domination." Senator Simmons regularly invoked the glory days of the white supremacy era and, as Cash suspected, worked secretly with Amos C. Duncan and national Klan officers and surreptitiously raised money to help the Klan finance its hate campaign. [30] But Smith Democrats gave as good as they got. Josephus Daniels' Raleigh *News and Observer* ran racist editorials, some on the front page, and large advertisements reminding readers of the horrors of Reconstruction during Republican rule. North Carolina Democrats imported Theodore Bilbo from Mississippi and Coley Blease, who engaged in their customary race-baiting. Blease told an excited crowd in Gastonia that "Mr. Hoover loves a Negro better than he does any white man in North Carolina." [31]

Cash, who earlier in the Charlotte *News* had sneered at the "Neolithic Blease," reported on Blease's racist outpourings in Cleveland County cautiously and without his customary indignation: "The pic-

29. *Ibid.*, September 20, 1928.
30. Watson, "A Political Leader Bolts," 538.
31. Deskins, "The Presidential Election," 88.

ture of black men crowding white women from the street and wantonly insulting them stirred the crowd's fire, and the Senator's promise that such activities in his own state would be greeted by men 'who know how to tie a rope to a tree and to the other end, too' brought laughter and whoops."[32]

Cash's attention was mainly on the national election rather than race, and as election day neared his editorials and columns became more subdued, more somber. A true party loyalist, he did not concede defeat, but there were hints that he predicted the outcome. On October 23, he editorialized, in a discouraged tone, that even if Cleveland County voters were determined to vote for Hoover and a government of the rich and for the few, they should at least help send Gardner to the governor's mansion and reelect their congressman, Major A. J. Bulwinkle, a Democratic stalwart. Cash had all but ignored Gardner, Hoey, and Josiah W. Bailey during the campaign, even though Hoey tirelessly supported Smith and in many circles Bailey "won acclaim for his unqualified assaults upon religious bigotry."[33] Apparently Cash could not bring himself to praise "Mr. Max" or any of the Democratic regulars, saying only that prudent self-interest alone should cause local voters to swell Gardner's numbers. Cash's silence and lack of enthusiasm for Shelby's own probably resulted from Gardner's lukewarm (but politically expedient) support of Smith. "I am a candidate for Governor of North Carolina," Gardner repeated, "not for President of the United States."[34] What little enthusiasm Cash could muster for local pro-Smith Democrats he reserved for Bulwinkle. (As it happened, in the Hoover landslide Bulwinkle lost to Charles Jonas, a Republican, who had waged an aggressive campaign.) Cash's political inexperience, his youthful passion for Smith, and his personal animosity toward Gardner and the party regulars—even though they supported Smith—left him unable to appreciate the practical problem confronting loyal Democrats. The electorate was openly hostile to Smith. The Charlotte *Observer* deserted its long-standing principles, supported the Republican ticket, and denounced Smith. In Shelby, even the ultraloyal *Cleveland Star* refrained from overpraising Smith for fear of hurting the ticket.[35]

32. *Cleveland Press*, October 30, 1928.
33. Watson, "A Political Leader Bolts," 530.
34. Quoted in Deskins, "The Presidential Election," 66.
35. Jack Claiborne, *The Charlotte "Observer": Its Time and Place, 1869–1986* (Chapel Hill, 1986), 189; Morrison, *Governor O. Max Gardner*, 50.

On election eve Cash all but conceded, but not before giving Mouzon, McNinch, and Hoover the back of his hand again. The imminence of Smith's defeat put Cash in a reflective, even prophetic mood.
In a lengthy "Moving Row" column Cash confessed that the campaign, which had begun in chaos and brought out the worst in the
bigots, had enabled him to see that although the election would not
prove anything final, there were signs beneath the surface that a fundamental shift was taking place in American politics. The two parties
would retain their names, but "what we are probably about to witness
is the formation of parties on strictly drawn lines of Conservatism and
Liberalism." Democrats, heirs to Jefferson's vision of human rights and
a government of the people, would become the "Liberals." Republicans might have embraced liberalism had World War I not sidetracked
Theodore Roosevelt's political and economic agenda into the Bourbon reaction of the 1920s. But now, Cash predicted, Hoover's reactionary views and policies would finish the job and make the Republicans thoroughly conservative.[36]

Such a transformation, Cash believed, would benefit the South and
the nation. Out would go the old clichés, along with the befogging,
misleading slogans and sham issues such as Prohibition. "The Bloody
Shirt, the Negro issue, The Grand Old Party, the Glories of Democracy—all the old watchwords, I think, are to be cast aside. In short,
we are going to quit battling over straw men and go after the things
that really matter to us." Mouzon and his ilk were crowing that the
liquor issue had been resolved, but it had only been postponed. There
would be a national referendum, and soon, said Cash optimistically, in
the same manner that he surveyed the changes he thought he saw on
the horizon. Sectionalism, as people had known it, would change.
The East would shove the South aside as the stronghold of the Democratic party, and the Republicans would increasingly look to the West
and parts of the South.[37] For all his doubts about the permanence of
prosperity, Cash, like most Americans, had no inkling that the Depression and the New Deal were at hand. But his predictions about the
evolution of political parties would one day come true.

The young piedmont pundit—Cash was twenty-eight that year—
even ventured to speculate that sectional shifts could, just possibly,

36. "The Moving Row," *Cleveland Press*, November 2, 1928; Editorial, "McNinch's Figures,"
November 6, 1928; Editorial, "Mouzon's Logic," *Cleveland Press*, November 6, 1928.
37. W. J. Cash, "The Moving Row," *Cleveland Press*, November 6, 1928.

mean that the race issue would evolve in ways quite foreign to the old alignments: "Because of the possible opportunity of the Negro to exert a balance of power, we may yet see the ultimately ironic spectacle of the Republican party raising the standard of 'white supremacy!'"[38]

In the wake of Hoover's victory, Cash was in no mood to concede anything. Hoover had executive strengths, one of which was honesty, "as he conceives honesty to be constituted," but the nation would once again witness the "cynical thievery" of the Harding years. "I opposed him before the election. I still oppose him. With that, the name of his party has nothing at all to do. Rather, I conceive him to be an apostle of Reaction. And, because I believe that, I regard even his strength with regret." The country needed and deserved a president for all the people, "but against that is his cry for the doctrine of do-as-you please in business, his training with the Coolidge pack. And I haven't much hope."[39]

Cash lamented that North Carolina had broken ranks with the Democracy and gone for Hoover—by nearly sixty-three thousand votes—as had four other southern states and the rest of the nation, save Massachusetts and Rhode Island. As for North Carolina, where Gardner won by more than seventy thousand votes—and swept Cleveland County by a wide margin while Smith carried it by only two hundred votes—Cash had no doubt that perceived prosperity and religious prejudice, inflamed by Simmons, McNinch, Mouzon, and Cannon, had been the determining element in the voters' minds, not Prohibition.

Whither Smith? Cash asked plaintively. On the eve of the election, Cash had predicted that even should Smith lose he would remain at the head of the party and bolters like Simmons and Alabama's Thomas Heflin would be sent packing by the Democratic party—as indeed they were. In the wake of Smith's defeat—which Cash minimized, pointing out that Smith had received more votes than any previous Democratic contender—Cash allowed himself a moment of sanguinary reflection. The values Smith represented would triumph in time: "It doesn't particularly matter about the fate of Alfred E. Smith, save as the fate of any brave and honorable man matters. It doesn't even matter a great deal whether or not the party called Democratic shall continue as it is. What does matter is that the Liberal cause, as

38. Ibid.
39. "The Moving Row," Cleveland Press, November 9, 1928.

represented—if too imperfectly,—by that party in this campaign, shall live. It will."[40]

Subsequent events vindicated Cash's brave words. Franklin Delano Roosevelt's victory in 1932 and the conversion of the Democratic party, at least the northern wing, to the welfare legislation of the New Deal shifted the party leftward. Southern Democrats lagged behind in their commitment to the New Deal's social planning and dug in their heels in opposition whenever the New Deal threatened to intervene on behalf of blacks, but the success of much of FDR's legislation depended on support from Dixie Democrats, and the South reaped the rewards of the lengthening arm of the federal government.

And then, seemingly in the twinkling of an eye, the prophetic, even hopeful mood that had informed W. J. Cash's words in November vanished. Once again, he fell sick and could not carry on. Once again, those debilitating "nervous symptoms" reappeared and brought him low: bouts of anxiety, lassitude, depression, fatigue. He appears to have been suffering from a psycho-physical ailment related to his chronic nemesis, hyperthyroidism, the endocrine disorder that left him nervous and despondent. On the advice of his physicians, "I retired to my native village." His name disappeared from the editorial page after November 19. The *Cleveland Press* limped along for a month or so before finally expiring shortly after the beginning of 1929.[41]

Looking back a few years later on the events of fall, 1928, Cash wrote Knopf that his passionate opposition to the religious bigotry of the campaign "quickly involved me in a bitter fight" that he could not handle emotionally. Though usually sympathetic to Cash, Joseph L. Morrison wonders whether "Cash may perhaps have overdramatized his fearlessness and independence in having stood out against religious bias."[42] Perhaps, if Cash's writings are surveyed from some Olympian journalistic perspective, he did overstate or "overdramatize" his role. But viewed subjectively, that is, from the perspective of Cash's inner life, his extreme personal sensitivity, and his tendency to "get sick" and have to "retire" momentarily from active life, his words ring true and take on an entirely different meaning. Throughout his brief editorial career in the fall of 1928 as politicians ranted and bishops and

---

40. *Ibid.*

41. Application for a John Simon Guggenheim Memorial Fellowship, October 20, 1932, in Morrison Papers.

42. *Ibid.*; Morrison, "Found," 42.

Klansmen issued scurrilous pamphlets and equated the election with Armageddon, a young, obscure country editor had sought to give voice to reason and decency. In that climate of hostility, young Cash needed all the psychic strength and courage he could muster. And in that region, for a young native son, living in a home where truth was lodged in the Baptist church, the mills, and the Democratic party, to smite bishops, the Klan, and The Senator, would require extraordinary courage and emotional strength. Cash's actions represented, in the Freudian sense, a recurrent slaying of the father. Killing the father(s) may be a prerequisite to becoming a man, as Freud said, but it can exact a heavy emotional price. If the price Cash paid was sickness, can the charge be sustained that he overdramatized his fearlessness or independence?

That question aside, Cash's words in the heat of the 1928 presidential campaign convey a profound alienation from his own people. Church news, sermon titles, profiles of pastors, glowing accounts of how many "souls" were "saved" at last week's revival—such were the staples of southern life. Religion honeycombed life. Prominent men taught Sunday School. Hoey's and Gardner's Sunday School classes frequently attracted more worshipers than the sermon and service that followed. Piedmont pastors, usually Baptists or Methodists, occasionally Presbyterian, prayed over new store openings, county fairs, and high school football games. Such was normal and good; such was assumed, unquestioned, and thus honored by being taken for granted. And all this Cash had rejected. He had, mainly by his intellectual quest and journey, emotionally distanced himself from that world of religion, the world of his father and mother. Was he aware? Did he know how great, how unbridgeable, the emotional gulf had become between his psyche and that of his people, the very people he was trying to lead? If he knew—and one suspects that his knowledge was nine-tenths intellectual and still beyond his psychic understanding—if he knew, then he also knew that anyone who attempts to speak a critical word of truth in a land where the mind is mired in myth, illusion, and racial prejudice—and enveloped in religious certainty—was fundamentally at odds with the very people he would lead. If that truth-teller happens to have, as Cash did, a passionate, one might even say religious, need to speak the truth, the way is made straight for sorrow, perhaps for tragedy.

W. J. Cash in 1917. *Courtesy Henry Cash*

The Kalliergeonian literary society at Boiling Springs High School, 1917–1918.
Cash is second from the left, second row. *From Boiling Springs High School Catalogue,*
1917–1918. Reproduced courtesy of Gardner-Webb College.

Publicity photograph of Cash taken in 1936. *Courtesy Harry Ransom Humanities Research Center, the University of Texas at Austin*

Charlotte *News* newsroom in 1938 or 1939. The man in the suit in front of the doorway is Tom Revelle. To his left, also in a suit, is Dick Young. To the right, sitting at the desk and facing the viewer, are Tom Pridgen and, in the visor, Brodie Griffith. Across from them with his back to the viewer is John Daly. Reed Sarratt is talking on the phone. *Courtesy Burke Davis*

W. J. Cash and Alfred A. Knopf at the Hotel Charlotte in March, 1941. *Courtesy Charles H. Elkins, Sr.*

Mary and W. J. Cash with Cash's parents, Nannie and John Cash, and his sister, Elizabeth (Bertie) Wilkins, 1941. The photograph was taken right before W. J. and Mary left for Mexico. *Courtesy Henry Cash*

W. J. Cash in 1941. *Courtesy Harry Ransom Humanities Research Center, the University of Texas at Austin*

5 / A Thinker in the South

Cash's neurasthenia, though real and recurrent, eased a bit once he was freed from constant editorial demands and the obligation to comment critically on the passing scene. Rest and recreation helped, too. By early spring of 1929 he felt ready to write again. On the advice of a friend, he expanded his rather extensive knowledge of Furnifold M. Simmons and produced a slashing essay designed specifically for H. L. Mencken's *American Mercury*. To his delight, Cash learned in May that Mencken, a strong supporter of Smith, liked the piece and wanted to publish it immediately. "Jehovah of the Tar Heels," as Mencken titled Cash's fiery diatribe, appeared in July. Mencken enjoyed discovering and nurturing young writers, particularly rebellious southern ones. His newest discovery's enthusiasm for the master's extravagant style added to his pleasure in publishing Cash. Mencken asked for more articles. Cash sharpened his pencil and whipped off a stunning tour de force he audaciously called "The Mind of the South." Again, Mencken liked it. The essay, appearing in October, foreshadowed most of the themes Cash would develop in other articles for Mencken and in his classic book. Five months later, in March, 1930, Cash reappeared in the *American Mercury* with "The War in the South," a sympathetic look at the Gastonia textile strike that had shocked North Carolina and the nation.[1]

1. W. J. Cash, "Jehovah of the Tar Heels," *American Mercury*, XVII (1929), 310–18; "The Mind of the South," *ibid.*, XVII (1929), 185–92; "The War in the South," *ibid.*, XIX (1930), 163–69. For Mencken and the South see Fred C. Hobson, Jr., *Serpent in Eden: H. L. Mencken and the South* (1974; rpr. Baton Rouge, 1978).

In just over a year, Cash had produced three highly professional, sprightly essays for one of America's finest magazines. In the meantime, he had told the prestigious Alfred A. Knopf publishing company that he was interested in writing a book on the "mind of the South" and that he was grateful to Mencken for suggesting his name and the idea for a book to the Knopfs. Cash was now brimming with ambition. He told his friends about his good fortune and immediately began to sketch out ideas for a book. He drew up lists of topics he hoped would interest Mencken. Thinking big and glowing with enthusiasm, he talked up various projects—essays, biographies, multivolume novels. Not yet thirty, W. J. Cash was obviously on his way to a literary career.

On receiving his first acceptance letter from Mencken, he rushed to his mama, hugged her generously, and poured out his heart. He felt wonderful. She was to ignore what she might hear about that man Mencken; he was a fine writer, about the most important editor there was. And never mind that he enjoyed baiting the South and had once pilloried Mississippi as the worst state in America. "Jehovah of the Tar Heels" was not his title, he explained, but it would do. To be in the *American Mercury* was a dream come true, Mencken paid two hundred dollars, and such articles were easy to write. Later that evening, sitting around the supper table with his family, Wilbur repeated his good news to his dad and the others, though in a more restrained manner.[2]

Wilbur walked over to Shelby to brag a little at the *Star*, where he had a few friends, and accept congratulatory handshakes. His friend Renn Drum was good for a firm handshake, a cup of coffee, and some spirited conversation about writing and the subject on everyone's mind, the South. His wife, Erma, who did a little bit of everything at the *Star*, was ecstatic and volunteered to type for Sleepy. They were an open-minded, good-humored couple who liked Mr. Cash, as Erma insisted on calling him. They even harbored some liberal notions.[3]

Drum heralded Cash's good fortune in his column, reminding readers that he and lots of folks around Cleveland County knew Cash could write and had long thought that "Young Cash would score heavily ere many years in the fields of higher writing." Cash's recent newspaper editorials "were of a type not exceeded by the most literary and

2. Interview with Elizabeth ("Bertie") Cash Elkins, August 6, 1984.
3. Telephone interview with Erma Drum, August 30, 1984.

philosophical editorial pages of the larger papers. In fact, and we can say it as a compliment, his philosophy in comment upon and in observance of current events was a bit more of the thoughtful magazine type than of the newspaper type." Since Simmons was up for reelection in 1930 and loyalists around Shelby knew that Democratic party regulars were rubbing their hands gleefully at the thought of bringing The Senator down, the July issue of the *American Mercury* was awaited with enthusiasm—"despite our frequent inclination to term Dr. Mencken, the editor, a sour-grape critic with a brilliant but diseased brain."[4]

Cash hitchhiked a ride to Charlotte and swaggered into the city room at the *News*, displaying with pride his letter from Mencken. That piece on Simmons, Cash drawled, the one he had said he was writing, would appear soon in the *Mercury*. (Cash's swagger is understandable. An acceptance letter from Mencken was like a victory banner. "Well, I had a letter from Henry Mencken today," Sherwood Anderson recalled. "You said it offhand, but in your heart you felt it was like being knighted by a king. You damn well knew the others felt the same.") One of the staffers, who was something of a maiden aunt to the younger writers, jumped up, grabbed Cash, and exclaimed, "I knew you'd do it, Bill Joe, I knew it." His buddy old Tom Revelle, the grizzled, one-armed city reporter, yelled out that an acceptance from Mencken called for a drink. The motion was seconded and passed, as was a proposed session at their hangout, the Little Pep Cafe, to be convened as soon as they got the paper out. Cash hurried upstairs to tell the others, especially his pal Tom Warren, the elderly proofreader, who was forever badgering reporters, young and old, to read Mencken and Walter Lippmann—"then maybe they would know how to write." Cash went to lunch with Dick Young and Tim Pridgen, reporter buddies who told him that he was a lucky dog to impress Mencken.[5]

Later that afternoon, Cash tagged along with the crowd to their nightly retreat at the Little Pep, a greasy spoon around the corner run by a good-natured Greek who was fond of Cash and the newspaper crowd. The Simmons piece had been easy to write, said Cash. He had looked up a few things and rummaged through the newspaper's files, but mainly he had spun it out of his head. Now he wanted to write that book for Knopf or tackle a novel, but he needed money. How was

4. *Cleveland Star* (Shelby, N.C.), May 15, 1929.
5. Katherine Grantham Rogers to Joseph L. Morrison, September 20, 1964, in Joseph L. Morrison Papers, Southern Historical Collection, University of North Carolina, Chapel Hill.

he to support himself and help his family now that he was out of a job? Perhaps a publisher would give him a royalty advance on a novel or on the biography of Lafcadio Hearn that Cash talked about writing. He felt torn between doing Hearn, a project he was sure he could complete quickly, and savaging the Fugitive-Agrarian writers for their conservative manifesto, *I'll Take My Stand*. Everybody was buzzing about it, but it totally misrepresented the South, Cash snapped. Mencken would love the piece he had in mind, a slashing essay à la the master himself, that would expose the Fugitive-Agrarians for the heartless reactionaries they were. Whenever he mentioned John Crowe Ransom, Allen Tate, Donald Davidson, or others in the Vanderbilt crowd, one of the group remembered, Cash "pronounced those names as if they were cuss words." "The tone was about the same that he always used in later years in speaking of Tom Wolfe—a tone that indicated three parts envy and six parts sneer."[6]

The envy is understandable. Tate and the Agrarians were his exact contemporaries, as was Wolfe, who in 1929 launched his acclaimed Brobdingnagian novel *Look Homeward, Angel*. As writers, they were his rivals. Cash was daring to measure his ability against theirs, daring to dream of matching them in reputation. An artist, Nietzsche said, cannot believe in himself too much. An artist has to believe in himself no matter how slight or even nonexistent the evidence and believe before he has any objective right to expect anyone to read one word from his pen. This was well and good, but in an artist as emotionally fragile and uncertain as Cash, one can certainly understand the sources, the hidden anger, the suppressed rage, and the fear of failure that can bring a sneer to the face. Not only were Tate and the Agrarians the competition, they were the enemy. Their love of tradition and of religion and their nostalgia for the Old South with its fixed social relations were anathema to Cash. Cash was keenly aware of Tate's ability and literary accomplishments. His work appeared in all the leading magazines. Among the Agrarians, his was the sharpest, most subtle, most creative mind; his "Ode to the Confederate Dead" (1927) had made his name as a poet. The year Cash broke into print in the *American Mercury*, Tate won a Guggenheim Fellowship on the strength of his slender biography *Stonewall Jackson* (1928)—"part Hemingway

6. *Ibid.*

and part elementary school primer," one critic has quipped—and used the year abroad to write an impressionistic biography of Jefferson Davis (1929).[7]

But for now Cash had an essay in the smartest magazine in America. "Jehovah of the Tar Heels" was brilliant pyrotechnics, worthy of the master himself. Cash mocks, scolds, overstates; the essay drips with sarcasm and cynicism. He swipes at "Buck Duke," "Dr. Wilson," the "essential sottishness of Democracy," and the "hymn-singing Charlotte *Observer*." And in aping Mencken's bold, intentionally provocative style Cash echoed Mencken's racial and ethnic slang. "Blackamoors" and "Ethiops" along with "wops" and "dagos" dot Cash's pages. And in chronicling Simmons' shameless exploitation of racism, Cash wrote: "On election day the coon shivered at home behind closed shutters and the Democrats swept back to power." Readers of the *American Mercury* were sophisticated enough to see that slangy flourishes underscored the ugliness of racism, but to modern ears, unaware of the journalistic context or the fact that Mencken (and Cash) used slangy epithets for every group—even their own—Cash's words sound like malicious slurs.[8]

Even so, Cash's essay embodied far more than Menckenian arm waving. Cash argued passionately, as he had while an obscure country editor, that Simmons was little more than a hollow reactionary, "the stateliest Neanderthaler who ever cooled his heels on a Capitol Hill desk." In fact, Simmons was a closet Republican. Never mind his protestations about party loyalty, his reputation as Mr. Democrat, or his well-known slogan "The party—from constable to President." Simmons' voting record, particularly his continued support for Republican-sponsored protective tariff bills, gave him away. His support for the highly protectionist Payne-Aldrich bill of 1909, to say nothing of his stand on inheritance tax laws in the 1920s, had set "the barons gurgling hosannas." Simmons had survived in North Carolina by staying in firm control of his machine, intimidating the state press, and

---

7. Richard H. King, *A Southern Renaissance: The Cultural Awakening of the American South, 1930–1955* (New York, 1980), 102; for incisive interpretations of Tate see Daniel Joseph Singal, *The War Within: From Victorian to Modernist Thought in the South, 1919–1945* (Chapel Hill, 1982), 232–64; Louis D. Rubin, Jr., *The Wary Fugitives: Four Poets and the South* (Baton Rouge, 1978), 64–135; and Michael O'Brien, *The Idea of the American South, 1920–1941* (Baltimore, 1979), 136–61.

8. Cash, "Jehovah of the Tar Heels," 313, 314.

aligning himself with North Carolina industrialists, the Cannons, the Dukes, and the Reynoldses. Simmons' biographer rightly dismisses Cash's contention that "The Senator" set the state on the road to Republicanism as so much bombast, though he makes clear, as Cash did, that Simmons' support for protective tariff laws and shrewd maneuvering on inheritance tax legislation saved the Duke Endowment, built on American Tobacco Company and Duke Power Company stocks, millions of dollars.[9]

"Jehovah of the Tar Heels" reveals Cash's entrenched political liberalism. He was a democrat, as well as a Democrat, and an idealist, although he tried to hide that—avowed idealists were scorned in Mencken's pages—and Cash derided "Dr. Wilson" and the "War for Humanity." But Cash reserved his full derision for his party's tradition of racism, his region's preachers and their anti-intellectualism and their susceptibility to recurrent bouts of nativism, and the GOP's tender regard for the tariff and business "barons."[10]

The July *American Mercury* appeared on North Carolina newsstands ballyhooing "Jehovah of the Tar Heels." Charlotte rushed to the newsstands; subscribers found themselves particularly popular with friends and neighbors. Cash, initially anxious about what people would think, was relieved and enormously pleased by the article's basically positive reception. He chuckled at the story that the local librarian had removed it from the shelves once she discovered what Cash had said about The Senator. She had a Christian duty to protect her town's morals, and blasphemy was blasphemy. The next spring, as the Democratic primary heated up and regular Democrats lined up behind Josiah W. Bailey, Simmons' opponent, Bailey's friends demanded that the magazine be returned to the shelves. But to no avail. The *American Mercury* was staying put—behind her desk, along with writings by atheists like Tom Paine, whose books she would not even catalog, let alone allow to circulate.[11]

Folks in Shelby, including The Senator's friends, could not wait to get their hands on Cash's sacrilege. Drum bragged that a local boy had a piece published by "America's best known and most widely cussed

9. *Ibid.*, 310, 311, 314, 316; Richard L. Watson, Jr., "Furnifold M. Simmons: 'Jehovah of the Tar Heels?'" *North Carolina Historical Review*, XLIV (1967), 179.

10. Cash, "Jehovah of the Tar Heels," 310.

11. Katherine Grantham Rogers to Joseph L. Morrison, September 20, 1964, in Morrison Papers.

critic." The piece was "a great article," full of "campaign thunder," said Drum gleefully, enough "to riddle the elderly senator." Lots of folks around Shelby knew what Cash knew, and some could actually write, but Cash had "the innards" to "write the plain truth about things, caring not a whit how much the Babbitts may bawl and whimper."[12]

Buoyed by his success, Cash surveyed "The Mind of the South" and had it ready for Mencken to publish in October. Of course, Cash had been preparing to write this piece for years, but still the essay's dazzling scope, to say nothing of its specific contentions, bespeaks extraordinary talent. The essay revolves around two overarching themes—that the contemporary southern mind was "basically and essentially the mind of the Old South" and that the fabled planters were usually nothing more than aggressive, rough-hewn farmers, one step removed from the frontier. Building on these two contentions, which he would restate more fully in *The Mind of the South*, Cash argued that it was an individualistic, romantic mind grounded in a "passion for the lush and baroque" and a never-ending religiosity.[13]

Whereas the previous generation—from Henry W. Grady to Edwin Mims—had heralded a New South of industry and rational consciousness, Cash saw a continuity of irrationality and fantasy. It was still a mind of the soil, not of the machine, of the countryside, not the city, of the folk, not the elite. By *mind* Cash meant a group mind, that cluster of assumptions and beliefs, fears and fantasies lurking in the unconscious and dominating life and what passed for rational thought. He meant, to use his later phrasing, "a fairly definite mental pattern . . . a complex of established relationships and habits of thought," not the ratiocinations of an intellectual class. "Its salient characteristic," Cash suggested in 1929, "is a magnificent incapacity for the real, a Brobdingnagian talent for the fantastic." As such, it was a mind "wholly unadjusted to the new industry"—unadjusted, as Cash would say more fully and perceptively in *The Mind of the South*, to the modern world.[14]

All this, as Fred Hobson has cogently pointed out, Mencken had said many times before. Cash not only imitated the master's style, he used Mencken's words. Certainly Cash's assertions that the southerner was unreflective and gripped by his passions reiterated Mencken. And

12. Renn Drum, "Around Our Town/Shelby Sidelights," *Cleveland Star*, June 26, 1929.
13. Cash, "Mind of the South," 185–89.
14. W. J. Cash, *The Mind of the South* (1941; rpr. New York, 1969), 429; Cash, "Mind of the South," 185.

like Mencken (and the New South liberals) Cash castigated the region's fondness for literary sentimentality and pap—Cash gave Thomas Dixon the back of his hand one more time—and the southerner's failure to read or appreciate anyone other than Scott, Dumas, or Dickens. Yet Cash was passionately serious in charging that the southerner's congenital fondness for unreality blinded him to the region's glaring hypocrisies. "He bawls loudly for Law Enforcement in the teeth of his own ingenious flouting of the Fourteenth and Fifteenth Amendments. He boasts of the purity of his Anglo-Saxon blood—and, *sub rosa*, winks at miscegenation." This blindness, when combined with his simple, congenital romanticism, deprived the southerner of critical thought. While mill owners and their apologists boasted about model villages, the majority of mill workers lived in houses that "are hardly more than pig-sties. The squalid, the ugly, and the drab are the hallmarks of the Southern mill town." [15]

Menckenisms abounded. "Lint-head," "romantic loon," "magnificent yokel," "mill-billy," and "peon" enliven Cash's pages. He had an important point to make—that the mill-billy was mired in history and, as a result, lacked any class consciousness or ability to understand his own deprivation—a controversial point that Cash would place at the center of his great book, *The Mind of the South*. But in 1929 a desire to shock (and perhaps to please Mencken) bedazzled Cash and threatened to trivialize his argument. The mountaineer–mill hand, he wrote, "is a still at heart a mountain lout, lolling among his hounds or putting about a moonshine-still while his women hoe the corn. He has no genuine conviction of wrong. His grievances exist only in the absolute. There is not one among them for which he is really willing to fight. And that is the prime reason why all Southern strikes fail." Such rhetorical flourishes gratified Cash's ego and made Mencken smile, but they obscured Cash's seriousness and his thoroughgoing modernism, particularly his reliance on Freud—that the mill-billy, caught in the web of history, is governed by his subconscious and pacified all too often by "the ego-warming backslap of the boss." For a writer with deeply moral intentions and serious arguments to make, Cash was at this time undergoing an unresolved, unconscious conflict between flippancy and moral argument. [16]

15. Cash, "Mind of the South," 186.
16. *Ibid.*, 187–89.

For all his extravagance, Cash's thesis has been underscored and echoed by other observers and historians. "At the core of the Southern mill workers' outlook on life," Paul Blanshard reported in the *Nation*, "are the Sunday school, the Star Spangled Banner, and personal friendship for the boss." In historian Irving Bernstein's view the southern worker was trapped in his "rural tradition, his ingrained individualism, his restless mobility, his apathy, his poverty, and his suspicions of northerners."[17] According to George B. Tindall, the striking mill hands, however mutinous, "seized upon the union as an instrument of protest rather than as an agency for long-range collective bargaining."[18]

Like Mencken and Gerald W. Johnson, Cash paid homage to the "civilized minority" of James Branch Cabell, DuBose Heyward and Julia Peterkin and their attempts to break free from southern sentimentality of the Thomas Dixon–Thomas Nelson Page variety. Cash also graciously saluted Howard Odum and William Louis Poteat. But "all of them are of that level of intelligence which is above and outside any group mind. They are isolated phenomena, thrown up, not because of conditions in the South, but in spite of them." The civilized minority was reasonable, the southern mind was emotional, a mind of fantasies and folk myths, much of which was locked in the subconscious far beyond the ratiocinations of any group.[19]

"One of these days," Renn Drum proclaimed, "Cleveland County may awake to the knowledge that it has produced another prominent writer—one who can already write rings around Thomas Dixon." Drum announced that the Knopfs had expressed interest in having Cash write a book. But what did those initials W. J. stand for, Drum teased. Had Cash been named for William Jennings Bryan? "Can it be that the young critic was named for the Great Commoner and so despises the Babbitts that he will never permit himself to write his name in full?"[20]

A week later, however, the *Star* editorially jabbed at Cash and reprinted chunks of a nasty editorial from a Virginia daily that berated him as a "callow" writer who "rarely cares to be hampered by the hard

17. Paul Blanshard, "One-Hundred Per Cent Americans on Strike," *Nation*, CXXVIII (1929), 556; Irving Bernstein, *The Lean Years: A History of the American Worker, 1920–1933* (Boston, 1960), 40.

18. George B. Tindall, *The Emergence of the New South, 1913–1945* (Baton Rouge, 1967), 350.

19. Cash, "Mind of the South," 191.

20. *Cleveland Star* (Shelby, N.C.), October 2, 1929.

reality of facts when lubricating for print."[21] Nearly a decade later, Cash exclaimed—with more than a touch of bravado—that fully fifty southern newspapers had laid into him for his words in the *Mercury* and that only Alabama's Grover Hall of the Montgomery *Advertiser* had anything nice to say about him, and he "proceeded to opine at great length that I was unmistakably an idiot." Letters abusing "me as a polecat, a hoss-thief, and a yellow dog" flowed in, too, "and some of them added admonitions to stay away from their part of the country on pain of a fast coat of tar and feathers."[22] Was Cash inventing? None of the vitriolic letters have survived, and a search of the major newspapers in North Carolina yielded nary an editorial comment, favorable or otherwise. Yet Cash's reputation for brilliance and bitterness had made its way into editorial offices. At the time Cash's critical piece appeared, Grover Hall suggested Cash's name to a Virginia newspaper editor who was looking for an associate editor. Hall, whose anti-Klan editorials had earned him a Pulitzer Prize, admired Cash but admitted that he was "'a bit sour in his outlook on the Southern scene.'" Cash, who probably never knew he was being considered, lost the job to another Tar Heel journalist. In 1938 Cash was still publicly smarting about the comments he had read, saying that in 1929 "my hide had not yet grown so tough as it is now."[23]

By late 1929 Cash, like everyone else in the region, had his attention drawn to labor unrest in nearby Gastonia and the wave of strikes and antiunion violence that swept the piedmont. Southern textile unions had made some gains during World War I, but by the mid-1920s unions had been nearly wiped out and the mill owners reigned supreme. In the words of one South Carolina boss, "We govern like the czar in Russia. We are monarchs of all we survey." But, says a historian, "a subterranean turbulence simmered in the mill villages of the piedmont" and erupted in 1928–1929 when Gastonia's Loray Mill, a Rhode Island–owned plant, increased work loads, cut wages, and fired rebellious workers. Incensed, the workers walked out and proclaimed the unthinkable, a real strike. The confrontation attracted worldwide attention when the National Textile Workers Union took charge in

21. Editorial, "Perhaps Cash Is Just Another Southerner?" *Cleveland Star* (Shelby, N.C.), October 9, 1929. The Virginia paper quoted is the Portsmouth *Star*.
22. Charlotte *News*, July 5, 1936.
23. John Kneebone, *Southern Liberal Journalists and the Issue of Race, 1920–1944* (Chapel Hill, 1985), 35.

late 1928. Then the communists arrived, led by Comrade Fred Beal, hoping to help and to make Gastonia "the citadel of the class struggle." By April, 1929, the strike had been busted, but a remnant, encouraged by militant labor leaders and communists, held out. Gastonia was shocked. The time-honored, ego-boosting pat on the back from the boss, as Cash would say in *The Mind of the South*, had failed to work. The culprits must be "outsiders." [24]

The outraged mill owners ran large advertisements in the local press warning against "world revolution, irreligion, racial mixing, and free love." Fears were exacerbated when the Gastonia police chief was killed during the storming of the strikers' "tent city." Following the mistrial of sixteen unionists for the sheriff's murder, an angry—and carefully prepped—mob roared through Gaston County in a "flying squadron" of Model T's, led by police, wrecking union property and terrorizing union sympathizers. And when a truckload of radical workers arrived at Gastonia's city limits in late September, 1929, they were turned back and fired on by the police and workers. In the mayhem, orchestrated by the police and management, young Ella May Wiggins, mother of five and a tent city balladeer, took a bullet in the back in clear daylight in front of fifty witnesses. After much foot-dragging her assailants were indicted, tried in Charlotte, and speedily acquitted by a jury that had heard the defense (supplied by the Loray Mill) argue that the defendants should be found innocent because the victim believed in communism. [25]

Journalists and writers North and South converged on Gastonia and the other strike centers to tell the world about "the madness at Marion," the "one-hundred per cent Americans on strike," or to discern "the lessons of Gastonia" or commemorate "Ella May's songs." Together they underscored the wretched mill conditions, the long hours, the low pay, and the fate of the die-hard dissidents. [26]

24. The mill boss is quoted in Tindall, *Emergence of the New South*, 333–39, 345. The authoritative work on the strike remains Liston Pope, *Millhands and Preachers: A Study of Gastonia* (New Haven, 1942).

25. Tindall, *Emergence of the New South*, 346–47; Pope, *Millhands and Preachers*, 239–95.

26. William Spofford, "Marion, North Carolina," *Christian Century*, XLVI (1929), 1502–1503; Paul Blanshard, "One-Hundred Per Cent Americans on Strike," *Nation*, CXXVIII (1929), 554–56; Paul Blanshard, "Communism in Southern Mills," *ibid.*, CXXVIII (1929), 500–501; Nell Battle Lewis, "Anarchy Versus Communism in Gastonia," *ibid.*, CXXIX (1929), 321–22; Margaret Larkin, "Ella May's Songs," *ibid.*, 383; Benjamin Stolberg, "Madness at Marion," *ibid.*, 463; Edgar W. Knight, "The Lesson of Gastonia," *Outlook and Independent*, CLIII (1929), 46; Benjamin U. Ratchford, "Economic Aspects of the Gastonia Situation," *Social Forces*, VIII (1929–30), 359–67.

By contrast, Cash's look at the war in the South was reflective, certainly more even-handed than his title implied. He concentrated mainly on the mill "baron," a simple man, Cash said acidly, "a horse-trader at heart," whose original intention of building mills to make money and to provide employment for the whites—Broadus Mitchell's argument from 1922—had turned into a full-scale social revolution. The new "hard-fisted" mill men had rudely shoved the planter aside as the head of the southern social order, a contention Cash would recant in his book. But the barons, being southerners, were an unreflective, simple lot and were now motivated only by greed, forever lost to noblesse oblige. Cash saw little reason to hope. The clergy and the barons were as one in their view of good and evil—a point Liston Pope would document in his classic work *Millhands and Preachers* (1942)—and all too eager to exploit the "hedonistic, shiftless" mill hands. With a notable exception here and there, the police, the courts, and the press were handmaidens of the mill owners. Even the murder of the Gastonia police chief was "undoubtedly precipitated by the badgering activities of his own officers." Beal and his comrades were "convicted before the hearings began." Cash's account squared with the facts fully established later by historians. The trial of the communists was "a heresy trial" at which the prosecution badgered the defendants with such questions as "Do you believe in North Carolina? Do you believe in good roads?" Ella May Wiggins' murderers had gone free, but Beal and the rest of the "outsiders" were found guilty of second-degree murder in one hour of jury deliberation.[27]

For the first time, Cash talked about violence. Citing the murder of Wiggins and how such murderers "must always go free," Cash argued that violence was the southern response to any serious criticism or attack. "The single best weapon for putting down the 'invader' and the 'renegade' is Ku Kluxery—the repressed sadism, the native blood-lust, the horrible mob-instinct, which smolders among the brutal and the ignorant everywhere in the South, and, above all, and ironically, among the mill-workers themselves." The workers' fears and prejudices were exploited by the "better South," the people and organizations dear to the heart of New South liberalism. In the following years, Cash would drive home the point that the real villains in southern

27. Cash, "War in the South," 165. Beal fled to Russia. He eventually returned, and was captured and imprisoned in North Carolina until pardoned by Governor J. Melville Broughton in 1942. See Tindall, *Emergence of the New South*, 347; Pope, *Millhands and Preachers*, 302–306.

violence were not the lintheads or the rednecks but the inflamed agents of what he would come to call "the ruling race" or "Proto-Dorians," he would say with a flourish, and their "savage ideal" of intolerance and brutal suppression of any serious questioning or dissent. [28]

The war at Gastonia and Marion (where six workers were killed and many more wounded) was over. The owners won hands down; the unions were busted. It would take a decade for the National Textile Workers Union to rebound in the mill country. But to Cash, the intellectual, the real war was still to be fought. The shortsighted barons were at war with the "New Industrialism," which looked beyond immediate profits, seeing that higher wages created consumer demand, which in turn stimulated production and even greater profits. Where Cash picked up this bit of basic Keynesian insight is unknown. "Consider," Cash wrote, "the possible effect on the over-production of cotton goods if the wages of the lint-head were so raised that he might change his underwear twice a week rather than once, as now the custom is!" But none of this would the old-time barons, trapped in their upbringing, understand. They were bound to go the way of the dinosaur and be shoved aside by a new race of "grand dukes" from "the commercial Babbitts of North and South alike." [29]

This time Renn Drum's pat on the back was less boisterous. His comments appeared in the form of a news article. Cash could make Mencken "flinch when he starts using sharp-edged adjectives and lance-like reviews," Drum wrote, and he defended Cash, saying that *baron* was the sort of word one had to use when writing for Mencken. (One wonders how the *Cleveland Star* would have reacted had Cash used Broadus Mitchell's term *fleshpots* or Gerald W. Johnson's *Lady Bountiful* for the mill owners' paternalism.) Drum still admired Cash's artistry and attitude, but he admitted that although "cleverly written," Cash's article "tends to give one the fidgets if the reader is not in sympathy with his views." [30]

The year 1929—so fateful for the nation as of Black Tuesday, October 29—had been a good year for Sleepy Cash. Other topics for Mencken danced before his eyes. Surely Poteat's courageous stand

---

28. Cash, "War in the South," 166.
29. *Ibid.*, 169; Tindall, *Emergence of the New South*, 348.
30. *Cleveland Star* (Shelby, N.C.), January 29, 1930; Broadus Mitchell, "Fleshpots in the South," *Virginia Quarterly Review*, III (1927), 161–76; Gerald W. Johnson, "Service in the Cotton Mills," *American Mercury*, V (1925), 219–23.

against the forces of darkness in North Carolina merited an admiring article, perhaps along the lines of Gerald W. Johnson's recent tribute to the University of North Carolina's Harry Woodburn Chase. Or perhaps the invigorating atmosphere of the university deserved an article. Certainly the Fugitives deserved a good going over. Lafcadio Hearn still sounded intriguing. Then there was that big book the Knopfs wanted.[31]

He thought he knew what he wanted to say in the book. In November, 1929, he detailed his ideas to Howard W. Odum, the acclaimed regionalist at the University of North Carolina. Cash repeated or refined his major points—the centrality of the past, the plantation past in particular; the barrenness of southern literature and art; the emergence of barons and mill workers; the region's sentimentality and romanticism; the undying significance of God; the emergence of a new industrial order based on Yankee notions of "hurry" and progress; and the coming triumph of Babbittry, both the "Yankeefied" and homegrown varieties. Conscious of Odum's congenital optimism, he admitted that the growing number of high school graduates, the proliferation of book clubs, and the increased sales of books were promising signs. But how much promise? Such signs surely "hearten the professional glad boys" like Edwin Mims, but he doubted whether the "civilized minority" even dinted the masses. "Who do North Carolinians follow," Cash asked plaintively, "Simmons or Harry Chase, Mouzon or Poteat? Who most perfectly represents their ideals and aspirations?"[32]

Cash's letter reveals how completely he had come to think of southern culture as an enmeshing whole, a closely woven texture, extending backward and forward in time, across class, sexual, and racial lines. Regarding race, however, he added little except to say that he wanted to find the reasons for the dominance of "Ku Kluckery" and that "I'm even more interested in the effect that the Negro has had on the thinking of the white man in the South." Cash was convinced that "the South" was no mere geographical expression. It was an engulfing emotional entity, an ever-present reality, a folk mind almost palpable, a mind, one might characterize—with a bow to Carl Jung—

31. Gerald W. Johnson, "Chase of North Carolina," *American Mercury*, XVII (1929), 183–90.

32. W. J. Cash to Howard Odum, November 13, 1929, in Howard Odum Papers, Southern Historical Collection, University of North Carolina, Chapel Hill.

as a "collective unconscious." To be southern meant to be enmeshed in that emotional reality.

"My thesis," Cash told Blanche Knopf in March, 1930, "is that the Southern mind represents a very definite culture, or attitude towards life, a heritage, from the Old South, but greatly modified and extended by conscious and unconscious efforts over the last hundred years to protect itself from the encroachments of three hostile factors: the Yankee Mind, the Modern Mind, and the Negro." This mind was "a combination of certain orthodoxies and a defense mechanism," said Cash, putting his reading in Freud to use. He intended in his discussion of the South's "Modern Mind," he continued, "to trace the conflict of the South with all those ideas dating from Darwin and after, and which together might be called the intellectual approach to life." Modern writers and thinkers had made some headway in the South, and they "will continue to make inroads . . . but I doubt that they will have any very considerable influence." In the end, leadership would, "in the very nature of things, continue in the hands of the charlatans." Ten years later, when he concluded *The Mind of the South*, Cash had not yielded one inch on this point.[33]

It was that "very nature of things," that unyielding folk mind, a mind that controlled the "charlatans" as they in turn controlled it, that Cash had set out to probe. It was a herculean task that called for a thinker in the South to stand both inside and outside the "nature of things." To fulfill the task Cash would need enormous ego and psychic strength.

On the heels of publishing three searingly critical pieces in the *Mercury* and telling Odum and Blanche Knopf what he intended to say about the South, Cash got sick again. His old nemesis, neurasthenia, laid him low again. He collapsed and had to be put to bed. On the advice of local doctors, he entered a hospital in Charlotte for rest and tests. He remained hospitalized for two months, but his physician, a urologist, could find nothing organically wrong except for a hyperthyroid condition. Why was Cash kept in a hospital for two months? Was his emotional condition that unstable? Was he being confined as a mental patient? If so, what treatment, besides rest (which he could have taken at home) did he receive? Electric shock was the standard

33. W. J. Cash to Blanche Knopf, March 3, 1930, in Morrison Papers.

and effective treatment in those days. Cash's physician, who had begun treating him in the late 1920s, remained convinced that Cash would have responded to proper psychiatric treatment, but Charlotte did not have a psychiatrist. The medical records have not survived, but after two months of some sort of treatment he was released and admonished "to refrain completely from writing and study of any kind, and, indeed, even from reading."[34]

Cash busied himself for the next few years "riding a bicycle, walking, swimming and cutting wood," and talking with cronies and town folks who had time on their hands. The specter of hard times was on the land. Tobacco prices were falling. His father's hosiery mill was feeling the effects of the Depression and could operate only one or two days a week at best. For the recovering son there was not much to do in Boiling Springs or Shelby except loaf and talk. He and the Reverend H. H. Honeycutt, an unemployed Baptist preacher, whose wife taught at Boiling Springs High School, frequently whiled away the hours talking about God and man in the South. Honeycutt was a sensitive, introspective man with an open, expansive turn of mind. Something of a maverick himself, he was a kindred spirit who sensed that beneath Cash's diffident exterior, often expressed in tough-guy talk, was a deeply passionate man, whose need to understand the southern past ran far deeper than the historian's usual interest in what happened. Sitting on the Honeycutts' front porch or in the kitchen, sipping cup after cup of coffee and smoking too many cigarettes, the two seekers frequently greeted the dawn with as much enthusiasm as when they began.[35]

During these years, in the early and mid-1930s, Cash became a familiar figure around Boiling Springs and Shelby. On warm afternoons he would frequently sit for hours in a cane-bottom chair, leaning contentedly against the courthouse, head down, apparently asleep, panama hat shading his eyes. On lazy, hot days he would doze in the manner of many leisurely southerners who did not have much to do, or anywhere to go, or any money to spend. He still lived with his folks. Most people considered him an odd fellow, a loafer pure and simple. His friends said Sleepy was thinking about things, and anyway he was "not well." Besides, he was not doing anybody any harm. Thus he

34. Application for a John Simon Guggenheim Memorial Fellowship, October 20, 1932, in Morrison Papers.
35. Interview with Jay Jenkins, August 11, 1984.

became one of Shelby's "characters" along with the perambulating preachers who staked out a corner on the square to "testify."

A good friend of Cash's in those days was a principal of the local school district. He was a fellow liberal, and there are "damn few liberals" around Boiling Springs and Shelby, the future Charlotte columnist Kays Gary remembers his father saying of his conversations with Cash. Young Kays would go to the picture show at the Webb Theater while his father and Cash talked about the plight of sharecroppers and mill workers and the operation of the local banks. Occasionally, Cash would give Gary's father some pages of manuscript to read and comment on. Once Gary asked his father what he had in his hand. "It's a book that'll never get finished," was the sad reply.[36]

Recovering emotionally and eager to get back to work, Cash followed local events avidly with an eye for possible articles. When Senator Lee Slater Overman died in December, 1930, and Governor Gardner appointed Cameron Morrison, a former governor, to fill the unexpired term, Cash pulled himself together sufficiently in early 1931 to sketch a profile of Morrison for the *American Mercury*. In "Paladin of the Drys" (published in October) Cash retained enough of his Menckenian style to dismiss the "Hon. Cam" as little more than a party hack who had been outmaneuvered by Simmons in claiming credit for North Carolina's white supremacy campaign and whose devotion to Prohibition had been tempered in 1928 by sensible party loyalty. Cash grudgingly listed Morrison's achievements, how as governor (1921–1925) he had continued the fight for public schools and the "good roads movement," part of what has been called "Business Progressivism." But mainly Cash lashed Morrison for having championed the antievolution forces in the state against Poteat and Chase of the University of North Carolina. That North Carolina did not go the way of Tennessee and become part of the laughingstock in the civilized world owed nothing to the "Hon. Cam," whom Cash criticized for his continued reviling of evolutionists even after he left office.[37]

Mainly, though, Cash suffered through his "breakdown." He mused about ways to escape the arid, tight little island that was Boiling

36. Telephone interview with Kays Gary, October 5, 1984.

37. Willard Gatewood, *Preachers, Pedagogues and Politicians: The Evolution Controversy in North Carolina, 1920–1927*, 100–146. For specific references to Cameron Morrison, see *ibid.*, 100, 108; George B. Tindall, "Business Progressivism: Southern Politics in the Twenties," *South Atlantic Quarterly*, LXII (1963), 92–106.

Springs. He reminded his parents that an ocean voyage and travel in Europe had helped in 1927. Perhaps another trip abroad would help. John and Nannie, now severely pinched financially by the Depression, reluctantly agreed and said they would help as much as they could. Looking forward to a seaman's berth on a merchant ship departing from New York, Wilbur said his good-byes and boarded the train. He made it to New York, where he collapsed in a hotel room. The long-suffering John Cash came to New York and brought his eldest son home.

Following a period of rest, Wilbur felt better by early 1932. On the advice and referral of his urologist in Charlotte, he went with his father to the Johns Hopkins Hospital for a checkup. The doctors, apparently unable to find anything wrong with him—no medical records survive—pronounced him fit, whereupon a much relieved young man traveled to New York to visit the Knopfs and refresh himself visiting with his friend Katherine Grantham Rogers, formerly of the Charlotte News.[38]

Cash was much better by the fall of 1932. He had been following the events at Chapel Hill, where the university's new president, Frank Porter Graham, was embroiled in controversy following the appearances on campus of Bertrand Russell and the acclaimed black poet Langston Hughes. Russell's visit followed closely on the heels of his recent iconoclastic book, Marriage and Morals, a red flag in the face of Bible-believing Tar Heels. Hughes's admirers aroused further hostility when they circulated some of his poems, including "Black Christ," with its line "Christ is a nigger on the cross of the South." North Carolina's fundamentalists, still seething over the loss to the evolutionists and "modernists," bristled at the thought of the university hosting "athe-istic radicals" and "nigger poets." The battle lines were drawn in September, 1932, as conservatives and reactionaries fought to oust the new president, who was "just as liberal" as the last one, Henry Woodburn Chase. But the trustees backed Graham, the beleaguered professors, and free speech.[39]

Surely Mencken, long an admirer of the university, would want to see an article from Cash that put the controversy in perspective and

38. Katherine Grantham Rogers to Joseph L. Morrison, September 20, 1984, in Morrison Papers; Joseph L. Morrison, W. J. Cash, Southern Prophet: A Biography and a Reader (New York, 1967), 56.

39. Warren Ashby, Frank Porter Graham: A Southern Liberal (Winston-Salem: John F. Blair Publisher, 1980), 125, 127.

got in some licks against Graham's enemies. But Mencken said no. To publish anything written during the crisis, he feared, would be "imprudent." The controversy had been widely reported in the newspapers, including the Baltimore *Sun*, and other accounts were sure to follow as new facts were discovered and events unfolded. "Thus it would be practically impossible to form an article in such manner that it would be proof against errors and omissions." Of course, Mencken asked, "What other ideas have you?"[40]

Cash then surprised Mencken and the Knopfs by announcing that he had decided to turn his full attention to writing a biography of the exotic Lafcadio Hearn. Cash needed money for travel so he was applying for a John Simon Guggenheim Memorial Fellowship, and he requested letters of recommendation. "It goes without saying," Mencken replied halfheartedly, "that I'll be delighted to endorse you." Cash was to have the foundation send its "usual blank and I'll fill it out." Mencken was plainly more excited about a piece on Charlotte that Cash had mentioned.[41]

What explains Cash's erratic behavior? Perhaps it might be traceable to his unhappiness with a quickly written draft of a major part of the book. "It contained some excellent ideas and some passages of good writing," Cash thought, but he had written "too rapidly." Overall it was unsatisfactory. "I knew a great deal less about the South," he acknowledged a few years later, "than I thought I knew, and above all I grew to dislike the attitude with which I had begun." It was, he told Knopf, "so hopelessly out of line with changes in my ideas and so unsatisfactorily organized, that the best thing to do was to scrap it *in toto* and start writing virtually from the beginning." It is tempting, given Cash's tendency to procrastinate, to second-guess him and feel anger or impatience with the man for throwing away pages and then avoiding working on a book that would become a classic. Cash was a master of avoidance behavior. But he was also a sound critic and presumably knew, if only dimly, what he wanted to write. Perhaps the manuscript was deficient and deserved to be scrapped. In any case, destroying the manuscript was a stark statement about the enormity of his task. All his uncertainties and fears welled up within him, and he responded by

40. H. L. Mencken to W. J. Cash, September 12, 1932, in H. L. Mencken Papers, New York Public Library, New York City.
41. H. L. Mencken to W. J. Cash, October 25, 1932, *ibid.*

thinking wistfully about another writing project, a life of Hearn, a book that would be "easy" and could be done "quickly."[42]

A book about Hearn also held out the promise of affording Cash a socially acceptable and perhaps profitable way to analyze himself. Hearn was a romantic, much like himself, and held an exotic appeal for Cash. Born in Greece in 1850 to Irish and Greek parents, raised in Dublin, educated in France and England, Hearn emigrated to the United States, finally settling in New Orleans in 1877, where he worked for a decade as a journalist, short story writer, novelist, collector of Creole tales, legends, and proverbs, orientalist, student of all things imaginative and fantastic, and critic of southern culture. He ended his days in Japan, having become a Japanese citizen. Here truly was a wandering romantic, and a Celt to boot. Hearn had deliberately uprooted himself, physically and psychologically, much like a character out of Cash's beloved Conrad.[43]

What Cash had in mind, he told the Guggenheim Foundation, was not "the gathering and setting forth of new facts" about Hearn "but the using of the known facts and his letters as a basis for the study of his psychological make-up, and, through him, *of the psychological make-up of romantics in general*" (emphasis added). A Guggenheim grant would enable him to "visit New Orleans for several weeks," then go abroad, "visiting Ireland and Wales, countries in which Hearn lived as a child, and increasing my somewhat sketchy acquaintance with London; then to take up residence in Paris, the capital of literary romanticism." The whole venture could be completed in just over a year, of that he was sure.[44]

When Cash entertained these dreams and fantasies in the fall of 1932, he was a recovering neurasthenic, age thirty-two, with no job and no desire, apparently, for one. He lived at home with his parents. When able to write, he sat alone in a back room at the Boiling Springs post office, where his Aunt Bertha, the postmistress, scrounged some spare sheets of paper he could use. When he felt like working, he sat alone under a single electric light bulb and pounded out pages on his trusty Underwood. On hot summer days he sweltered. On cold winter

42. Application for a John Simon Guggenheim Memorial Fellowship, October, 1936; W. J. Cash to Alfred A. Knopf, November 27, 1935, both in Morrison Papers.

43. Beongcheon Yu, *An Ape of Gods: The Art and Thought of Lafcadio Hearn* (New York, 1964).

44. Application for a John Simon Guggenheim Memorial Fellowship, October, 1936, in Morrison Papers.

days he worked huddled in coat and hat. He knew what people whispered, what they said after church, that John and Nannie's boy—never mind his age, he was a boy—had always been odd. It was difficult for him to maintain the dignity a writer ought to have. Mischievous youngsters would crowd around the window at the rear of the post office and pester him without mercy. "We haunted him," one of those young cretins remembered with remorse. "We would slink up to the window, stick out our tongues and leer at him. Failing to get attention in that manner, we pecked tantalizingly on the glass with our fingers." Finally, when Cash had had enough, he would chase the little wretches away with a Niagara of profanity seldom heard in Baptist country.[45]

By late 1932 John Cash was finding it more and more difficult to keep his small mill operating. To economize, he moved his family to a much smaller house in Shelby, rented out his house in Boiling Springs, and traveled back and forth to work. By early 1933, with his mill at a standstill and bankruptcy staring him in the face, he sold the house in Boiling Springs, salvaged a few machines from the mill, and moved to Shelby, where he hoped to find work or outlets or individual customers for his handwoven socks.

A Guggenheim grant would have provided Wilbur Cash with the necessary funds to escape this bleak, despairing world. While waiting to hear about the fellowship, Cash kept in touch with Mencken, wrote and rewrote an article on Charlotte, scrapped his piece on Chapel Hill, and began to consider Mencken's suggestion that he muckrake "Buck Duke's" university. He also continued mulling over how he might write a critical and salable piece on the Agrarians. All the while he brooded about his and the South's failures, sat up late talking with Honeycutt, puffed away on too many roll-your-own cigarettes, and slipped over to Shelby and Charlotte, where someone would be good for a bootleg drink or two. The Guggenheim Foundation said no. Disappointed but not devastated, Cash waved good-bye to Hearn and returned to writing articles.

By February, 1933, Cash had the Charlotte piece up to Mencken's standards. It was published in April as "Close View of a Calvinist Lhasa," a title Mencken suggested but did not particularly like.[46] Cash wrote with furious indignation, portraying Charlotte, where the anti-

45. Interview with Jay Jenkins, August 11, 1984; Morrison, *W. J. Cash*, 89.
46. W. J. Cash, "Close View of a Calvinist Lhasa," *American Mercury*, XXVII (April 1933), 443–51; H. L. Mencken to W. J. Cash, February 1, 1933, in Mencken Papers.

Smith hysteria found its center, as a citadel of bigotry and obscurantism, in love with Presbyterianism, Babbittry, and the Duke Power Company. Rotary ruled. Charlotte was an "old Tory town," where "life is one continuous blue-law" and life—having degenerated to a "dreary ritual of the office, golf and the church—becomes nearly unbearably dull even for Presbyterians not wholly pathological." In Charlotte, Cash charged, as he enumerated the city's sins, the anti-evolutionary zealots, the Committee of One Hundred, had formed with an eye toward "throttling" the University of North Carolina's appropriations unless the school fell in line. Charlotteans originated the Tatum petition to remove from the university library "the works of Darwin, Freud, John Watson, Bertrand Russell, and, indeed, of everybody who has had anything to say since 1800." Charlotte inspired Gastonia reactionaries to shoot and burn out the communists and was the site where they were "formally and legally lynched." And in 1932, when the Socialist Norman Thomas got on the presidential ticket and spoke in North Carolina and Langston Hughes read poetry at Chapel Hill and elsewhere, Charlotte "stood on its head and tore its shirt and screamed for gore."[47]

There were scattered glimmerings of hope. Charlotte had repudiated Cameron Morrison in 1932. There was a Little Theater group, a cosmopolitan younger generation, and the liberal Charlotte News. The city even supported a fledgling symphony orchestra, which "at least allows one Italian fiddler to eat regularly and to wear a pair of sound pants—surely no mean success for a fiddler in Dixie." But mainly, Cash's piece was grim, angry, almost sour—far closer to Thomas Wolfe's attack on Asheville in Look Homeward, Angel than to Gerald W. Johnson's gentle deflating of Greensboro, published several years earlier in the southern magazine the Reviewer. Cash reported Charlotte "for what it is: the chief enemy of civilization" in the South. "Let the future answer for itself."[48]

There was nothing in Cash's personality to allow him to write jovially about Charlotte, whose motto was "After Edinburgh the Greatest Church-going Town in the World." Cash's Charlotte friends, particularly the crowd at the News, where drinking and skepticism toward self-righteousness went hand in hand, constantly snickered at

47. Cash, "Close View of Calvinist Lhasa," 444–45, 448–49.
48. Ibid., 449–50; Gerald W. Johnson, "Greensboro, or What You Will," Reviewer, IV (1924), 169–75.

what they considered the city's smugness and blue-nosed religiosity. At the *News* Cash and "old Mr. Warren" liked to yell out whenever they got an audience: "No modern civilized parent would send children to Sunday school."[49]

They got no argument from their buddy lawyer-reporter Tom Jimison, a defrocked Methodist minister, who called Charlotte "the lowest-kneeling, loudest-praying, tightest-fisted, hardest-drinking clan of Scotch Presbyterian[s] that ever staggered to the polls to vote dry." A lean mountaineer who daily swigged moonshine for his "stomach's sake," Jimison was a banty rooster in a red bow tie. After being stripped of his clerical collar, he had become a liberal lawyer who defended blacks. He had helped in the defense of the communists at Gastonia. Charlotte's high crime rate and self-righteousness prompted Jimison to proclaim: "They'd crucify Christ again right in front of the First Presbyterian Church if ever he dared to show up here."[50]

Cash's carving up of Charlotte was "quite daring" stuff to his friends at the *News* and to young Tar Heels at Chapel Hill, who read him eagerly in the *Mercury* and "knew who Cash was." Cash's visits to the *News* or to the Little Pep were commented on, observed. Young journalists, themselves daring to dream of becoming writers, craned their necks to have a look at the slightly balding, chain-smoking writer. "That's Cash over there," someone would whisper excitedly. "He's writing a book."[51]

Well, he may have been. In the spring of 1933 he was following up on Mencken's suggestion to "make some mention of the situation at Duke." Mencken, who reveled in sneering at the newly built Duke University as "the Methodist Rolling Mill" and "a great Fundamentalist college for yokels," had heard that a dean there had publicly protested against the mistreatment of Negro convicts. This was capital stuff, Mencken whooped, and, he told Cash, "must be a bitter pill to the 100% patriots who counted on Duke to counteract the evil influence of Chapel Hill."[52]

At first, Cash had difficulty shaping the article to satisfy Mencken. In May, 1933, Mencken pointed out that Cash had begun by saying

49. Katherine Grantham Rogers to Joseph L. Morrison, September 20, 1984, in Morrison Papers.
50. *Ibid.*
51. Interview with Harriet Doar, September 17, 1984.
52. H. L. Mencken to W. J. Cash, November 30, 1932, in Mencken Papers. Mencken on Duke is quoted in Hobson, *Serpent in Eden*, 115.

that the "opposition of old Buck Duke will be overcome," but "toward the end you seem to show it prevailing." Mencken was sure that in time the administration of President William P. Few and Dean William Wannamaker would "disappear and the university will move away from the Methodist demonology," as the medical school was already doing. Cash loyally followed Mencken's lead and produced a lively, irreverent, slashing polemic.[53] It was not for the tender-minded or for easily offended traditionalists. But it contained some extraordinarily good writing—some of the best Cash ever did—and concluded with the prediction that the day would come when the university would liberalize itself and become "a militant champion of civilization and a dangerous critic of the *status quo*."[54]

Along the way Cash got in his licks describing the late benefactor, James B. ("Buck") Duke, as one who "remained to the end essentially what he was at seventeen, a red-headed shambling Methodist-jake out of Orange county, North Carolina—which is to say, a sort of peasant out of the Eleventh Century, incredibly ignorant, incredibly obtuse, incredibly picayune." But old Buck understood profits and keeping his money. In creating the Duke Endowment, he successfully placed millions beyond the taxing arm of the federal government with the aid of a windfall inheritance tax of 1926 helped through the Congress by Furnifold M. Simmons. Now, said Cash sarcastically, millions were safely set aside for "building Methodist churches in the sticks," as well as for hospitals, orphanages, and a university that would be conducted, as Duke had charged, "'along sane and practical, as opposed to dogmatic and theoretical lines.'"[55]

"That," said Cash mocking Duke's shrewdness, "ought to hold the Legislature, eh? The theorists wouldn't get far there, heh?"

But theorists were within the gates, signing petitions protesting the treatment of black convicts and defending Norman Thomas.

"What would Mister Duke say, hunh? What would Mr. Duke say, hunh?" Cash, who was seldom humorous, was clearly having fun.

There was not much Duke's heirs or assigns could do about it. If reprimanded, the heretics would take jobs elsewhere and "write pieces

---

53. W. J. Cash, "Buck Duke's University," *American Mercury*, XXX (1933), 102–10; H. L. Mencken to W. J. Cash, May 22, 1933, in Mencken Papers.

54. H. L. Mencken to W. J. Cash, May 22, 1933, in Mencken Papers; Cash, "Buck Duke's University," 110.

55. Cash, "Buck Duke's University," 104; Watson, "Furnifold M. Simmons," 179.

about it for the *New Republic*." The new university with its imposing Gothic spires and proud tradition of academic freedom (in 1903, the college had stood firmly behind historian John Spencer Bassett's right to speak his mind freely about blacks) could not afford negative publicity. "There will be no lynchings at Duke." Bassett had eventually gone north, but professors even more liberal, Cash chortled, had gotten into the place, and more would come.[56]

Pleased with himself, Cash ripped into the Agrarians for Mencken in August, 1933. "This is a magnificent refutation of Tate, Ransom and Company," Mencken replied, "but I can't convince myself the *American Mercury* is the place to print it. Basically, it is part of a debate between Southerners, and though the suggestion may seem preposterous, I think it should be printed in the South." Did Cash have any connections with Nell Battle Lewis of the Raleigh *News and Observer*? Mencken was sure she could help. "Needless to say, I agree with you thoroughly," Mencken closed. Cash put the essay back in his drawer and later published bits and pieces of it in the Charlotte *News* and a fuller, much more restrained version in *The Mind of the South*.[57]

Five months later, in January, 1934, Cash was back in the *Mercury* with "Holy Men Muff a Chance," a satirical jab at the clergy's failure to revive the faithful by citing the stock market collapse and the bread lines as proof that the Second Coming was at hand. The problem was that the people remembered 1928 and the preachers' assurance that Hoover had been hand-picked by God. Still, the people were "hankering for certainty as a shield against the cold, harsh winds of immensity." But the real problem was that the preachers no longer really believed, "and because they don't believe, nobody really believes." The pastors stand in their pulpits and "look down into the round, fat, go-getting faces of the audience and think about their wives away at the beach and the preposterous bill the electric company sent them last week." Being human, with groceries and gasoline to buy, they "are trying to fill up their emptiness and, perhaps, to convince themselves that they are earning their money."[58]

Cash's words are startling, and startlingly inaccurate, one guesses, given the continued religious feelings and faith of southerners. But his

56. Cash, "Buck Duke's University," 104–106.

57. H. L. Mencken to W. J. Cash, August 26, 1933, in Mencken Papers.

58. W. J. Cash, "Holy Men Muff a Chance," *American Mercury*, XXXI (1934), 112–18, quote on 116.

astounding contentions, in addition to tickling Mencken and his clientele, were based on his extended conversations with disaffected clergymen, his own observations, and the climate of opinion at the *News*. Moreover, the essay reflected Cash's wide reading in contemporary thought and sheds light on his mind. He acknowledged an irony of his generation—that a great many people, including some of the era's prominent writers, still longed to believe in something permanent or something that promised some meaning as a "shield against the cold, harsh winds of immensity." He had in mind the New Humanists and the Neoplatonists, in America and abroad, and the celebrated Catholic converts of his generation, Gilbert Keith Chesterton and Hilaire Belloc, and their legion of followers. But being Cash, he could not resist adding, "and what do you suppose is the true meaning of Rotary and Kiwanis?"[59]

In "Holy Men Muff a Chance," his seventh and last major article for the *Mercury*, Cash's style, Fred Hobson has argued, had become "stale," and "instead of effective satire, the article was a bitter indictment that betrayed the personal feelings of the author." Cash's personal feelings are evident, and the essay is shallow. But it has the ring of sincerity, of a striving for detachment, the quality that had been missing from Cash's other, better writing for Mencken, the quality Hobson cogently argues must be there for the Menckenian style to be effective.[60] All along, Cash had reflected, perhaps even "betrayed," his deepest feelings. Earlier, he may have subordinated or sacrificed those feelings—meaning his passions, his ideals, his convictions—to satisfy Mencken and to achieve a flamboyant "style." (Cash had tailored "Buck Duke's University" to Mencken's ideas.) By the time "Holy Men Muff a Chance" appeared, his journalistic style had become stale because his thought had become stale.

In writing about "holy men" Cash was searching for something to write about, rather than plumbing his own feelings and experiences. Cash had always been a victim of his own talent for imitation, the easy, seemingly effortless writing in a Menckenian vein. "It was," in Hobson's view, "as if the young newspaperman had read Mencken so often and had quoted him so frequently that the same words, the same rhythm, even at times the exact phrases reverberated in his mind; thus, when he sat down to write, in the years before 1935, he wrote

59. *Ibid.*, 116.
60. Hobson, *Serpent in Eden*, 115–16.

pure Mencken. The words came from a different typewriter, but they were charged with the authority of the master." But by 1935 he was growing out of his Mencken phase.[61]

It was just as well, then, for Cash, that Mencken sold his magazine and retired from the field of battle in 1934. Knopf, continuing as the publisher of the *American Mercury*, announced that henceforth the magazine would concern itself far less with "the lower inhabitants of the Bible Belt." Appropriately, Cash's last essay, in May, 1935, was a short, straightforward overview titled "Genesis of the Southern Cracker" in which he undertook, with sympathy, to show how the "cracker" must be understood as a sorry product of southern history. But the ghost of Mencken still guided his hand. The vicious, neurotic cracker was "a pig quite capable of incest—in brief, everything that William Faulkner and Erskine Caldwell have made him out to be, and perhaps something more." Snared in the ancient pattern, the cracker is blind to the "implacable fact: to succeed in revolt he must join forces with the Negro. And rather than to do that, he prefers to starve and to rot."[62]

Preoccupation with Cash's style, his lack of detachment, his slavish devotion to Mencken, however important, obscures the greater problem Cash faced. He was an intellectual, a critic, a prober, a thinker passionately absorbed in his subject. In truth, he never wanted to be detached, certainly not as scholars understand the word and not if it meant that his style and thought would flatten out and lose their vibrancy. The South was mysterious and irrational, ensnared in an "ancient pattern" of racism, hedonism, puritanism, religiosity, and violence. To pursue that mystery, to get to the bottom of it, to plumb that "collective unconscious," and to do so in an engaging style that would attract readers was an extraordinarily difficult task. How could he stand outside the mind he would explore—in short, become de- tached—and yet avoid a ponderous, academic style? With Faulkner's genius for creating a literary vehicle to fit his purpose, Cash might have turned to fiction, as he continued to dream about doing. But Cash was, intellectually, a rationalist, trying to fathom and portray ra- tionally a mind that was rooted in an emotional religion deeply sus- picious of reason.

61. *Ibid.*, 112–13.
62. W. J. Cash, "Genesis of the Southern Cracker," *American Mercury*, XXXV (1935), 105–108, quote on 108.

None of this was theoretical to Cash. It was an ever-present conflict, particularly because (like Faulkner and unlike Wolfe) he sincerely liked the very people he felt compelled to criticize. It was no mere rhetorical flourish when he wrote in 1929 as he surveyed "The Mind of the South" that "a thinker in the South is regarded quite logically as an enemy of the people who, for the commonweal, ought to be put down summarily—for to think at all, it is necessary to repudiate the whole Southern scheme of things, to go outside God's ordered drama and contrive with Satan for the overthrow of Heaven." What was Cash to do? He knew that thinking in the South "involves unpleasant realities, unsavory conditions; and happily, there is no need for it, since, as everything is arranged by God, there is nothing to think about." What darker hell could exist for an intellectual than to reside where there was "nothing to think about"?[63]

63. Cash, "Mind of the South," 191.

6 / On the Authority of My Imagination

But wait, as W. J. Cash himself might have said. The case for Cash's psychological malaise has been exaggerated. In 1935 he was alive and well, writing and making a dollar here and there. The two hundred dollars from the *American Mercury* for "Genesis of the Southern Cracker" was of some help to him and his parents. The Baltimore *Evening Sun*, where Mencken and Cash's friend R. P. Harriss worked, bought two free-lanced pieces in the late summer of 1935—one a stinging indictment of the role of the "best people" in a North Carolina lynching and a second on a proposed federal antilynching law. Cash opposed such legislation on the traditional grounds that any attempt to coerce the stubborn South would only make matters worse for blacks by inflaming whites.[1]

By early 1936, all those long, lonely, seemingly fruitless writing sessions at the Boiling Springs post office and in the small brick house on Tryon Street were bearing fruit. On January 23, he mailed the Knopfs 306 manuscript pages. He had another chapter all but finished, he said, some 38 pages, which he was revising. That and a concluding 150 to 175 pages would soon be forthcoming, Cash promised. Not only was Cash at work, but his work was good. The 306 pages dealt expertly and provocatively with the frontier origins of the Old South, including its vaunted aristocracy and the emerging "mind" shaped by

1. W. J. Cash, "North Carolina Faces the Facts," Baltimore *Evening Sun*, August 29, 1935; W. J. Cash, "Will Any Federal Anti-Lynching Law Help Curb the Mob?" *ibid.*, September 11, 1935.

the frontiers of time, conflict, the Yankee attack on slavery, and a social structure based on slavery.[2]

February passed, but no word was heard from Shelby. To show good faith, Knopf mailed a contract in early March along with the encouraging word that Cash's manuscript was "the best picture of the South, I think, that has ever been done." The contract was standard for first-book authors: 10 percent of the net profit but no advance against royalties. Cash signed it and returned it along with excuses, apologies for his slow progress, and a promise to be finished by July 15. But could he have a modest advance, he asked plaintively, say $250? "I have sufficient income to take care of bare living expenses, but I owe $150 (of which the main part represents a balance on my typewriter) which must be met within the next 60 days, and I need the rest for incidental expenses." He could probably get the money by "turning out some articles for magazines and newspapers," but naturally he preferred to give the book his full attention. Knopf agreed and said he looked forward to seeing the concluding pages and Cash's response to an in-house reader's suggestion that he attempt to support his sweeping, bold generalizations with more specifics.[3]

April passed. No manuscript arrived. Letters came periodically from Cash bearing various excuses and explanations that he was having trouble revising some pages and, in the case of the promised chapter, "finding a way to clarify and shorten it." At one point, neuritis had "pursued" him for at least five weeks. He did find time to have his picture taken, to submit a glossy photograph, and to give some thought to his preference in binding and typeset.[4]

In mid-May Cash replied, in a somewhat aggrieved, hurt tone, to the reader's suggestion for greater specificity. "I am painfully aware of the fault in the manuscript which the reader calls attention to," but he thought it was more concrete and specific than the critic had said. Then Cash put his finger on the real issue. His book was no ordinary history, no scholarly compendium of facts marshaled to buttress impersonal arguments. Such additions as Knopf's reader wanted, Cash

2. W. J. Cash to Alfred A. Knopf, January 23, 1936, in Joseph L. Morrison Papers, Southern Historical Collection, University of North Carolina, Chapel Hill. Cash's manuscript pages make up the first 161 pages of the Vintage paperback edition of *The Mind of the South.*
3. Blanche Knopf to W. J. Cash, March 2, 1936; W. J. Cash to Alfred A. Knopf, January 23, 1936; Alfred A. Knopf to W. J. Cash, March 2, 1936; W. J. Cash to Alfred A. Knopf, March 9, 1936, all in Morrison Papers.
4. W. J. Cash to Alfred A. Knopf, April 27, 1936, *ibid.*

thought, would make the work too long. The real problem was that he had decided from the beginning "that ultimately the book is one man's view—a sort of personal report—which must rest in large part on the authority of my imagination and understanding at play on a pattern into which I was born and which I have lived most of my life." Stung by the reader's mild criticism, Cash went on at length to explain that he had already cut fifteen thousand words that would, if now added, clutter up the text with information others had treated in scholarly monographs. Most of the specifics could be relegated to running notes, he thought, "though I see that I may have made a too thorough job of the stripping, and that much of the stuff eliminated probably ought to go back into the body of the thing." He saw "no difficulty" meeting the reader's suggestions, Cash replied, but his defensive tone suggests otherwise, as does the admission that he had been "horribly stuck for nearly three weeks."[5]

June passed. No manuscript reached New York.

On July 3 Cash wrote that he had been busy inserting "concrete references" into the section on the Old South but had been having trouble shaping the next two chapters. In late August the Knopfs learned that another batch of pages was on the way, but they turned out to be revisions and additions. Cash had earnestly taken the critic's advice to heart and had added about four thousand words "of the kind of material I understand him to mean." He would make sure that the third and concluding section would be satisfactorily specific. But once again he confessed that he had been "stuck" several times and had discarded half a dozen different approaches to troublesome sections. His slowness was "irritating," and he, too, knew the desirability of getting the book out as soon as possible. "But the thing has quite genuinely had me balked—unable to get it into form which did not seem to me intolerably weak and confused."[6]

In October his story was the same. He had spent the last three months writing and rewriting, he confessed to Blanche Knopf, but without "getting much closer to a satisfactory solution—or at least it seems so to me: I'm so worried out with the thing that it is hard for me to judge." He was continuing to work on old and new sections with the critic's suggestion in mind and would soon have additional manu-

5. W. J. Cash to Alfred A. Knopf, May 17, 1936, *ibid.*
6. W. J. Cash to Alfred A. Knopf, August 28, 1936, *ibid.*

script ready. Another fifteen to eighteen thousand words would finish the job. He looked confidently to a spring, 1937, publication. Did the Knopfs fear that he had been loafing? Nothing was further from the truth, he assured them.[7]

A week later, on October 12, Cash replied soulfully that he hoped the Knopfs did not interpret his words to sound like "the Great Artist Reluctantly Surrendering His Soul to Crass Commercialism." He was anything but that. But he did "hate books which are inadequately woven into a piece, and the thought of turning out such a book." The Knopfs were right: now was the time to finish. He intended to wrap the whole thing up immediately. To do that he was going to get completely away from the writing for a week "in the hope that I'll be able to stop spinning around in dead center when I return to it."[8]

Then Cash nonchalantly announced that he was filling out an application for a Guggenheim Fellowship, which would make it possible for him to write a novel. He thought Italy and Germany would be an ideal location. He had in mind, he told Blanche Knopf blithely, chronicling "the growth of a Carolina hamlet into an industrial town, and what happened to the lives and characters of several people, mainly members of two families, in that process and *milieu*." He also hoped to observe fascism up close, "with a view to the possible writing of a sort of anatomy of the system." He had listed her, "Mr. Knopf," and Mencken as his "chief witnesses." Mencken was "willing to testify to the belief I'll make a good job of it," Cash concluded airily. He hoped the Knopfs would agree. Alfred Knopf sighed and agreed.[9]

His book for Knopf would be finished by spring of 1937, Cash assured the Guggenheim Foundation, and he had a "particular interest in the Nazi regime and movement as a historical phenomenon." For that reason he proposed to stay mainly in Berlin and Munich. Should Germany be at war by May, 1937, he thought England would be an acceptable place to write his novel, "regardless of war." The plot and theme he outlined to the Guggenheim Foundation, however, were not those he had told the Knopfs. The novel he now had in mind would be a realistic portrayal of the Old South, quite different from what the "legend-mongers have made it out to be." At the center would be a "stout young Irishman," the aggressive, self-made planter,

7. W. J. Cash to Blanche Knopf, October 4, 1936, *ibid.*
8. W. J. Cash to Blanche Knopf, October 12, 1936, *ibid.*
9. *Ibid.*

whose achievements Cash had portrayed in the opening pages of the soon-to-be-completed manuscript of *The Mind of the South*. Cash's protagonist, Angus Carrick, had ended his career as a major in the Confederate army and fathered five children. Their stories would have to be told, along with those of other plantation families, as well as "the no-count Martins, a family of so-called 'white trash.'" Cash, thinking big, was planning a sprawling family saga reminiscent of a Thomas Wolfe novel. Confidently, he expected to write the novel in one year.[10]

The differing plots, time periods, and characters Cash outlined to the Knopfs and in his application to the Guggenheim Foundation suggest that Cash did not have a clear outline for a novel in his mind and that he was living in a make-believe world with regard to his writing plans. Once again, the Guggenheim Foundation turned him down. The house of Knopf would not hear again from W. J. Cash for two years.

During that time, he fretted over his stillborn book and tried his hand at free-lancing. Ideas for novels danced before his eyes. He loafed, read, and talked politics with his friend Everett Houser, a local newspaperman and Superior Court clerk in Shelby. Cash and Lindsey Dail, a friend from the *Cleveland Star*, strolled through nearby cemeteries and talked for hours about the mills, unemployment, falling tobacco prices, southern demagogues, the Shelby dynasty, the Baptist church, the South. Cash drank a few beers with Cameron Shipp of the *Star*, cursed Prohibition, went to the picture show at the Webb Theater, lolled contentedly on the courthouse square, loafed on the bench outside Stephenson's Drug Store, or meandered inside to stand at the magazine rack and leaf through the *Atlantic* or *Harper's*. Now and then he bicycled or hitched a ride to Charlotte to see the crowd at the *News*.[11]

With a book contract to his name, Cash was something of a minor celebrity around Shelby, but he was also something of a curiosity, one of those sensitive, big fellows who, folks whispered, was "a burden to his parents." He had no job—did he even want one? The Depression was deepening, and lots of people were out of work, of course. But the bespectacled Cash, with thinning hair and widening waist, could hardly be missed when he sat on the courthouse square dozing in the

10. Application for a John Simon Guggenheim Memorial Fellowship, October, 1936, in Morrison Papers.

11. Interview with Lindsey Dail, October 28, 1985.

noonday sun. Thirty-six years old and still living at home in 1936, Wilbur contributed precious little to his family. Kinfolks and town busybodies remembered that just a few years earlier Wilbur's brother Allen had had to drop out of dental school for three years to live with his brother Henry and work thirteen hours a night at a nearby hosiery mill.[12]

In mid-November, 1935, just two months before he mailed his first pages to Knopf, an opportunity arose for Cash to do some regular writing and earn a steady, if modest, income. Earlier that fall, Cameron Shipp, formerly city editor of the *Star*, had joined the Charlotte *News*, an afternoon daily, as literary and drama editor. He immediately began urging Carey Dowd, the publisher, and his brother J. E. ("Bill") Dowd, the editor, to give Cash a job. The Dowds, intriguing mixtures of southern conservatism and New Deal liberalism, admired talent. They agreed wholeheartedly that Cash could write, but could he be trusted, and could Shipp keep Cash's radical ideas in check? The *News* was a "liberal" paper in its opposition to Prohibition and blue laws and its willingness to talk openly about rural poverty, illiteracy, and Charlotte's and the South's crime rates. Certainly the *News* was liberal when compared to the Charlotte *Observer*. But Carey and Bill Dowd were loyal southern Democrats—unlike the *Observer*, the *News* had stood firmly for Al Smith in 1928—and at one with their countrymen (and subscribers) on most social and racial issues. The Dowds were ambivalent toward Cash's acerbic pieces in the *American Mercury*. Still, the thought of adding an accomplished writer with a reputation to their staff was intriguing. Shipp's friend could write editorials on international affairs, said the Dowds, agreeing to take Cash on. But he was not to write about local matters or state politics. Shipp had to make Cash understand that.[13]

Shipp had little trouble persuading his buddy to join the paper. The salary of thiry-five dollars a week was lousy, Shipp agreed, but Cash could continue living at home. Write about Hitler, Mussolini, and Franco, Shipp told him—lay into the Nazis and fascists or anything in Europe or abroad that Cash cared to run on about. On the Sunday book page, Cash could have an even freer hand. Old-hand journalists knew that no one seemed to pay attention to what was said in the literary section. Anyway, Shipp told him, his duties would be light. He would have time to work on his book.

12. Interview with Allen Cash, August 7, 1984.
13. Interview with Charles A. McKnight, September 15, 1984.

Cam Shipp was a big, robust man with blond hair and attractive blue eyes. He smiled readily, told jokes with style, teased affably, and drank generously with his friends. Home was wherever he was, and he made others feel the same. Young and old hands at the *News* liked him, admired him, and marveled at how quickly he turned out good readable copy without ever seeming to furrow his brow or chew on his pencil. To Shipp, Jack Cash was a home boy who had a big book in him, if only he would write it. Shipp teased, cajoled, and sometimes hollered at Cash to write that book—behavior Cash would not have tolerated from anybody else, an old friend remembered. Shipp introduced his pal to the readers of the Charlotte *News* on November 17, 1935, saying, "I commend to you the Cash lucubrations, which, whether you always find them agreeable to your notions, are always amusing. This Cash is now in Shelby completing 'The Mind of the South,' a performance that is certainly far and away above any contribution I know of attempting to explain why we think like we do."[14]

For the next five years, while Knopf waited with growing impatience, Cash wrote regularly for the *News*. He penned brief, hard-hitting editorials on the tumultuous scene in Europe, mused on a variety of literary matters and authors past and present, and reviewed an array of new books. When Shipp was not joshing him and needling him to write "that book," he encouraged him to meander across the contemporary and classic literary landscape and write about whatever or whoever interested him. One week found Cash ruminating on the joys of reading William Hazlitt—particularly Hazlitt's ironic "On the Disadvantages of Intellectual Superiority," one of Cash's favorite texts and one of his pet topics of conversation. The next week he was celebrating Remy de Gourmant on style, exploring Tolstoy's contention that art must be moral, meditating on *Hamlet*, Ecclesiastes, *Don Quixote*, or the worlds created by Chaucer and Pepys. Pepys, Montaigne, and Chaucer, Cash once observed, "show us the stuff of our common humanity in its full truth, and yet without bitterness—and without any of the dreadful Freudian convulsions which beset our introspective moderns."[15]

Was Cash procrastinating, engaging in the time-honored practice of avoidance behavior when he might have been finishing his book? No

14. Harriet Doar to author, November 17, 1984; interview with Charles A. McKnight, September 15, 1984; Charlotte *News*, November 17, 1935.
15. Charlotte *News*, May 15, 1936.

doubt he was. He was also, as he frequently admitted, a "lazy fellow." But having embarked upon a book that was "a sort of personal report" resting largely "on the authority of my imagination," Cash had to draw upon himself, upon his own perceptions. His task required that he plunge deeply into his feelings for an understanding of his people. He was, in short, his own authority. He had no notecards to fall back on, no graphs or charts or statistics to fill up pages and "prove" that this or that was true. For a writer of Cash's tender psyche, this was a herculean task, made all the more excruciating because he had undertaken a sweeping critique of his own people.

As a newspaperman Cash had to produce words for someone else, not his book. During his five-plus years with the *News* Cash contributed some 260 pieces that either bear his byline, appear in his scrapbook, or sound unmistakably like his voice—the latter being mainly brief editorials. At the end of two years with the newspaper—from November, 1935, to November, 1937, when he moved to Charlotte to become an associate editor—Cash had contributed 131 pieces (80 in the first year, 51 the second). During the following year (November, 1937, to October, 1938) Cash continued at the same pace, contributing 68 pieces as well as doing editorial work. By fall of 1938, after he had been in Charlotte for a year, he was finally making progress on his book. On December 14, he mailed Knopf sixty pages of new manuscript, and additional pages were ready by February. Then he lapsed into another dry spell and did not have any significantly new material ready until June, 1939, and would not complete the project for another year. From late 1938 until June, 1940, when he made major progress on his manuscript, Cash was writing far less for the newspaper, approximately 51 pieces, many of them slight (28 the first year, 23 the second). Obviously, his newspaper writing kept him from his book. But it is also true that Cash did substantial work on his manuscript *after* his duties with the newspaper increased significantly and *after* he had moved out of his parents' house and into an apartment in Charlotte.

During his first two and a half years with the paper, when he apparently made little or no headway with his book, Cash's major journalistic topics were literature, novels mainly, implying, perhaps, that his dream of writing a novel still held him in its thrall, or perhaps that when he was stymied and could not make progress on his history he turned for solace to his abiding love, literature. From his first appearance in the *News* on November 17, 1935, his compelling interest was southern fiction, the work of his own generation, which came to be known as the Southern Renaissance. Readers of the Charlotte *News* were regularly treated to Cash's spirited discussions of Thomas Wolfe, William Faulkner, Erskine Caldwell, James Branch Cabell, Paul Green, Allen Tate, and the Agrarians. Nor did Cash neglect Hamilton Basso, Evelyn Scott, Margaret Mitchell, Lillian Smith, and Paula Snelling. In addition, Cash returned regularly to Joseph Conrad and William Hazlitt and commented on Mark Twain, Sinclair Lewis, Ernest Hemingway, and others. Given Cash's intense interest in creative literature, his recurring dreams and abortive plans to write a southern novel, and his seeming lack of interest in works of southern history or the key works of social comment or anthropology that appeared in the late 1930s, his dream of becoming a "real writer" was at least partially responsible for his failure to buckle down to finish his book.[16]

Cash held no "literary theory." Such fancy, high-brow talk would have brought instantaneous hooting and guffawing from Shipp and the rest. Cash had something better—an intense, passionate love of books and an abiding conviction that literature mattered in people's lives. Further, he shared with his generation, North and South, a complete rejection of the sentimental, costume romance novel of the Thomas Nelson Page–Thomas Dixon variety. In their place Cash hoped to see a "realistic" literature on the order of, say, Theodore Dreiser's *Sister Carrie*, one of Cash's favorite novels. Yet Cash was impatient with "mere realism." He hoped to see a southern novel embodying the great European romantic notion of the nobility of man. Cash came to this view through an intense reading of European masters, notably Conrad. Couple that with his early acceptance of Darwin, his absorption in Freud and Nietzsche, and his familiarity with Marx, and one sees his literary journalism as an amalgamation of traditional and modernist assumptions. Cash's modernism included an awareness of the centrality in man's makeup not of reason but of ego, of irrationality, of emotions, social and personal; of the universe as unpredictable; of the importance of social class and the inherent certainty of conflict both

16. One of the few history books Cash reviewed was Benjamin B. Kendrick and Alex Matthews Arnett, *The South Looks at Its Past* (Chapel Hill, 1935), Charlotte *News*, December 8, 1935.

in individuals and in the social order; of the need for a critical mind capable of living with ambiguity, irony, and paradox.[17]

Cash's personality, his immersion in the gods of modernism, and his wide reading in what his generation considered the best that had been thought and said gave his literary views an intensely subjective quality that, paradoxically, communicated his conviction that the classics embodied an objective standard. His own standards were high, perhaps too high, as Louis D. Rubin suggested in noting how Cash judged southern writing against masterpieces. True, Cash doubted whether any of his contemporaries, even Thomas Wolfe (whose novels were widely acclaimed) or William Faulkner or his beloved James Branch Cabell, were truly exceptional, worthy of a place in the American literary pantheon of Poe, Hawthorne, Whitman, Melville, and James, to say nothing of the European masters. But Cash's literary journalism also reveals that his feelings often collided with his intellect as he sorted out his thought and came to understand that for all his rebelliousness, for all his emancipation, he and his generation were, as Lillian Smith said, "forever southerners."[18]

The South "is grinding out new books faster than any other equal portion of the United States," Cash observed in early 1936 in one of his first full-length pieces on southern literature for the News, "and a new writer bounces on the scene at least once in every thirty seconds or so." Mencken's "Sahara of the Bozart" was blooming luxuriously and unpredictably. Still, Cash fretted. The Southern Renaissance was falling "into a few rigid and narrow patterns." The Caldwell-Faulkner school—"the prevailing one at the moment"—seemed fixated on violence, on the very dregs of life. The North Carolina dramatist Paul Green and his followers were breathing life into old local color stories, and white authors such as Julia Peterkin, DuBose Heyward, and Howard W. Odum were striving to portray the "real Negro." Thomas Wolfe's brilliance threatened to deluge readers "with not less than fifty mighty odysseys of the lonely souls of tortured young men in the south."[19]

17. Daniel Joseph Singal, *The War Within: From Victorian to Modernist Thought in the South, 1919–1941* (Chapel Hill, 1982), 6–8; Carl Becker, *The Heavenly City of the Eighteenth-Century Philosophers* (New Haven, 1932), 15.

18. Louis D. Rubin, Jr., "The Mind of the South," *Sewanee Review*, LXII (1954), 683–95; Charlotte *News*, August 8, 1937.

19. Charlotte *News*, February 9, 1936.

Like other lonely, tortured young men in the 1930s, Cash prized Wolfe—but with reservations. When *Of Time and the River* appeared in 1935 to acclaim and hallelujahs that here was the Great American Novel, better even than *Look Homeward, Angel* (1929), Cash's response was tempered. Wolfe was a "very great talent"; he "towered over" Faulkner, Caldwell, and Hemingway, not one of whom "is remotely his equal in force, in color, in accurate observation, in beauty." Wolfe had not written a masterpiece, surely, but he was the only southern writer likely to be read after his death, said Cash in late December, 1935. Later the next year, when he was stalled on his own book, Cash was less taken with Wolfe's rhapsodic, epic style. His stories rambled and lacked subtlety; his rhetorical flights now seemed "embarrassingly" southern.[20]

Two years later, stunned by Wolfe's death at age thirty-seven, Cash reversed himself in two memorials. Wolfe "was undoubtedly the ablest novelist of his generation," perhaps "the greatest master of rhetoric the United States has ever produced." (Had Cash forgotten Whitman?) Cash said little about Wolfe's books, concentrating instead on Wolfe, the recorder of their generation's "bewildered adolescence." If Wolfe's novels were "formless and chaotic and verbose," as Bernard De Voto said in a savage attack, so were their generation's experiences, Cash countered. "The standards of the fathers were going, and strange, exotic standards were pouring in upon us. We, whose people had been simple people with a relatively fixed set of notions ever since their coming to these shores, found ourselves overwhelmed by a new torrent of ideas and whole systems of ideas. And so the result was that we weltered and plunged and sank and rose in a sea of sensation and indecision."[21]

Cash admired Wolfe's artistry and thought his protagonist Eugene Gant superbly molded out of Wolfe's life, much as George Webber would be another autobiographical transmutation in *You Can't Go Home Again* (1940), but Cash identified more strongly with Wolfe's conscience than with his artist-heroes, suggesting that Cash read with the eye of an intellectual, rather than as a novelist-to-be. Having himself been reviled for attacking Charlotte, Cash sympathized with

20. *Ibid.*, December 15, 1935, November 8, 1936.
21. *Ibid.*, November 16, 1938.

Wolfe's sensitivity to complaints from Asheville—Wolfe's "Altamont" was clearly Asheville—for being "indecent and ungentlemanly." One could be a gentleman or tell the truth, Cash concluded sadly—such was the plight of the southern artist—and "Wolfe very rightly chose not to be a gentleman."[22]

To Cash no southern writer symbolized the contrast between artist and gentleman better than Erskine Caldwell. Caldwell's novels of degenerate poor whites wallowing in filth, drunkenness, and incest infuriated respectable opinion. But Cash thought *Tobacco Road* and *God's Little Acre* were honest, refreshing attempts to be realistic, to tell the truth in a region where unreality and a demand for literary niceness prevailed. Caldwell's "appalling poor whites are automatically a part of [the] scene, a big part—and the fellow is a magnificent reporter and increasingly a master of drama," said Cash in 1936 as he sought to delineate the patterns of southern writing.[23]

"I like Caldwell a great deal," Cash wrote three years later. "And for all his faults he has a sardonic sense of humor that sometimes raises old Jeeter Lester and the rest of his brood to Rabelaisian proportions." *Tobacco Road* was "a near-great comic novel. Maybe you have to go to Dr. Freud to get a theory of comedy to fit that view of the matter, but the fact that comedy is cruel does not deprive it of its comic nature," a point, said Cash, Rabelais and Aristophanes understood. Yet Cash understood the objection to Caldwell's stark realism. "I am pretty sick of detailed photographs of nigger lynchings which are exactly like the other 211 I have read. I'd like to see my poor whites through some other eyes than Caldwell's—and I'd like to see the country represented as being populated by somebody besides those poor whites and the coons."[24] For all his newspaperman's tough talk, his slangy irony, Cash wanted a realistic and sympathetic portrayal of whites and blacks, rich and poor.

Though willing to defend Caldwell's realism as a salutary force, Cash remained concerned lest the new realism prove nothing more than the old romanticism in a new guise. In his first piece in the Charlotte *News*, which Shipp headlined as "Realists Are Haunted by

22. *Ibid.*, October 30, 1938. For the response in Asheville to Wolfe's first novel, *Look Homeward, Angel* (1929), see David Herbert Donald, *Look Homeward: A Life of Thomas Wolfe* (Boston, 1987), 213–18.

23. Charlotte *News*, February 9, 1936.

24. *Ibid.*, February 12, 1939, February 9, 1936.

Personal Devils," Cash announced that Caldwell and Faulkner were really romantics. Faulkner yearned to write as realistically as Dreiser, and his descriptions of poor whites were accurate, yet "his fundamental pattern is in every case extravagant and melodramatic—which is to say romantic." So too was the South—a contentious point Cash was struggling to drive home in *The Mind of the South*. But Faulkner's romanticism was undisciplined, a "jejune" extravagance "far beyond what is merely necessary in order to render the land accurately. It exists, in large measure, and plainly, for itself—a naive delight in hearing the horses gallop and the guns bark." Faulkner was one of those "disillusioned romantics at eternal war with themselves, the emotions ranged on one side and the intellect on the other"—a sentence that could also stand as a self-portrait.[25]

Cash's view of Faulkner fluctuated. He was no genius as some were saying by the mid-1930s, but he writes "with gripping power, and his single primary theme of violence is authentically part of the southern scene." In 1936 Cash had not yet read Faulkner's recent and heatedly discussed *Absalom, Absalom!* but he liked the violent, depressing *Sanctuary* and admired *The Sound and the Fury* and *As I Lay Dying* enough to reread them and to praise Faulkner fulsomely. But in 1939, the year Faulkner published *The Wild Palms* (which Shipp dismissed as "confusing," "badly written," and "silly" in places), Cash reiterated that Faulkner and Caldwell were mainly "old-fashioned 'romanticists' of the South in reverse, dealing with obscure poor-whites instead of lordly ladies and loyal old slaves but dealing with them in essentially the same spirit with an eye for the gaudy."[26]

As he would on many occasions when discussing Caldwell and Faulkner, Cash complained that neither put his characters in context or grounded his stories in southern history. Proletarian or Marxist novels like Grace Lumpkin's *To Make My Bread* (1932) and *A Sign for Cain* (1935) were not the answer—"better they had never been written"—though he did think that a southerner should write a novel stressing class. He could "dispense with the much touted performances of T. S. Stribling without too great a pang" because Stribling was primarily interested in background. But Faulkner, for all his talent for characterization, "avoids any consideration of social forces as sedu-

25. *Ibid.*, November 17, 1935.
26. *Ibid.*, November 8, 1936, February 12, 1939.

lously as he would the smallpox." Cash detected the influence of Emile Zola's notions of the scientific or naturalistic novel on Faulkner and other American writers but contended that their appropriation of Zola was "uncritical." That, combined with Faulkner's deliberately insular style, Cash complained in 1936, suggested that he had little sympathy for his characters or his readers.[27]

Cash's problem with Faulkner was mainly personal—Cash could not find himself, or the self he yearned to be, among Faulkner's characters. Young Bayard Sartoris throws his life away in drink, depression, and eventual suicide; Horace Benbow is an ineffectual, dreamy would-be poet, half in love with his sister Narcissa; Quentin Compson's unfulfilled lust for his sister drives him to kill himself; and Jason Compson survives, a critic has said, by "becoming a kind of super-Snopes himself." Reading Faulkner made Cash feel as though he had been plopped "in the middle of a ward for far-gone mad psychopaths." Faulkner's gentlemen "are brutal and some of them soft, but all of them are contemptible and essentially decadent."[28] Did Cash unconsciously see more of himself in Faulkner's "gentlemen" than he dared admit, even to himself? There is no suggestion that Cash was ever tortured by incestuous longings or guilty of miscegenation—two of Faulkner's recurring themes. Cash idolized women, but like many of Faulkner's protagonists, he was more than a little afraid of them and generally uncomfortable in their presence, particularly if he did not know them well.

Cash was not alone in undervaluing Faulkner and in failing to see that an intense historical consciousness was central to his fiction. To many critics, even those who praised Faulkner's maddeningly convoluted style, the creator of Yoknapatawpha County, Mississippi, was the exponent of a new "cult of cruelty," whose world, said Granville Hicks, resounded "with the hideous trampling march of lust and disease, brutality and death." After reading *Sanctuary*, *The Sound and the Fury*, and *As I Lay Dying*, Thomas Wolfe complained that Faulkner had created "Pop-eye horrors, pederasts, [and] macabre distortions." In 1938, C. Vann Woodward, eight years Cash's junior, disparaged Faulkner and criticized him for "pulling his characters out of a well."

27. *Ibid.*, April 5, 1936, November 31, 1937, November 24, 1935, April 5, 1936.
28. *Ibid.*, April 5, 1936; William Faulkner, *Sartoris* (1929; rpr. New York, 1961), introduction by Robert Cantwell, xi.

Like Woodward, who later completely and brilliantly reversed himself, Cash was too close to his generation to see that one of Faulkner's greatest achievements was his creation of a world in which history honeycombs every remark, every gesture, every aspect of life.[29]

Cash read his contemporaries as a self-absorbed intellectual, not as a novelist, a creator of imaginary worlds, who can distance himself from his creation. Thus when he looked up from reading *Look Homeward, Angel* or *The Sound and the Fury* or other contemporary novels, he instinctively pondered his generation's social predicament, not their artistic achievements or possibilities. The result was not all bad, by any means. Cash emerged with a heightened sense of history and a probing awareness of his own southernness. He announced in 1935, for instance, that in attempting to throw off sentimentality and embrace realism and naturalism his generation had become ensnared in a regressive romanticism. "All of us who grew up in the south in the first two decades of the 1900's—in that south with its heroic rhetoric, its gyneolatry, its continual flourishing of the word noble, and its constant glorification of the past—were fore-ordained to the thing." Their sacred primer was Thomas Nelson Page's "Two Little Confederates." Their great historical myth was the Civil War and its doleful aftermath. "Ten thousand times [we] stepped into the breach at that critical moment on that reeking slope at Gettysburg, and with our tremendous swords, and in defiance of chronology, then and there won the Civil War."[30]

These were hardly hollow autobiographical musings. He went to the heart of the current fascination with the South's quite un-American experience with "frustration, failure, and defeat." In this, Cash's feelings were distinctly generational. Had Cash lived to read *Intruder in the Dust* (1948) he might have smiled knowingly on reading Faulkner's famous line: "For every Southern boy fourteen years old, not once but whenever he wants it, there is the instant when it's still not yet two o'clock on that July afternoon in 1863 . . . it hasn't happened yet, it hasn't even begun yet, it not only hasn't begun yet but

---

29. Hicks quoted in George Tindall, *The Emergence of the New South, 1913–1945* (Baton Rouge, 1967), 656; Wolfe quoted in Donald, *Look Homeward*, 354; John Herbert Roper, *C. Vann Woodward, Southerner* (Athens, Ga., 1987), 117; C. Vann Woodward, *The Burden of Southern History* (Baton Rouge, 1960), 22–25.

30. Charlotte *News*, November 7, 1935.

there is still time for it not to begin. . . . *This time. Maybe this time* with all this much to lose and all this much to gain." [31]

Their generation's rebellion against the sentimental tradition— "designed to bolster up the ego of the south against the assaults of Yankeedom," Cash told his readers—had even engulfed his first and great love, James Branch Cabell. Cabell, said Cash in 1937, is "the most complete stylist, by common consent, who has ever practiced in America, with the possible exception of Henry James." The great Virginian was "by long odds the most eminent of southern writers yet the least read." When Cash began reading Cabell in the early 1920s, he had just created *Jurgen* (1919), his fabulous medieval province of Poictesme, peopling it with lords and ladies. Cabell's fantasies represented a naughty romanticism—*Jurgen* had been banned for a while—but few of Cash's countrymen shared his (or Mencken's) enthusiasm for Cabell. Cabell's baroque style reveled in irony, paradox, and melancholy, all subversive, all forbidden, in the land of Progress, said Cash—no matter that Cabell was southern to the core, that Poictesme was really Virginia and Cabell's heroes and heroines were derived from myths of the Cavalier. [32]

In spelling out his longing for a literature that combined realism (the logical conclusion of modernism) with an exploration, perhaps even a celebration, of man's longing for some higher truth, Cash suggested the debt his romanticism owed to Cabell. Literature, Cabell said in his romantic credo *Beyond Life* (1919), another of Cash's favorite books, need not avoid the "distasteful." Rather, southern writing should embrace the essence of romanticism: man's "charity," "symmetry," "beauty," "tenderness," and even "urbanity." Realists need not despair. A true romanticism denied none of life's "running sores," from "dungheaps" to "syphilis." [33]

Aided by Cabell and Dreiser and a host of moderns, Cash concluded that great literature kept faith with all of man's life and desires, including his dreams, as foolish and as doomed as they might be. Was such a literature possible? "I point you to Joseph Conrad's magnificent *Lord Jim*," said Cash, "and his scarcely less magnificent *Victory*. Here are two of the finest romantic novels ever written in the world." [34]

31. Woodward, *Burden of Southern History*, 19; William Faulkner, *Intruder in the Dust* (New York, 1948), 194–95.
32. Charlotte *News*, July 11, 1937, February 6, 1938.
33. *Ibid.*, October 18, 1936.
34. *Ibid.*

Cash's reverence for Conrad, particularly the early Conrad of *Lord Jim*, *Victory*, and *Heart of Darkness*, clarifies Cash's notion of true romanticism. Landbound but with a constant longing to be somewhere else, Cash was fascinated with Conrad, the seafaring Pole, who had emigrated to England and mastered the language to write haunting tales of wandering, displaced white men living in distant corners of the world among half-caste and oppressed men and women of other races. Lord Jim, an English officer in the Arabian Sea, deserts his ship after it springs a leak. Though legally innocent of misconduct, he retreats into the Malaysian jungles in self-imposed penance. Lesser men might have fled to Canada or the United States to begin again, said Cash, but not Jim. Like Hamlet, another of Cash's heroes, Jim's high-mindedness and fine conscience demanded the severe code of moral retribution.

Cash was similarly moved by Axel Heyst in *Victory*. Self-exiled on "Samburan" island, Heyst rescues the mistreated Lena and takes her to a remote island, where he tries, in vain, to protect her from evil men. Like Jim, Heyst has an inflexible code of honor that renders him out of place in an immoral world, removes him from humanity, and precipitates tragedy, which he accepts uncomplainingly. Such was Heyst's bitterly ironic "victory." To Heyst, honor was everything, as it was to Conrad and to Cash.[35]

Cash, who knew his Conrad from "lid to lid," as his family said about his knowledge of the Bible, was drawn to Conrad for literary as well as personal reasons. As a writer Cash appreciated Conrad's personal yet detached multiple styles that rendered a composite voice consistent with the disciplined southern rhetoric Cash used in *The Mind of the South*. Cash thought his contemporaries should emulate Conrad's detachment, his ability to stand back from his characters, portraying them with empathy. Moreover, Conrad's probing, subtle romanticism could easily be accommodated to a fading aristocracy; so, too, could the realism of *Heart of Darkness*, a searing indictment of racism intertwined with capitalism and its ability to corrupt even the best intentioned of masters. Cash reacted passionately to Kurtz, the shadowy main character in *Heart of Darkness*. Although Kurtz had gone into the Congo "to elevate the lesser breeds," as an obedient agent of The Company, he, too, helped rape the land of its ivory and

35. *Ibid.*, April 3, 1938.

exploit the natives. Ravaged by work, disease, and isolation, dehumanized by the jungle and his own impossibly high ideals, Kurtz went mad and died, crying out, "The horror, the horror." His tragedy, said Cash in a tribute to Conrad in 1938, was that at the end Kurtz could believe in nothing, save Force. His lament that Kurtz was contemporary man, divorced from honor or any ideals, points to a widening stream of pessimism in Cash and, at the same time, underscores Cash's romanticism and consuming passion to believe in honor or other ideals.[36]

Did Cash see, or yearn to see, a version of himself in Jim and Heyst? Heyst and Jim are perfect alter egos for a romantic idealist at odds with an immoral world. Then, too, Conrad's heroes are made to order for an ironist. Perhaps Cash saw, or feared that he saw, a bit of Kurtz in himself. To keep his sanity, Kurtz jealously guarded his scribbled account of life in the heart of darkness much as Cash scribbled an account of his people. No doubt Cash also identified with Marlow, the hard-headed but empathetic narrator, who recognizes the disastrous consequences of Jim's and Kurtz's inflexible idealism.

Picture Cash in the late 1930s. He was nearly forty, a balding, pot-bellied bachelor in Charlotte, near—if not at—his own heart of darkness; he lined his shoes with cardboard and made do on a paltry salary. His father walked the streets peddling handwoven socks. Cash wrote ranting editorials damning Hitler and fascism and churned out "literary" columns for an obscure newspaper whose readers could not pronounce half the names he mentioned. Novels, poetry, philosophy, essays—these were a lonely bachelor's companions in Presbyterian Charlotte, a city he had dismissed in the *American Mercury* as "one continuous blue-law," where the gentry lived out their days in the "dreary ritual of the office, golf, and the church." Each week, he held forth on writers who would never read him or even know whether he wrote a word. All the while he struggled to write a book no one thought he could finish—a book that damned the darkness yet found little light or honor anywhere.

How old-fashioned, and southern, Cash sounds as he sings in praise of honor. In *The Mind of the South* honor stands at the center of the southern psyche, but it was an honor distorted first into a defense of slavery and then into a perverted chivalry. Thus degraded, honor was

36. *Ibid.*, October 3, 1937, April 3, 1938.

expressed in the code of the swaggering hothead, and all too often it degenerated into violence. As he hacked out literary columns or worked on his book, Cash had no illusions that southerners would ever again embrace true honor. His mind, shaped by modernism, told him that cherished beliefs were transitory, mere illusions of permanence—fragile expressions of a human, all-too-human desire (said Nietzsche) to make sense of an evolving, unknowable world. His heart and mind told him that honor was the last thing worth safeguarding— Conradian honor, the honor of men and women who know, deep in their hearts, that honor is an imperative illusion, at bottom a curious mixture of selflessness, ego, conscience, and foolhardiness. "Honor," wrote Jacob Burckhardt, "is often what remains after faith, love, and hope are lost."[37]

But for all his love of masterpieces, Cash never became a literary curmudgeon. He praised Hamilton Basso's political novel *Court House Square* in 1936 and Evelyn Scott's *The Wave* the following year, saying the latter was the only novel to deal honestly with the Old South. In making his case for Scott, who knew "that there was never any such South as Thomas Nelson Page and his successor in the tradition, Mr. Stark Young, have so assiduously portrayed," Cash relied on the language of modernism. The Old South of myth, "spawned in Cloud-Cuckoo land," was and is "a defense mechanism, invented almost purely out of whole cloth by way of soothing the South's uneasy ego and conscience, first before slavery and the Yankee's assault on slavery, and afterward, before the poverty and defeat of the postbellum period."[38] Then, too, Cash's willingness to read his contemporaries, even the frightening Faulkner and the shocking Caldwell, suggests that he could learn from and admire them without enshrining them. For all his love of masterpieces, Cash knew with Nietzsche that by constantly judging everything against masterpieces, art could be used to kill art.

In 1937 he revised his opinion of *Gone With the Wind*, saying the runaway best-seller was far more realistic than many thought. It was no masterpiece, contrary to the views of various southern tom-tom beaters, because "its passions are too naked and simple, and its characters, indubitably having a kind of reality, yet have only such reality as

37. Jacob Burckhardt, *The Civilization of the Renaissance in Italy* (London, 1929), 428.
38. *Charlotte News*, October 25, 1936, October 24, 1937.

belongs to the better sort of moving picture." Margaret Mitchell's portrait of social conditions was far more authentic than her detractors were saying. "With a nose easily offended by the slightest whiff of Meh Lady," Cash wrote, "or that ineffable coon, Billy, I am unable to discover much truth in the charge."[39]

Cash's breezy tolerance for slangy racist-sounding talk should not obscure his emerging sympathy for writers, black or white, who were moving away from racial stereotypes. One of the most compelling literary developments of recent times, said Cash in 1936, was the fresh, emancipated writing by and about blacks. The old stereotype, the cruel caricature of the Negro as either Uncle Tom or that "banjo-picking, heel-flinging, hi-yi-ing coon" or "as a menace, a sort of cosmic fiend forever waiting for unsuspecting virgins" was giving way to realism. Julia Peterkin's *Green Thursday* (1924) and *Black April* (1927) had started the trend, Cash thought, followed by novels by DuBose Heyward, particularly *Porgy* (1925) and *Mamba's Daughters* (1929), and Howard Odum, *Rainbow Round My Shoulder* (1928), which had, for the first time, "told the truth about the black figure behind Jim Crow." Little of this was new in Cash's thinking. He had, as had Gerald W. Johnson, saluted Peterkin and the rest in the *American Mercury* several years earlier, but Cash continued to prize the new spirit of openness he detected in the southern writers of the 1920s. Scholars today detect lingering racial stereotyping, particularly in Odum's novels, but the writers of the 1920s had taken giant steps beyond the racism of Dixon and Page, as Cash and his generation knew.[40]

Cash knew, too, that none of these writers had truly explored the Negro soul. For that, he told the readers of the *News*, one had to turn to contemporary black writers, "whose names are legion." He urged his readers to go beyond Phillis Wheatley's poems or Booker T. Washington's *Up from Slavery* or the poetry of Paul Laurence Dunbar. Cash recommended the prose and poetry of Wallace Thurmond, Langston Hughes, Claude McKay, Jean Toomer, Countee Cullen—"a lyric poet of high order"—or James Weldon Johnson, author of the "intensely absorbing" *Autobiography of an Ex-Colored Man*. These young writers

39. *Ibid.*, May 16, 1937.

40. *Ibid.*, July 26, 1936; Gerald W. Johnson, "The Horrible South," *Virginia Quarterly Review*, XI (1935), 201–17; Joseph M. Flora, "Fiction in the 1920s: Some New Voices," in *The History of Southern Literature*, ed. Louis D. Rubin, Jr., Blyden Jackson, Rayburn S. Moore, Lewis P. Simpson, and Thomas Daniel Young (Baton Rouge, 1985), 282–85.

were exploring the lives of common blacks and not just those who had succeeded. "Many are hysterical in their absorption with race consciousness and nearly all are obsessed with the white man," but their pride in being black "was a healthy sign." No black writer had yet made it into the first rank of American letters, Cash said in 1936 as he surveyed the literature of the Negro, but one was "bound to one of these days."[41]

The next year, taking stock of the Negro and his poetry, Cash uttered pure heresy: "There is precious little support left in the world for the view, still often and complacently mouthed in these parts, that the negro is incapable of any independent intellectual or creative achievement" or that at best black writing was an imitation of the white man's. In confronting the stars of the Harlem Renaissance, Cash had learned that the "New Negro" was different from the myth and was filled with bitterness, "a bold, uncompromising, direct, explicit bitterness." To illustrate his point and to show his appreciation for the gifted Harlem writers, Cash quoted liberally from Jean Toomer's "Georgia Dusk" and Langston Hughes's "Song for a Black Girl."[42]

In praising black artists as well as southern whites who were trying to emancipate themselves from racism, Cash was making his own escape from the prison of racism. He reached out for support from many sources. He read Franz Boas on the fallacy of thinking of pure races and was always on the lookout for scientists and writers who undercut the old racial orthodoxies, most of which, he said in 1937, rested on power, whether political or social, rather than on truth. This Cash learned from his wide, open-minded reading and from Shipp and young Reed Sarratt, who reviewed and commented favorably on black writers.[43]

But Cash's openness had its limits, particularly when writers offended his politics or his sense of history. Such was the case with the Agrarians, self-styled Fugitives from the modern world, who doted on the glories of the past. Foiled by Mencken's refusal to be interested in his views of Allen Tate, John Crowe Ransom, and the rest of the Vanderbilt literati, Cash squared off against them in 1936 in a long review of Tate's *Reactionary Essays on Poetry and Ideas*. Cash liked Tate's poetry, could tolerate his "not wholly bad" biographies of Stonewall

41. Charlotte *News*, July 26, 1936.
42. *Ibid.*, April 11, 1937; Johnson, "Horrible South," 201–17.
43. Charlotte *News*, July 12, 1936, October 3, 1937.

Jackson and Jefferson Davis, but could not stomach his fondness for the Old South. Tate's admiration for a stratified society and an established church was so much "muddled Medievalism." Tate "likes to fancy that if only he had been fortunate enough to have been born in those fine glamourous old times, he'd have been the Sieur Alain at least, swinging gloriously back and forth from singing in the courts of love and praying in the gorgeous twilight of Chartres or Cluny." The brutal truth, said Cash, was that Tate would likely have been a serf, condemned to hard labor on the "dungheap."[44]

Despite his strong feelings, Cash was moderate when publicly discussing the Agrarians. When they issued a second manifesto edited by Herbert Agar, a newcomer from Kentucky, Cash greeted *Who Owns America?* (1938) graciously. He praised Tate's poetry again and noted that among the Agrarians' newer recruits was a very able writer named Robert Penn Warren. But their ideas remained repugnant to Cash: "I still don't know how they propose to get the land into the hands of the Southern masses," Cash wrote, "nor even how they propose to stop industrialism." He suspected that for all their talent and sentimentality they were another version of the Populists. True, they were miles removed from Populists in politics, but both were animated by hostility toward "a somewhat nebulous monster crouching in Wall Street called the Money Power."[45]

In *The Mind of the South* Cash continued to scold Tate and the rest as the "spiritual heirs of Thomas Nelson Page." But he defended them against the charge that they "consciously inclined to Fascism" or that they were moved simply by nostalgia. Their chief fault, said Cash (who, in reality, had little aesthetic appreciation for their work, even Tate's), was that in their sentimentality they failed to see any blemishes in the Old South. "But it is probably fair to say that this has been well balanced out by their services in puncturing the smugness of Progress, in directing attention to the evils of *laissez-faire* industrialism, in their insistence on developing a sensible farm program for the region, and in recalling that the South must not be too much weaned away from its ancient leisureliness—the assumption that the first end of life is living itself—which, as they rightly contend, is surely one of its greatest virtues."[46]

44. *Ibid.*, March 29, 1936.
45. *Ibid.*, May 29, 1938.
46. W. J. Cash, *The Mind of the South* (1941; rpr. New York, 1969), 390, 391, 393–94.

Whether holding forth on the Agrarians, Faulkner, or even Con-rad, Cash's literary musings in the 1930s and in his great book suggest that he was obsessed with the South and what it meant to be southern. His immersion in the Southern Renaissance and in the world of great literature had left its mark. As he said in a generous tribute to Lillian Smith and Paula Snelling, two other writers who struggled to come to terms with their land and its traditions: "For better or worse, all of us who were born here are forever southerners, that by no process of taking thought can we really turn ourselves into Frenchmen or Ger-mans or Italians or even Yankees, that our destinies are at last and incurably bound up with the destinies of this land." Now he could see that his generation had been so busy reacting against the region's "sen-timentality" that they had slipped into an "unreasoning hatred" as "sterile as unreasoning love."[47]

All this prepared him to write in *The Mind of the South* that his gen-eration "hated the South a good deal less than they said and thought. Rather, so far as their hatred was not mere vain profession designed to invite attention to their own superior perception, they hated it with the exasperated hate of a lover who cannot persuade the object of his affections to his desire. Or, perhaps more accurately, as Narcissus, growing at length analytical, might have suddenly begun to hate his image reflected in the pool."[48]

47. Charlotte *News*, August 8, 1937.
48. Cash, *Mind of the South*, 386–87.

7 / The Camaraderie of the Newsroom

In the fall of 1937 several jobs and promotions became available at the Charlotte *News*. Shipp, ever mindful of his friend Jack Cash, persuaded the Dowds to take Cash on full time as an associate editor. The position meant a pay raise—up to the lordly sum of fifty dollars a week—and a chance, finally, to escape Shelby, live in Charlotte, and assist his parents a bit more. The eldest son was now thirty-seven, too old to be living at home, to be wearing shiny pants and lining his shoes with cardboard, never to have a dime and with nowhere to go but uptown, two blocks away, to sit on the courthouse square and doze in the noonday sun.

Cash joined the Charlotte *News* at an exciting time. The Dowds had an eye for talent and relished the daily competition with the *Observer*. Joining Cash in 1937 were Burke Davis, whose beat was sports but who would go on to a prolific career as a successful writer and popular historian of the South, and Reed Sarratt, a local lad, fresh from Chapel Hill's School of Journalism and full of enthusiasm and liberal ideas even on the race question. The three new writers—Cash, Davis, and Sarratt—and two new photographers were introduced to the public in a group photograph in November, 1937. Sarratt, youthfully earnest, stands erect with just a trace of a smile, hair parted in the middle. The two young photographers smile nonchalantly, accustomed, apparently, to having their picture taken. Cash and Davis stare out stony faced—no hint of a smile—from beneath wide-brimmed hats, looking like two tough guys from a grade B Hollywood gangster movie.[1]

1. Telephone interviews with Burke Davis, October 1, 1984, and Reed Sarratt, November 28, 1984.

Other staff members in the late 1930s included Harriet Doar, poet and future literary editor of the *News* and then the *Observer*; Walter Spearman, who later as a literary columnist and professor of journalism at Chapel Hill would help train generations of journalists; and young Charles A. ("Pete") McKnight. In time, McKnight and Sarratt, whose book *The Ordeal of Desegregation* (1966) challenged many southern racial myths, became outspoken critics of segregation. In hiring Shipp, Cash, Sarratt, McKnight, Doar, and Spearman the *News* justifiably took pride in its brashness and its power to attract bright, creative young writers. Here, Cash's iconoclastic bent was not only tolerated but admired, encouraged, and expanded.[2]

Despite a few added duties after 1937, Cash's job remained far from arduous. It consisted mainly of writing editorials, book reviews, literary pieces, and the occasional column and helping Bill Dowd lay out the editorial page. (The Dowds may have been slightly paternalistic toward Cash, though he would have bristled at the suggestion and pointed an accusing finger, as all the *News* editors and staffers did, at the niggardly salary the Dowds paid most of them.) Mainly, Cash sat at his desk, read newspapers and magazines to keep abreast of international news, and mulled over editorial topics and new books and writers. His mates knew when an idea started to germinate in his mind. He squinted. He rubbed his forehead vigorously. His cigarette burned dangerously close to his lips. Once the idea had taken shape, he reached for a legal pad, furiously brushed off the cigarette ashes, and started scribbling. Unlike Shipp, Cash fussed and fussed with his copy before handing it to a typist, showing it to Shipp, or passing it to Dowd.[3]

Jack Cash enjoyed the fishbowl that was the small, cramped editorial office and newsroom. He sat just outside Bill Dowd's glassed-in office, where, everyone said, the editor could keep an eye on him. Unlike the other staff members, Cash reported directly to Dowd, who liked Cash but thought it best to keep him on a short rein. At the *News*, the challenge and fun was scooping the morning paper, the larger, better-known *Observer*, which everyone around the *News* considered as stuffy as Charlotte itself. The managing editor at the *News*

2. Interview with Harriet Doar, September 17, 1984; Burke Davis to author, December 18, 1984; Reed Sarratt to author, December 12, 1984; Reed Sarratt, *The Ordeal of Desegregation* (New York, 1966).

3. Telephone interview with Reed Sarratt, November 28, 1984.

was Brodie Griffith, a South Carolina farmboy, who liked a clear, crisp, lean sentence, a swig of whiskey—in the 1940s he became a tee-totaler—the Democratic party, the American Legion, and reminiscing about his days in the infantry during World War I. This old-time southern newspaperman surveyed the world from beneath a green eyeshade and through a haze of cigarette smoke. He scowled at young reporters. But he could also offer fatherly advice and be courtly, particularly around ladies. He was a "yellow dog" Democrat, he liked to tell newcomers to the paper, meaning he would vote for a yellow dog should the party nominate one. He saw nothing irregular about the fact that his crack reporter, John Daly, was deeply involved in local Democratic politics and regularly served as campaign manager for local congressional candidates.[4]

Griffith was respected and liked. But Uncle John Dickson was loved. The city editor was a slight, diminutive man—all of 5'2"—with a high, squeaky voice and wispy hair that would not stay combed. He was "Uncle John" to boy and woman alike. Uncle John was as huggable as his clothes were rumpled; surely he slept in those suits, Cash and his cronies laughed, but then the disheveled Jack Cash was not one to talk. Uncle John, in suspenders and with his characteristic green eyeshade, worked with his hat pushed back on his head, a cigarette dangling precariously from his lips, a half-empty bottle of Coca-Cola on his desk, and a bottle of whiskey in his drawer. He carelessly dropped ashes on his desk, on his trousers, on the floor. When his cigarette threatened to singe his fingers, he casually lit a new smoke with the old one and tossed the used one over his shoulder—somewhere in the vicinity of the wastebasket. Those on target frequently touched off fires which sent everyone scurrying to grab a cup of water or Uncle John's bottle of pop to douse the flames. Merriment twinkled in Uncle John's eyes. When a news tip came in, he leaned back in his chair, took a drag on his cigarette, looked in the general direction of some reporter, and said there was a fire over on such and such a street. "Maybe someone should go over and check it out." Nothing bothered Uncle John save pomposity, prohibitionists, Republicans, limp sentences, factual inaccuracies, men of God, and Presbyterians in particular. He loved fast-paced works of history, adventure yarns, and historical novels. His style was relaxed and lively. He had an eye for a

4. Burke Davis to author, December 18, 1984; telephone interview with Reed Sarratt, November 28, 1984.

well-turned ankle and drank far too much—perhaps, some said, because he was unhappily married.[5]

Uncle John reserved a special fondness for two of Cash's buddies on the paper, John Daly, who was "a beaver for digging for stories, good and bad," Burke Davis remembered, and Tom Revelle, the one-armed mountaineer journalist, a giant of indeterminate age, "who had been a reporter forever," it seemed to youngsters like Davis and Spearman. Big Tom Revelle loved mountain ballads, strong drink—though beer and wine would do in a pinch—and writing dog stories. A favorite piece of lore at the *News* was that the imposing Revelle would hire himself out to the Women's Christian Temperance Union to serve as its "horrible example" of drink. Big Tom would sit sober and straight-faced on the stage, staring blankly ahead, while Charlotte's Carry Nation adumbrated the many terrors of drink.[6]

Shipp, Revelle, Daly, and John Harden, whose beat was city news, were Cash's pals and unofficial professors of journalism. In the evenings the thirsty bachelors Revelle and Cash would frequently drop by Harden's house to talk, sip wine or beer, and smile ruefully at Charlotte's hypocrisies. Harden and Big Tom regaled Cash and wide-eyed rookie reporters with stories of riding with the police when they periodically raided the local hotels to run the prostitutes out of town, keep the bootleggers on their toes, and put the fear of God in the local respectable men sneaking around to patronize the women of the night. To hear Harden and Revelle tell it, Charlotte's call girls said that "not even in Chicago" had they had requests for such perversity or seen such vice, including narcotics.[7]

Cash drew upon his newspaperman's inside knowledge of the seamier side of southern life in his book. Prohibition, Cash wrote in *The Mind of the South*, had intertwined with human nature and the South's congenital Puritanism to produce a sordid, back-alley culture in which bootleg liquor and prostitution flourished, often with a racial twist conveniently ignored by the "better sort." Bootlegging had become the province of whites; distributing it, particularly in the cities, the province of blacks, "especially in the hotels, where the black bellboys

5. Burke Davis to author, November 1, 1984; telephone interview with Reed Sarratt, November 28, 1984; telephone interview with Marion Hargrove, October 10, 1984.
6. Reed Sarratt to author, December 12, 1984; Burke Davis to author, December 18, 1984.
7. Telephone interview with John Harden, December 3, 1984; Katherine Grantham Rogers to Joseph L. Morrison, September 20, 1984, in Joseph L. Morrison Papers, Southern Historical Collection, University of North Carolina, Chapel Hill.

enjoyed an almost complete monopoly of the business—keeping out competitors from outside by threats of betraying them to the police." That, combined with the closing down of red-light districts, pushed liquor and streetwalkers, both under the rule of black pimps, into the hotels, turning "most Southern hotels into public stews." The black bellboys were powerful enough to demand and receive from their white prostitutes "all the traditional prerogatives of the pimp, including not only a large share of their earnings but also and above all the right of sexual intercourse—often enforced against the most reluctant of the women, again under the threat of betrayal to the police." As the gulf between the South's professed Puritanism and its hedonistic practices widened, there arose "a horde of raffish blacks, full of secret, contemptuous knowledge of the split in the psyche of the shamefaced Southern whites."[8]

By the mid-1930s the Charlotte *News* relentlessly documented and criticized the worst features of southern white racism. In news articles and editorials the newspaper exposed and criticized the Ku Klux Klan. The leaders of the "Karolina Klan plan to ride tonight, burning crosses, and intimidating innocent blacks," the paper announced on August 26, 1936, in a typical editorial. The Klan leaders were well known, "having been prominent in various organizations of a statewide nature." In the spring of 1937 the *News* carried a front-page photograph of the Klan in Atlanta. In July, 1937, the editors denounced the invisible order's strength in Spartanburg, South Carolina, calling the Klan and its activities "anarchy." In April, 1940, the *News* lashed at the Klan's activities in Georgia and praised Fulton County for indicting seventeen Kluxers for murder. The following week, a *News* editorial called the KKK a "sadistic gang of masked hoodlums."[9]

Along with denunciations of the Klan went equally forceful condemnation of lynchings. By the 1930s the number of lynchings had declined greatly since the gory pre-1914 days, prompting many boosters to say proudly that racist violence was not only declining but disappearing. But to the *News* folks the time had not yet arrived for celebration or undue self-congratulation. Any lynchings were a source of shame, particularly since they always occurred in the South and the

8. W. J. Cash, *The Mind of the South* (1941; rpr. New York, 1969), 320–21.
9. Charlotte *News*, May 5, 1937, July 23, 1937, April 20, 28, 1940.

victims were almost always black. In 1937 there were eight lynchings in America—all of blacks, all southern. "It is a shameful record," said the *News*, "and one for which as Southerners, we hang our heads." Furthermore, one of the lynching victims had been put to death, not by rope or even shotgun blasts but by blowtorch, slowly and "fiendishly." As usual, the *News* cried, "the sheriff says he could not recognize any of the mob." The paper dwelt on such grisly barbarities, editorialized against racial violence, and began a drumbeat of editorials that finally laid the blame for racial lynchings at the feet of the "best people" and their compliant servants, the police. The *News* was not alone in this dramatic turn from New South liberalism, which always blamed the unwashed, white masses for such barbarities. The editors not only graphically publicized lynchings—which even openly racist newspapers had done for years, often as a way of pandering to the white public's cravings for sensationalism—they insisted on fair and forceful punishment. The editors and writers knew that lynchers were seldom arrested, let alone convicted. In the first thirty years of the twentieth century only twelve lynchers had been brought to justice. The *News* maintained that the police could stop lynchings immediately. The police were simply following the tacit orders of the "best people."[10]

Such was Cash's view, too. Indeed, he had forcefully indicted the "best people" and the police in the summer of 1935, just before joining the *News*. In August, a lynching in tiny Louisburg, near Wake Forest College, had touched off considerable public comment. The sheriff and his five deputies watched a crowd of twenty-five unmasked men forcibly grab the prisoner and administer mob justice in broad daylight. A gaping crowd had watched. But afterward no one could recall a single name or face or remember any license plate numbers. "The fact is overwhelmingly plain," Cash wrote in the Baltimore *Evening Sun*. "The hands which actually manipulated rope and trigger at Louisburg may very well have been those of the degraded poor-whites." But the real culprit, "the force which really lynches everywhere in the South—was and is the force of public opinion," that of the "good people," as the Charlotte *News* had been saying for some time. In 1935 Cash was not sanguine, but he was pleased to report

10. *Ibid.*, December 28, April 14, 1937; Cash, *Mind of the South*, 310; Pete Daniel, *Standing at the Crossroads: Southern Life Since 1900* (New York, 1986), 58. Editorials in the Charlotte *News*, April 4, 1937, and May 15, 1938, are representative.

that the Raleigh *News and Observer* and the Greensboro *Daily News* were voicing similar views. Even the Charlotte *Observer*—whose policy "has always been one of uncompromising Southern apology"—had charged that it was the "good people" who were the real lynchers.[11]

His years at the *News* confirmed and deepened Cash's notion that southern lynchings were related to class but only superficially to the lower class. In the book he was fitfully working on, Cash argued that lynchings were never really the work of the policeman, who was "everywhere a simple soul primarily interested in keeping his job," or the easily inflamed "white trash." They merely did what their betters wanted or encouraged them to do. "The common whites have usually done the actual execution, of course, though even that is not an invariable rule. . . . But they have kept on doing it, in the last analysis, only because their betters either consented quietly or, more often, definitely approved." The blame for lynchings rested squarely with the "ruling race."[12]

To Cash, the decline of lynchings hardly proved that racism was decreasing or that enlightenment had finally arrived in Dixie. Members of the ruling race had discovered that lynchings and violent outbursts of racism were potentially threatening to their power over the masses. As the South urbanized and industrialized and fell in love with progress and the dollars progress promised, the better sort saw that lynchings were bad for the South's image and for maintaining control of the workers. Moreover, the machine, the symbol of progress, required order; lynchings and race riots represented disorder. To prove his point, in *The Mind of the South* Cash singled out North Carolina, a relatively urbanized and industrialized state, where lynchings had all but disappeared, and Mississippi, the most rural state and the one with the highest lynching rate. The machine, the love of money, the desire to maintain social control *over whites*—these, not goodwill or even old-fashioned southern paternalism, led the ruling race to demand better race relations.[13]

Cash's years as a newspaperman sharpened his awareness of southern violence. And when it came to violence, Charlotte—Presbyterian Charlotte, "after Edinburgh the Greatest Church-going Town in the

---

11. W. J. Cash, "North Carolina Faces the Facts," Baltimore *Evening Sun*, August 29, 1935.
12. Cash, *Mind of the South*, 310–11.
13. *Ibid.*

World"—took a backseat to no other city or region in the South or the nation. The Queen City's murder rate was so shockingly high that the Dowds and the liberals on the paper tallied the figures and maintained a running commentary on the shameful facts. Charlotte was "the murder capital of the United States," the paper traditionally announced at the beginning of each new year. With 55 homicides in 1936 and a population of 90,000, Charlotte was relatively the most violent city in the United States. That year, Grand Rapids, Michigan (population 168,592), recorded 2 murders. Charlotte's murder rate was that of a city of 2 million. To match New York City's 329 murders, Charlotte's population ought to be 1,250,000, the editors calculated.[14]

Each month the *News* tabulated Charlotte's violence, its crime and homicide rate, noting (whenever possible) that the city had either maintained its supremacy or slipped slightly behind some other southern city. "No murders in Charlotte during November," an editorial wisecracked in late 1936. Early in 1938 Atlanta threatened to dethrone Charlotte as the queen city of murder, the *News* said mockingly, but by August Charlotte had regained the lead and maintained it to the end of the year. At the beginning of 1940 the editors proclaimed cynically that with 35 murders Charlotte had nosed out Atlanta and Montgomery, Alabama—the latter with 30 murders and a population of 66,000—and retained its ignominious title as the nation's murder capital for 1939. Two thirds of the way through 1940 the paper noted that with 36 murders the city had already surpassed the previous year's total and had a chance to outdistance all competitors.[15]

Critics howled in protest. The *News* was airing the city's dirty linen and hurting Charlotte's image. The truth had to be told and faced, the editors replied. Charlotte's chief of police echoed the defiant view of many whites when he charged that blacks were responsible for the city's murders and crimes. The editors countered by citing other southern cities with equal if not larger black populations. Comparable cities such as Durham, North Carolina, and Columbia, South Carolina, had far fewer murders. The editors acknowledged that most of Charlotte's murderers and victims were black. But that proved only that the root of the problem lay in social conditions. Slums, poverty,

---

14. Charlotte *News*, November 25, 1937.
15. *Ibid.*, December 6, 1936, November 28, 1939, October 20, 1940.

and ignorance create an environment that fosters violence. The dominant white society could act to improve the social and economic position of blacks and thus reduce crime and violence significantly.[16]

The *News* charged that for too long whites had tended to shrug their shoulders at black crime when the victims were black, which was usually the case. Such attitudes and practices actually encouraged crime and betrayed a pernicious racism. Blacks who robbed or were guilty of assault or murder should be punished to the full extent of the law, the *News* argued. It was a cruel irony of southern history that the editors of the Charlotte *News*, along with the region's liberal journalists, would find themselves trying to help blacks and combat white racism by arguing for swift and harsh punishment for blacks. The editors, whose reports of the horrors of executions in North Carolina's "Gas Room" suggest an aversion (if not opposition) to capital punishment, dutifully reported in 1937 that a Negro had been put to death for killing a black girl.[17]

However ironic the *News*'s position, it presented an argument, as well as an attitude and a grouping of facts, that Cash learned and spelled out explicitly in *The Mind of the South*. "Often," Cash wrote, "a Negro murderer of another Negro drew no heavier penalty than that commonly meted out to a chickenthief. And when in North Carolina in 1937," Cash recalled of Shipp's vigilance at the *News*, "such a murderer was actually condemned to execution and ultimately dispatched, it so startled one editor that he was moved to investigate and discover that it had been twenty years since another case of the kind had happened in the state."[18]

Cash underscored the point that the South was a murderous place and drew on the facts and figures used by Shipp and the others with telling effect. The South's murder rates rose throughout the 1930s and consistently exceeded the national figures. And the rates for southern cities were even more dramatic. The region's urban murder rate in 1937 proved that "Southern cities were over five times as murderous as those of either the North Central area or the Far West, over six times as those of the Middle Atlantic country, and over eighteen times as those of New England!"[19]

16. *Ibid.*, March 30, May 9, 1936, June 11, July 30, 1937, March 7, 1938.
17. *Ibid.*, July 30, 1937.
18. Cash, *Mind of the South*, 425.
19. *Ibid.*, 424.

Early in 1937, a few months before Cash moved to Charlotte, the *News* startled the community and much of the region by publishing, under commanding front-page headlines, a slashing exposé of the city's slums. The muckraker responsible was Cameron Shipp. For four unrelenting days in February the *News* documented Charlotte's living conditions as some of the worst in America. With a photographer at his side, Shipp had gone into the most wretched parts of the city, the slum sections, Blue Heaven, Black Bottom, and Sugaw Creek. He went looking for facts, for the truth, not the conventional racist wisdom or Chamber of Commerce facts. He found and reported filth, disease, fetid conditions, lack of sanitation, and dilapidated shotgun houses—hovels, really—teeming with poor, downtrodden people. He stood in run-down, windowless houses, pitch dark even in the middle of the day. He saw despair, depression, and desperation.

"Strike a match in this hut," Shipp's first installment began, "to see a black child dying of tuberculosis." Everywhere Shipp went he found poor people, perhaps as many as seven thousand, huddled in misery, suffering in filth, dying from "tuberculosis, gonorrhea, syphilis, and colitis." Here were the wretched of the earth—in the Queen City.[20]

"Murder Lives in the Slums," shouted the eight-column, front-page headline that assaulted Charlotte on the third day. Murder, like disease, had a social cause, and that cause, that germ, grew in the slums and was transmitted by social conditions. Shipp was angry. Change the way blacks are forced to live, the *News* demanded. Change living conditions for the oppressed and everyone will gain.[21]

On the fourth and last day, Shipp and the *News* headlined another awful truth: "White People Exist in Areas of Misery." Shipp knew that many readers—perhaps even Brodie Griffith and the Dowds—might, in their secret hearts, think that blacks deserved what they had. White readers might also be able to dismiss the whole nasty story by repeating the litany that blacks were lazy, shiftless animals who lived like brutes because they were innately slovenly, ignorant, and immoral. Such was actually the public pronouncement of the president of Charlotte's Queens College in April, 1938.[22] For decades, Charlotte's uptown elite had shunned and made fun of the "degraded" mill hands, who were white. Cash himself had, in the *American Mercury*,

20. Charlotte *News*, February 7, 8, 1937.
21. *Ibid.*, February 9, 1937.
22. *Ibid.*, April 15, 1938.

pilloried the mill workers as shiftless galoots and had come dangerously close to suggesting that the South's wretched, white or black,
had congenitally defective characters. But Shipp's liberalism was of
sterner stuff, born of a conviction that ugly social realities trap and
shape people, destroy their souls, sap their hope, making them appear
congenitally shiftless or inferior.

Shipp meant to shock and scare. He had convinced the Dowds that
he had to tell the truth to awaken Charlotte, its churches, its civic
groups, its Men's Bible Classes, and its Ladies' Literary Societies.
Shipp's thunderbolts startled Charlotte. Citizens' Leagues, white and
black, rolled up their sleeves and went to work to rid the city of slums.
Churches and social organizations sponsored frank discussion of Shipp's
revelations. The civic-minded pressured their congressmen to ensure
that Charlotte received its share of the New Deal's Wagner-Steagall
Act with its millions of dollars for slum clearance.[23]

The piedmont awoke. Gastonians demanded that their tenement
sections be condemned as slums. By late 1938 Charlotte's city council
was pressing the city's housing authority for action. A year latter, Gastonia and Charlotte were actively winning federal funds and building
low cost housing. But the task was staggering. In early 1940 the *News*
reported that after all that had been done there were still more than
five thousand dwellings in the Queen City without proper toilets and
more than ten thousand without bathtubs.[24]

Shipp's courageous journalism left its mark on Jack Cash. In the
concluding pages of *The Mind of the South* Cash saluted the new, intelligent, realistic journalism of the 1930s and singled out J. E. Dowd,
Shipp, and the *News* for special recognition. Shipp's crusading exposé
was "the most uncompromising and thorough survey of local slum
conditions ever carried out in a Southern town." Out of slums, said
Cash, remembering Shipp's biting series, "grow virtually every epidemic of such scourges of childhood as measles, whooping cough, scar-
let fever, diphtheria, and colitis, of such scourges of child and adult
alike as dysentery and influenza." The Negro in the slums was the obvious cause, Cash admitted, but slum conditions were the real culprit.
Slums breed ignorance and crime. In cities like Atlanta and Charlotte—"the two which had the highest murder-rate for the South,"

23. *Ibid.*, March 11, August 29, 1937.
24. *Ibid.*, January 26, 1938, January 23, 1939, March 6, 1940.

said Cash, echoing *News* editorials and feature articles—"the incidence of crime occurs in exactly the slums where unemployment, crowding, squalor, and want are most prevalent."[25]

J. E. Dowd even finally allowed Cash to do a bit of social commentary. In early 1939 Cash recounted the "plight of the sharecropper." Ever the historian-publicist, Cash could not pass up the chance to argue, as he had for Mencken and would again in his book, that southern whites, no matter how great their wealth or social station (or lack of social standing), sprang from a common, humble source. The majority of the Old South's "aristocrats" and the New South's "best families" had evolved from the same stock. "Go into almost any county in Dixie," Cash told readers of the *News*, "and look about you a little and you'll find the same family names shared both by the leading gentry and the sharecropper." The sharecropper side of the first family had been "degraded" by the plantation and "its tendency to hog all the good lands before the War, and carry on through all the evils of our cotton—and tobacco—economy since the Civil War." But Cash's mind, molded by a pervasive sense of history and a probing social psychology, was far from believing that once exposed, social ills could be easily eradicated. He confessed that the sharecropper "must somehow be rescued," but he was "quite unable to say what ought to be done."[26]

Could this be the same sassy W. J. Cash who had been such an insensitive know-it-all in the *American Mercury*? Where were the Menckenian smart-aleckiness, the extravagant style, the blustery tone? For the moment, they were gone. Jack Cash was growing up. And it would show in the book he was struggling to finish.

In June, 1939, Cash penned a stinging exposé of the wretched conditions at the local tuberculosis sanatorium. The place was dark, dank, and poorly ventilated. Patients were jammed together. There were too few nurses. The ceiling and floors were rickety and unsafe. The building was not fireproof. In the white sections, "seven to eight people use each bathroom." The building was so constructed that everyone had "to pass through the sick wards to reach the convalescent wards, and for patients in the convalescent wards to reach the bathrooms."[27]

The segregated blacks suffered even more. Thirty-three blacks, men and women, many of them waiting to die, shared "one toilet, one

25. Cash, *Mind of the South*, 383, 425, 427.
26. Charlotte *News*, January 15, 1939.
27. *Ibid.*, June 11, 1939.

bathtub, one wash basin," with "just walking space between the cots." What passed for an isolation ward was a tiny corner barely big enough for the three tightly crammed-in beds it held. "They put the far-gone cases there either to take a change for the better or to die—usually to die. If they die audibly, and they do die audibly nearly always, the other patients hear their rattling gasps, their moans and their mutterings. Most of them can see their contorted faces and bodies as they struggle for the last precious breath. The bodies of the dead must be carried out under the eyes of the whole ward." Despite the wretched conditions for blacks, the sanatorium always had a long waiting list. Unlike most white patients, Cash reported, few blacks survived. Many died before they could gain admission to the hospital; many arrived at a terminal stage of illness. "Every year, an appalling number of blacks is literally condemned to death by the fact that the hospital has no way to take care of them." [28]

For whites, or anyone else, who might say the sanitorium and blacks with hacking, wracking coughs were no affair of theirs, or declare they would pay no more taxes, Cash detailed the chilling medical and social facts: tubercular blacks, each "a walking source of infection," trod Charlotte's streets, entered daily into white homes "for the preparation of the food eaten there, or for the care of white children." The hospital superintendent's findings were stark: of all blacks recently admitted "over half have been employed in domestic service, and many of them were so employed right up to the time of their admission." [29]

Perhaps had Cash been given free rein at the News—and had he not by 1939 been devoting his main energies to his book—he might have become even more outspoken on social issues, even the race question. But one must keep in mind that the News's racial liberalism had its limits and must be understood within the context of the times. One staffer remembered that editor Dowd tolerated racial liberals at the News but that "some of his prejudices, as against blacks, were so unreasoning to be absurd even in that clime and time." [30] The News attacked slums, inadequate hospitals for blacks, and blatant white racism, particularly violence. The paper had taken several steps away from the racist language that had characterized southern newspapers for decades. Furthermore, the paper campaigned for blacks to serve on

28. Ibid.
29. Ibid.
30. Burke Davis to author, December 18, 1984.

grand and petit juries and on city commissions and authorities. But there was a line the editors did not cross. It was the unwritten law of white supremacy: racial segregation. At no time during the 1930s did the *News* attack either racial segregation or disfranchisement of blacks any more than did such liberals as Virginius Dabney at the Richmond *Times-Dispatch* or Ralph McGill at the Atlanta *Constitution*. The *News* routinely reported black crime in sensationalist front-page headlines and news articles that would certainly sound racist to modern ears. Darkey cartoons appeared now and then and editorials and articles lapsed into darkey dialect on occasion. It was a different day, to be sure, and dialect or the word *nigger* could be used, as Cash did regularly, for effect, often in a way intended to expose racism.[31]

Important manifestations of the racism of the times were subtle and hidden from most people's view. For instance, whenever blacks were mentioned in white southern newspapers, and the *News* was no exception, they were routinely identified as such, usually called "colored." They were referred to by their given names, frequently their nicknames, like "Honey Boy," "Dancin' Man," or "Lucky Boy." Only rarely were blacks referred to as Mr. or Mrs. or Miss. Positive news of blacks seldom got reported; when it did it was usually tucked away inconspicuously on the inside pages. Little of this was talked about; it was taken for granted. Yet none of it was happenstance. Being "colored" or black was *the* stigma in the South. And should the *News* ever err and identify a white person, especially someone of prominence, as Negro or colored, the publisher had a policy in place. Someone from the editorial office was to contact the offended person immediately and apologize profusely. Should that not mollify the offended white, financial compensation was to be offered on the spot. By all means, the newspaper wanted to show private contrition and avoid public embarrassment.[32]

The unwritten but understood and enforced rule at the *News* was "No pictures of snakes or niggers."[33]

Cash had heard talk like that all his life and much that was far worse. Like most humane, benign white southerners who were in the

31. John Kneebone, *Southern Liberal Journalists and the Issue of Race, 1920–1944* (Chapel Hill, 1985), 74–96, 196–214.

32. Telephone interview with Reed Sarratt, November 30, 1984; Reed Sarratt to author, December 19, 1984.

33. Telephone interview with Reed Sarratt, November 30, 1984; Reed Sarratt to author, December 19, 1984.

process of extricating themselves from the many forms of racism, he made his daily allowances for people he liked and knew to be better than their public pronouncements. He would surely have agreed with Jimmy Carter's remark that sensitive white southerners, whatever their own emancipation, could hardly withdraw from the human race.

That aside, Cash enjoyed the camaraderie of the newsroom where some curmudgeonly editor's cussing pierced the hazy air blue with cigarette smoke. It was difficult, even for Cash, to remain too serious when Uncle John's wastebasket flared in flames or when Pete McKnight, drawling in true southern Baptist cadence, quoted from a faith healer's sermon, or Big Tom Revelle wisecracked about the busy bootleggers and overworked prostitutes in Presbyterian Charlotte, or Shipp intoned sonorously that the pride of Shelby, the Reverend Tom Dixon, had, "Thank God Almighty," decided to quit writing "those preposterous novels" and was prayerfully considering running for public office on the "Re-pub-li-can" ticket, the party of Lord Hoover or Alf Landon. Jack Ca-ash, as Shipp liked to drawl out his name, was not one of the office merrymakers, but he allowed himself a sheepish grin when Shipp loudly announced to visitors or newcomers to the staff that they were to remember that Mr. Jack Ca-ash, formerly of Shelby, was somebody, that he was writing a book for Mr. Knopf—"you are writin' on that book, aren't you Mr. Ca-ash?"—and had pleased old Mencken in his day. Why, Mr. Ca-ash, Shipp would drawl, was probably at this very moment worrying himself into a sick headache about Nietzsche's Superman or whether Spengler had it right, and would the Western world at least survive until *The Mind of the South* somehow got itself composed or, just as important, until quitting time rolled around so that everyone could meander over to the Little Pep for food and drink.

8 / Love and Deadlines

Spring, 1938, proved to be a wonderful, and therefore rare, moment in W. J. Cash's life. The occasion was the first Carolinas Book Fair, conceived and planned by Cameron Shipp. The four-day event in May was a rousing success. The mayor turned up to welcome the assembled literati and introduce Paul Green, the opening speaker. "Governor Clyde R. Hoey was invited two months ago to make the opening address," Shipp explained teasingly in the News, but "he stalled so long that we stopped asking him. He was probably right: no votes at a book fair." No votes, maybe, but lots of good book talk, convivial partying with publishers' representatives and fellow writers, and browsing among the more than five thousand new books on display. The most popular book was *Pose, Please*, a book of nudes. "We had to assign a special man to watch it day and night," Shipp quipped, "lest leaves be torn out." Margaret Mitchell followed her usual practice of refusing to attend such functions but sent "personal regards" by Macmillan's representative. DuBose Heyward had other plans but sent greetings. The aging Thomas Dixon was not invited.[1]

Marian Sims, the reigning Charlotte novelist, was much in evidence, sharing the speakers' table with Paul Green, Jonathan Daniels, and the "one critic" Shipp had invited to speak. There was considerable talk about Sims's novel-in-progress, *The City on a Hill* (1940), set in Charlotte and, she said, centering on the heated question of prohibition. Tim Pridgen of the News, fresh from his triumph "Courage:

---

1. Charlotte News, May 15, 1938; Joseph L. Morrison, *W. J. Cash, Southern Prophet: A Biography and a Reader* (New York, 1967), 82.

The Story of Modern Cock Fighting," was in fine form answering questions. Daniels and "his lovely wife" were a popular couple and the recipients of much laudatory comment about his new book, *A Southerner Discovers the South*. There was much buzzing that Daniels' book was sure to be a selection of a major book club. Green, the loyal Tar Heel, got off a much appreciated jab at the "two mountains of conceit" to the north and south of North Carolina when he remarked that since "the valley of humility" had "no past to speak of," North Carolina "therefore turns its eyes without regret wholly on the future." Cash, one of Green's most ardent admirers, agreed that the state's humble past was "certainly gorgeous stuff for the novelist and the playwright who is able to deal with it directly and as it was and is, rather than through the veil of literary conventions." Fiction was the proper medium for southern writers, more than one writer nodded, when W. T. Couch, director of the University of North Carolina Press, remarked that he "did not expect social-minded literature to be popular now that the people are turning against Roosevelt."[2]

The four-day talkfest was great fun, Shipp reported. "All the writers got along beautifully, no fights." The talks were upbeat, the mood good. Over late-night coffee at the Hotel Charlotte with the Danielses and a group from the fair, Cash shied away from commenting on his own stalled book but predicted that President Franklin D. Roosevelt's recent remark that the South was the nation's number one economic problem would mean a large readership for Daniels' book. Cash enjoyed the book talk, the gossip, and the chance to meet or renew acquaintances with other writers. But he could turn churlish. A young, wide-eyed staffer from the *News*, who had been in awe of Cash for some time, came up to him and said admiringly, "You have a book coming out, too, don't you Mr. Cash?"—only to be told curtly that the manuscript was nowhere near finished.[3]

Cash's mood at the Book Fair improved remarkably when Shipp took him by the arm and said he had a young lady, one of his cousins, and "one of your admirers, Jack," he wanted Cash to meet. "She likes intellectuals," Shipp whispered as they approached Mary Bagley Ross Northrop. Cash had already noticed her in the crowd several times.

2. Charlotte *News*, May 8, 15, 1938; Morrison, *W. J. Cash*, 82. The "one critic" Shipp invited was Ruth Hinman Carter of Georgia.
3. Telephone interview with Emery Wister, September 16, 1984.

He was also sure that he had seen her watching him. He had been hoping to meet her for some time, having heard about her from some of his Charlotte friends and seen her picture several times on the book page of the *News*. She had won the local Writers' Club annual short story contest five years running. Perhaps she had some literary talent, Cash thought as he mused ruefully on his suspicion of ladies' literary groups. He had enjoyed reading her occasional reviews and pieces on the book page; she wrote in a peppery style without sounding silly or childish. She must have some ability. She had, he knew, gotten the editing job with the Federal Writers' Project that he had sought. Talented or not, up close she was a dark-eyed brunette fully as attractive as her picture.[4]

Mary Northrop (she still used her former husband's last name) had been wanting to meet him, too. She had known of him as a writer since 1932 when she had begun reading him in the *American Mercury*. At the time she was recovering from tuberculosis in the Charlotte sanitorium—the very one Cash would muckrake in 1939—and ending a mutually unsatisfying marriage. A friend had brought her a copy of the *American Mercury* with Cash's delicious dissection of Charlotte. A self-consciously liberated person herself with a boisterous disdain for Charlotte's smuggery, and one of Mencken's admirers, she liked Cash's audacious writing style, she had told several of her friends when she started reading him again in the *News*. A Charlotte native from a settled Episcopalian family, she was nonetheless, at age thirty-two in 1938, uncomfortable with the conventional notions of southern womanhood and wanted to break free. She smoked cigarettes, enjoyed a drink or two, wisecracked (sometimes in a loud voice), and had no intention of being an empty-headed southern "belle." As a divorcee with a vivacious, perhaps boisterous personality, she would have had little success pretending to be a southern lady. Mary "was very much a breezy and easygoing person," wrote Joseph Morrison, who knew her in her later years. "In these respects, her temperament was directly opposed to Cash's, and perhaps for that reason she was all the more attractive to him." She respected him and saw beyond the "shiny broad suit" he was wearing when they met, seeing the truly interest-

---

4. For a photograph of Mary Ross Northrop and the news of her winning the prize in 1936, see Charlotte *News*, August 9, 1936; Morrison, *W. J. Cash*, 83.

ing, original thinker he was, which is to say that Mary Northrop was about as close to being the ideal woman as Cash was likely to find.[5]

To judge from his writing, Mary had concluded, Cash was probably some "crusty and sassy old gentleman." And standing before her at the Book Fair was a "rather badly dressed fellow with a small pot [belly] developing, going bald and sporting a terrible haircut for the sake of the few remaining bristles on his crown." But he was neither old, crusty, nor sassy. He was rather shy, but he had a twinkle in his eye, and a bemused, even smitten look flitted across his roundish face.[6]

Both were smitten. It was one of those wonderful chance meetings (thanks to cousin Cam) that romantics like Jack Cash and Mary Northrop dream about. "The first attraction," Mary remembered years later, "was instantaneous and was nothing more than the old Boy Meets Girl business. As I came to know him, the second attraction showed up in his genius with the spoken words: he was a wit and a spellbinder." The morning after their first meeting Mary told her mother confidently: "Last night I met a fat country boy I am going to marry." Within a month or so, Cash, the thirty-eight-year-old pudgy bachelor, was telling her he wanted to marry just as soon as he could finish that cursed manuscript. Then he could get a good job or perhaps make his way as a writer. "Being in love," he confided to a friend, "was one of the nicest things that civilization has produced."[7] Here, thought Mary, was someone who had a mind, who liked to listen to her and loved to ramble on about writing, books, the South, southern literature—all the things she found fascinating. Jack Cash, or Cash, as she always called him, was refreshingly different from her first husband, a handsome but languid man, mainly interested in talking about yachting.

In truth, few women had ever been attracted to Cash. "He looks like somebody's uncle" was the common response of women after meeting the shy, taciturn fellow with the nicotine-stained fingers. "He never says anything," one woman exclaimed in exasperation after having

5. Mary Cash Maury, "Recollections," n.d., MS in Joseph L. Morrison Papers, Southern Historical Collection, University of North Carolina, Chapel Hill. Cash's widow, née Mary Bagley Ross, had been married and divorced when Cash met her and was called Mary Ross Northrop. After Cash's death, she married again and went by the name Mary Cash Maury (Morrison, *W. J. Cash*, 83).

6. Maury, "Recollections," in Morrison Papers.

7. *Ibid.*; Morrison, *W. J. Cash*, 81–83; telephone interview with Erma Drum, August 31, 1984.

been introduced to Cash at a social occasion. When one young woman was told, somewhat defensively, how smart Cash was, she blurted out, "Well, he certainly doesn't *look* smart." But Mary touched off a spark of animation in Cash; she charmed him and brought him out of his shell. When Cash was not talking and gesturing with his left hand, the one holding the ubiquitous cigarette, as he punctuated the air to make some point, he sat and actually listened to her. He wanted to know what she thought.[8]

They began seeing each other almost nightly. They met regularly after they got off work to relax and dine at the Little Pep. On other evenings Cash visited Mary and her mother at their apartment, which was comfortably spacious compared to his two-room efficiency at the Frederick. To the end of her days, Mary beamed whenever she thought of those summer nights as they sat around the kitchen table drinking coffee and smoking, or sat on the front porch listening to music or talking about books and ideas. "We were a pair of people fascinated by all that was or might be or might have been, by all we saw and knew or suspected and didn't know, and the talk went on and on and there never seemed to be any right time to break it off," Mary recalled of those first glorious days. Under the sunshine of Mary's admiring smile, his shyness melted away. He regaled her with stories about his youth: about Gaffney, Boiling Springs, the Baptist church, his parents. The story she liked best, the one that left both of them howling with laughter, was about his one and only football game, "an actual game against an opposing team, with townspeople watching him gallop mindlessly all over the field, anywhere, everywhere, in response to no signals and regardless of the ball or the teams." Write about that, she told him; it was priceless. Make that into a short story, she said wiping tears of laughter from her eyes.[9]

But what about her stories? Cash asked. He wanted to read them. You might not like them, she said; you are a real writer. Don't be silly, he replied. She knew that he had, at first, half suspected that her prize-winning pieces were sentimental "women's stories," but he smiled knowingly when she told him she needed the twenty-five-dollar prize. At the dinner table one evening she thrust a sheaf of pages into his

8. Maury, "Recollections," in Morrison Papers; interview with Harriet Doar, September 17, 1984; telephone interview with Erma Drum, August 31, 1984.

9. Maury, "Recollections," in Morrison Papers.

hands. Here, she said, were her various short stories she had titled "Women's Ward." He started reading. Mary and her mother picked quietly at their food, fearful lest their chatter disturb the critic. First came that telltale twinkle in his eyes; then he began chuckling and nodding. He liked what he was reading. Daughter and mother finished dinner while Mary's gentleman caller continued reading and nodding until he had read all the sketches. Yes, he liked her stories, he said, liked them very much. Mary sighed. She had passed the test.[10]

What about your book? Mary asked. He had put it away, he murmured, but he had been thinking about it. He thought he could write now that he had someone who really cared for him. He told her about Peggy Ann and confessed that his youthful failure had left him afraid that he would never know true happiness with a woman. He was sure that his earlier sexual fiasco had contributed markedly to his recurring neurasthenia. But now all that was behind him; he was ready to write.

That summer of 1938 his boss at the *News* added two extra weeks to his regular one-week vacation. Buoyed by romance and time off, Cash possessed himself in resolve and went to work. By October he had 508 typed pages ready for Knopf. It was not all new—the first 306 were revised pages—but the new parts were good and took the story down through the rise of the cotton mills and the politics of the late nineteenth century, including those nefarious South Carolina demagogues Pitchfork Ben Tillman and Coley Blease. At this point, Cash thought he had only a chapter and a half to write to complete the book. He was wrong.[11]

Once again, the Knopfs were thrilled with what they received and delighted to think that the rest was coming soon, that publication was on the horizon. They had sent the manuscript to Odum, who replied excitedly that they should publish it as soon as possible; "the body of the text not only approximates a brilliant interpretation, but reads like a story." In place of Cash's "commonplace introduction" entitled "To Begin With—" Odum suggested that Cash "pen a very fine little preview note" and call it "Preview to Understanding," which in time he did. Odum cautioned the Knopfs not to ask Cash to make many changes: "Better take it while it is moving smoothly."[12]

10. *Ibid.*; Morrison, *W. J. Cash*, 84.

11. In W. J. Cash, *The Mind of the South* (1941; rpr. New York, 1969), this material goes through Book Three's Chapter II, Section 8, p. 273.

12. Howard W. Odum to Alfred A. Knopf, November 8, 1938, Alfred A. Knopf Papers, Harry Ransom Humanities Research Center, University of Texas at Austin.

In late November, Cash answered that he, too, was eager to finish "and that I'll give you the whole just as rapidly as I possibly can." He had been laid up for two weeks "with the worst cold I have ever had." He had no objection to submitting the manuscript to Odum, Cash said somewhat petulantly, but he had not heard from him. Both Alfred and Blanche Knopf replied instantly, urging him to finish and expressing mild, exasperated surprise that Odum's letter had not reached him. [13]

Cash replied with disheartening words: "This thing, somewhat to my horror, is stringing out to greater length than I had planned." He had another sixty pages done, but he knew a great deal more had yet to be written. He promised to hurry, however, and was confident he would be done by January, 1939. "If you want an absolute date, say February 1 as the final deadline." He would give an earlier date, but the Christmas holidays were at hand, "and I know from experience that it is virtually impossible to work in this country at that time." Blanche Knopf replied that she hoped he could finish earlier because waiting until February 1 would make spring publication difficult. [14]

For their pains, the Knopfs learned from Odum that Cash had never replied to his letter and from Cash that he had yet to hear from Odum. The disbelieving, exasperated Knopfs patiently sent Cash a carbon of Odum's letter. They received in return an apology and another excuse. "We had a cold day down here, and, coming out of the apartment house, I slipped on the ice, fell down the stairs, and smashed my face up pretty dreadfully." From groveling, he switched to some lame good old boy humor: "Fortunately, my head seems to be pretty thick and so there were no serious results." He was just as "irritated" by the delay as they were, and he would work as hard as possible. Once more, the Knopfs' reply conveyed impatience and mild irritation. [15]

Cash was maddening. In mid-February he mailed fifty-one pages of manuscript but neglected to include a cover letter or a single word of explanation. Several days later he wrote that the recent batch of pages was the sixty he had mentioned back in December—"considerably

13. Alfred A. Knopf to W. J. Cash, November 28, 1938, saying gently that he was eager to set a publication date; Cash to Knopf, November 23, 1938; Knopf to Cash, December 9, 1938, all in Morrison Papers.
14. W. J. Cash to Blanche Knopf, December 14, 1938; Blanche Knopf to W. J. Cash, December 19, 1938, *ibid.*
15. Howard Odum to Alfred A. Knopf, December 31, 1938; W. J. Cash to Blanche Knopf, January 4, 1939; Alfred A. Knopf to W. J. Cash, January 9, 1939; W. J. Cash to Alfred A. Knopf, January 4, 1939, *ibid.*

trimmed down." In between, Blanche Knopf fired off a letter asking whether the fifty-one pages was the final installment. He was not finished yet, his belated cover letter indicated, but he had arranged a two-week leave from his job, and he was sure he could wind the whole thing up by March 3.[16]

"Am I to take it that we will have the complete manuscript by March 3 definitely?" Blanche Knopf asked. March 3 came and went. Not a sound came from Charlotte. "Will you please let me know how much material we are still to get from you and when we will have it," Blanche Knopf inquired cryptically in early April. "Others' books will be coming out on the South and it seems to me that we had better get yours quickly."[17]

The Knopfs, hoping to coax the rest of the book out of Cash in time for their fall list, arranged to come to Greensboro and meet with their gifted but tardy author. Wisely, they arrived in an avuncular, non-scolding mood. Everyone was graceful and charming. At a convivial meeting at the O. Henry Hotel on April 15, Cash assured them that another sixty pages were done. These pages were finished, merely needing to be typed, which he was having done. Encouraged to the point of delight, the Knopfs agreed to an additional advance to help with his typing and other expenses. On arriving in New York, they received a letter from Cash asking whether they could raise that advance to two hundred dollars. He would understand if they refused, "but I think it will help in getting the book finished."[18]

Knopf mailed the larger advance immediately. Cash received it, cashed it, and spent it. But the Knopfs received no reply, not even an acknowledgment of the check, let alone those sixty pages they had been led to believe constituted the concluding section. In late May, after prodding from Knopf, Cash replied lamely that he was sure he had posted a thank you letter via the office secretary. About the sixty pages, he spun a convoluted story about his typist's husband having been sick, but he fully intended to find another typist. He was sure he could finish in two or three weeks.[19] Yes, Alfred Knopf sighed, a new typist was in order. If Cash could keep his word, the book could be

16. Blanche Knopf to W. J. Cash, February 15, 1939, *ibid.*
17. Blanche Knopf to W. J. Cash, February 20, April 6, 1939, *ibid.*
18. W. J. Cash to Alfred A. Knopf, April 22, 1939, *ibid.*
19. Alfred A. Knopf to W. J. Cash, April 25, 1939; Cash to Knopf, May 31, 1939, *ibid.*

brought out in the fall. Knopf was off to London in June, he told Cash, and having the completed manuscript in hand before departure would lift his spirits mightily. "Mrs. Knopf, of course, will be here ready to give you no peace at all if you don't come across."[20]

In mid-June, Cash asked nonchalantly if the Knopfs would like to see the completed "Preview to Understanding." By all means, Knopf wired. But where was the rest of the manuscript? The house would have to have it by June 20 to ensure a fall publication. On June 19 Cash mailed the seven-page Preview to Understanding and ninety-three additional pages. But the book was not completed. This new batch was what would turn out to be the next to last chapter. No, he was not quite finished, he explained in an aggrieved tone. "I am quite as sorry as you are that I couldn't hand over all the manuscript by tomorrow. However, what I promised was to get to work on the job and stay at it until it was completed. I have kept that promise, and am keeping it. And I shall not hold up the preparation of the book longer than is absolutely necessary. Mostly, it has again turned out to be a little longer than I had hoped. And I cannot write it faster than the time at my disposal will allow. The end is in sight, and I am giving it every minute I can. That's all I can do."[21]

The end was not in sight. Learning that upon returning from London, Alfred Knopf replied coldly: "I don't think I ever had to annoy anyone quite as much as I have had to you, but for every reason this manuscript should be delivered now. Please do tell me what goes on about it." The kindly, patient Knopf had another reason to be irritated. He was not entirely sure where the last ninety-three pages—which Cash had simply titled "Chapter Two" (by which he meant Chapter Two of the concluding third section)—went in the manuscript.[22]

Cash cleared up that question quickly, but the nettlesome one of why he had not finished required explanation. He had been ailing with "chronic bronchitis" for an entire month. "I am thoroughly depressed about the delay. But the matter has been out of my control, and at least the delay is about over." In mid-September, having heard

20. Alfred A. Knopf to W. J. Cash, June 2, 1939, *ibid.*
21. Alfred A. Knopf to W. J. Cash, June 16, 1939; W. J. Cash to Blanche Knopf, June 19, 1939, *ibid.*; Cash, *Mind of the South*, Preview to Understanding, vii–x; the ninety-three pages took the book to page 350.
22. Alfred A. Knopf to W. J. Cash, August 10, 1939, in Morrison Papers.

nothing from Charlotte, Blanche Knopf wrote that she hoped "very much that you will let me know immediately that the manuscript is finished and on the way to me."[23]

Cash replied that his bronchitis had held on a month longer and had kept him from working. Like a little boy, Cash lowered himself to say that "Mr. Dowd, the editor here, will bear me out in that." But he was back at work and hoped "to send it to you within a very short time." The Knopfs were speechless. Again, Cash was reduced to pathetic excuses: "That chronic bronchitis has held on all this time." He was truly sorry and would submit the final pages in "in about ten days or two weeks at the most." He hoped everyone knew that he was "even sicker of the everlasting delay than you are."[24]

What was Cash up to? What had gone wrong this time? He may have been laid low with bronchitis or a respiratory ailment—he was a heavy smoker living in a hot, humid region and forced to live and work in non-air-conditioned buildings. To make matters worse, Mary was away in the summer of 1939. Her job with the Federal Writers' Project had taken her to Asheville. Cash visited her in June and wrote two or three times a week. He missed her greatly and desperately needed a steady flow of letters from her, though his letters (which have not survived) were brief and to the point, Mary recalled. Cash was moody and restless without her. But given his long-standing tendency to avoid working on his book at the first feeling of anxiety—he turned out a moving feature piece on Thomas Wolfe after visiting Mary and visiting Wolfe's grave, where tears had streamed down his face—other reasons for Cash's exasperating delays in finishing the manuscript must be found.[25]

The dark, menacing war clouds hanging over Europe in the fall of 1939 intensified Cash's long-standing alarm at fascist aggression in Europe into an ominous, obsessive rage against Hitler. For some time, the international scene had filled Cash with growing alarm. The result had been a string of informed, biting editorials denouncing Japanese aggression in China, Mussolini's invasion and conquest of Abyssinia (Ethiopia) in late 1935 and early 1936, and Hitler's ranting national-

23. W. J. Cash to Blanche Knopf, August 10, 1939; Blanche Knopf to W. J. Cash, September 13, 1939, ibid.

24. W. J. Cash to Blanche Knopf, October [1939]; Blanche Knopf to W. J. Cash, October 24, 1939; W. J. Cash to Blanche Knopf, October 31, 1939, ibid.

25. Maury, "Recollections," in Morrison Papers; Charlotte News, July 30, 1939.

ism and occupation of the demilitarized zone of the Rhineland in March, 1936. Each instance of blatant aggression filled him with anger and foreboding. The Western democracies' failure to do anything made him angrier and angrier. "I am not interested in the gentle and polite world of books today," he wrote on August 29, 1937, "for I cannot forget the thing that the Japanese pigs did in Shanghai last Monday. Whether the shell which exploded at the busiest street corner in the world outside New York and London came from a Japanese gun or a Chinese gun I don't know and I don't care. Wherever the shell came from, the deed is still the deed of the militarists who rule Japan." Later, thinking about Japan's recent aggression in China, Cash denounced the "swinish war gods of Japan." [26]

By fall of 1938, after Hitler's invasion and annexation of Austria not only went unchallenged but actually brought the European democracies to embrace England's policy of appeasement, Cash's editorials grew even more incisive and prophetic. He had nothing but contempt for the architect of appeasement, Neville Chamberlain, whom he routinely called Mr. Bumble. Hitler was not going to be content with Austria; Cash predicted that Czechoslovakia would be next, then Poland. While Chamberlain and others were telling themselves that Hitler, though obviously a cad, was just another nationalistic politician who would settle down once he had gained certain victories, Cash wrote angry editorials that won acclaim far beyond the boundaries of North Carolina. In late September, 1938, Cash recalled Oswald Spengler's prediction in *The Decline of the West* that the Western countries would lapse from civilization into barbarism. "It has happened, first in Italy, and now, even more thoroughly, in Germany. Neither country is any longer a civilized nation in the sense we have understood the word since the Renaissance. They are states organized as barbarian states are organized, strictly on military lines for the purpose of rapine and plunder, and the barbarian notion of 'glory' that goes with success in rapine and plunder." [27]

As war loomed in August, 1939, Cash observed the foreign scene with a despair born of an awareness of how calamitous Hitler and war would be for the Western world. "The price will be the lives of mil-

---

26. Charlotte *News*, March 8, 1936, November 30, 1935, July 11, August 29, October 3, 1937.
27. *Ibid.*, September 12, 17, 25, 1938.

lions on millions of men, and in all probability economic ruin for all of us," Cash observed sadly. When Hitler invaded Poland on September 1 and the Western world plunged into the second world war of the century, Cash denounced Hitler as a fanatic "who identifies himself with God, who believes that he is resistless, and who meant all along to have his way even though it involved a world war and the deaths of millions on millions." Nazism was a philosophy invented "by a gang of criminals" to take the world back to barbarism.[28]

Cash could fathom Hitler's real aims and personality because he had read *Mein Kampf* carefully, with pencil in hand, jotting his fearful observations in the margins. In several lengthy columns Cash spelled out in detail that Hitler was a racist, an anti-Semite, a blood-thirsty militarist, and a power-mad nationalist. Cash's few references to the fate of German Jews suggest that like most people in the United States he did not fully fathom the depths of Hitler's demonic anti-Semitism, but he sensed as early as 1936 that Hitler's racism had dire consequences for Jews.[29]

By late 1939, with his fears fixated on Hitler, the merest mention of the dictator's name caused Cash's anger to flare. He would begin by rubbing his forehead vigorously and squinting his eyes. Then he would start pacing, muttering about Hitler's villainy. Then his voice would rise as he flailed his arms in denunciation. When reading something disturbing about the international scene, he would at first sit staring at his newspaper or magazine. Then he would jump up, fling the paper on the floor, and grind it under his heel. Hitler was a demon, a filthy monster. Cash would stand staring at the giant wall map at the *News*, carefully and silently tracing Hitler's movements. Then he would begin to scream epithets: Hitler was a madman, a maniac, a Ku Kluxer, white trash. Cash's screams could be heard throughout the newsroom and beyond. When his fits began, his mates would avert their eyes or bury themselves in their work, but his tantrums were frequently so loud and disturbing that a hush came over the newsroom as everyone stared at him in pity and horror. When he was raging, no one went near him. Nor did anyone try to counsel or console him when he had calmed down. Cash was not one who invited such gestures. How often

28. *Ibid.*, August 19, September 1, 1939.
29. *Ibid.*, January 3, 1936, September 5, 1937, March 20, September 8, 1938, March 5, 26, November 19, 1939.

and how many times did Cash become a raging volcano? No one counted. But to a person, his friends from his newspaper days vividly remembered those terrible outbursts. Everybody at the paper talked about his fits, worried about them, but considered them one more manifestation of a complex man's very odd behavior.[30]

Yet if one caught Cash in a relaxed mood, he could be teased a little, even about those things that angered him. One day a newcomer to the paper approached him hesitantly, and said, "I've got a brilliant idea for an editorial for you, Mr. Cash." Cash nodded, and the young man blurted out: "Adolph Shitler." To everyone's relief, Cash laughed uproariously and thanked him.[31]

Cash's preoccupation with Hitler was obsessive and strange, clearly neurotic. Normal people did not (and do not) act as Cash did. But maybe "normal people," in their capacity to stay "balanced" whenever they thought about Hitler and the coming of a catastrophic war, were deficient. Perhaps their ability to live calmly in the same world as such a monumentally evil man was neurotic. Perhaps Cash had a greater capacity for moral outrage than most people, even writers and editors like the Knopfs, who would in time publish book after book detailing the monstrous horrors of the Nazi evil.[32]

Cash was one of those people who are always in the presence of their emotions and frequently captive of their passionate feelings. He

30. Telephone interviews with Burke Davis, October 1, 1984, and Reed Sarratt, November 30, 1984.

31. Telephone interview with Emery Wister, September 16, 1984.

32. The historian David Thomson writes of the democracies' failure to understand Hitler: "The politics of appeasement had failed because it was based upon a fundamental misconception of the nature of National Socialism in Germany and of Hitler himself. Had Nazism been a normal nationalist movement, guided by utilitarian considerations and realistic views of national interest—had the Nazi leaders been even averagely normal men of reason and sense—Chamberlain's policy might have succeeded. It was impossible to set limits to the expansion and tyranny of Nazism other than by destroying it; it was impossible to make any terms with Hitler because he would never be bound by them. Nazism and Hitler were caricatures of the depths of cynicism and mistrust to which lack of respect for treaty obligations or promises had reduced international relations. The movement and its leaders were nihilistic—bent upon total destruction of the liberal matrix of civilization which they detested, and if in this they failed, they were bent upon self-destruction. Statesmen acclimatized to the more rational, humane ways of democracy found—with few exceptions—such a movement virtually incomprehensible. They shut their eyes to it as long as they could, submitting to its seductive propaganda and its incessant self-pity; and even when they were forced to look at it straight, they were still so sickened by the thought of general war that they went on deluding themselves with the hope that its dynamism might be spent, its limits found. But the lust for power and further conquest fed on success, the hoped for limits constantly receded, until the thing had to be confronted in its full horror" (*Europe Since Napoleon* [New York, 1957], 716).

felt things deeply; tears easily welled up in his eyes and streamed down his face. In June, 1939, when Mary was away and he was having serious problems writing, his kid sister, Bertie, was married. Knowing how much he prized her, she pleaded with him to take part in the ceremony. No, he said over and over again. He knew himself all too well, he told Bertie. He would start bawling the moment she entered the church. And how would it look for her big brother to stand up in front of the congregation blubbering like a baby? At the wedding Cash sat beside his mother struggling to keep his composure as tears streamed down his face.[33]

Cash had a long history of excessive emotionality, which worsened whenever he faced a stressful situation. In 1939–1940 he was pushing himself to finish a book that filled him with extreme anxiety. Is it possible that Cash's hysterical reactions to Hitler, however real and awful, were a subtle, uncontrollable way of avoiding finishing the book? Cash thought, and so have others, that his worrying about Hitler kept him from finishing the book. Perhaps it was the other way around. Perhaps Cash was directing the anger he felt toward the book—and by extension, toward himself—onto Hitler, the ultimate symbol of evil. Even in Charlotte, loathing and ranting against Hitler, while odd and disturbing to some others, were acceptable. Maybe his raging denunciations provided a psychological safety valve. If so, what he really yearned to do in those "fits" was to abuse himself—and, given the heights his blood pressure must have reached during those rages, he was probably succeeding. None of this is meant to question or diminish the moral depths of Cash's hostility toward Hitler, but his raging outbursts point to a mysterious problem in his psyche.

In addition, Cash was drinking too much by 1939 and 1940 as he struggled to finish his book. As in his earlier days, he drank beer mainly and a little sherry and wine now and then. Most of the News crowd, with the exception of the young Reed Sarratt, drank a good bit, even on the job, but mainly after work and at parties. Cash drank with cronies from the newspaper, with Mary, a heavy drinker "who could handle her liquor," and with their Charlotte friends. A few drinks loosened Cash up and made him much more sociable, more likable; he became chatty, talking freely, sometimes with spellbinding

33. Interview with Elizabeth ("Bertie") Cash Elkins and Charles Elkins, August 20, 1984.

clarity. He was unable to tolerate drink, however, and its influence on him was unpredictable. Sometimes he became loud and garrulous, given to bragging and boasting. He could also become irritable, surly, or unusually morose.[34]

A more ominous sign was that, after a few beers or several glasses of sherry, and occasionally something stronger, Cash was drunk and would stagger around clumsily. When he overdid his drinking, as he was doing with alarming frequency by late 1939, he had to be helped back to his room at the Frederick. No one kept count of how much he drank, and most of his contemporaries who admit to having enjoyed an occasional social drink with Cash and remember hearing stories of him drinking and seeing him drunk claim that they never drank to excess with him. It appears, also, that Cash did a good bit of solitary drinking. Again, how much, how often, or with what regularity cannot be verified. Several of his newspaper friends who roomed at the Frederick recall that when they came in at night, usually on weekends, they would hear his old phonograph playing the same record over and over again, and loudly, a sure sign that Cash had passed out. His close friend Pete McKnight, who often drank with Cash, frequently let himself into Cash's apartment (Cash had given him a key), turned off the record player, and helped Cash off the floor or couch and into bed.[35]

Numerous people from the newspaper saw him in his cups more than once, bleary-eyed and slumped in his chair or with his head on his desk as though he were napping. It was common gossip, from editor Dowd on down, that Cash regularly drank too much. Sometimes he came to work barely able to function or completely unable to write. In the time-honored fashion of the newsroom, his friends covered for him when possible. One morning Cash staggered in late and slumped in his chair. His editorial was due in a matter of minutes. When editor Bill Dowd stepped out of the office, one of Cash's buddies rushed him out while another scurried around and found someone who had the time and the ability to write an editorial in Cash's style. Then there were Cash's all-too-frequent Monday absences. At one point, an exasperated Bill Dowd showed Burke Davis a ledger book indicating that

34. Harriet Doar to author, November, 1984.
35. Interview with Charles A. (Pete) McKnight, September 15, 1984; telephone interview with Burke Davis, October 1, 1984.

Cash had missed between thirty and forty Mondays during the last year or so he worked at the paper.[36]

Was Cash an alcoholic? The term is slippery and vague, with too many elusive definitions to make it a useful label, particularly for someone whose drinking habits cannot be known precisely. Pete McKnight said Cash drank far too much and that alcohol ruined his life. Cam Shipp, who enjoyed a drink as much as anyone around the *News*, once said sorrowfully that Cash drank all the time and was "hopeless" and beyond anybody's help—and that he would never finish his book. In short, Cash frequently drank to excess. According to Mary, his drinking increased significantly during 1939–1940. More ominously, he began drinking whiskey, much of it potent bootleg whiskey.[37]

Cash's long-standing pattern of avoidance behavior, his continuing inability or unwillingness to write, and his recurring bouts of depression when he thought about his book make it hazardous to suggest that drinking or anything external to his troubled psyche was the principal reason why he was so maddeningly slow in writing his book in 1939–1940. Certainly his heavy weekend drinking, when he might have been writing, and blue Mondays slowed his progress.

Doubtless, that albatross called the book, that great, seemingly never-to-be finished task, contributed to his drinking. Liquor, like any drug, dulls the senses, blots out thoughts about disagreeable duties, and cushions the ego against unpleasant demands. For Cash it was an escape from an extremely onerous, depressing task. But the reasons for Cash's drinking were deeper, more wide-ranging, and subtly intertwined with other features of his personality and psyche. He was a lifelong depressive, frequently so depressed that he could not work or even think about it. One sensitive friend who knew Cash and Mary well said that Cash always seemed depressed and lonely. Many depressives drink—and drink alone in secret. Moreover, his drinking, which was meant to banish the guilt he felt about his book, caused further bouts of guilt and depression. No one raised as he was, in a family to whom drunkenness was one of the cardinal sins, and with his

36. Harriet Doar to author, November, 1984; telephone interview with Burke Davis, October 1, 1984.

37. Maury, "Recollections," in Morrison Papers; telephone interview with Burke Davis, October 1, 1984.

personality, could have faced the morning, after having passed out in a drunken stupor the night before, without feeling an extra burden of guilt. True, he was a liberated man who worked and moved in liberated circles in which drinking, in Presbyterian, bone-dry Charlotte, was the thing to do. Drinking helped Cash to relax and rebel—against his upbringing and his book. (Significantly, there is no evidence that he ever drank or appeared even slightly drunk in the presence of his family, particularly his mother and father.) As is true of many depressives who drink too much, life looked better to Cash when viewed through an alcoholic haze. Cash, then, may be labeled an alcoholic.[38]

Alfred Knopf did not know about Cash's problems, but by early 1940 the publisher threw up his hands in desperation. Cash's continued excuses seemed "quite incredible," Knopf announced sternly in January, and further delay in publication was "making us both appear rather silly." Knopf proposed "a definite deadline" of mid-April, at which time the house would publish whatever material it had from Cash. His procrastination left no alternative.[39]

Cash replied three weeks later with more excuses. He had been "terribly ill" with influenza and had been in "foul shape" all fall and winter. But now he had the decks cleared to finish without further delay. He agreed with the Knopfs' suggestion that some fifteen to twenty thousand words, perhaps more, needed to be cut from the manuscript, and he gave the Knopfs carte blanche to make the necessary excisions. "If you care to go ahead and begin setting it up, with the understanding that if the material lacking isn't on hand by the date you name, you can publish it anyhow—that will be all right with me," Cash replied humbly to Knopf's ultimatum. "However, the material will be there, early in February, I am confident."[40]

Again, the material was not produced. February and March passed, and so did the April deadline. As before, there was no word from Charlotte. Baffled, the Knopfs quietly retreated from their threat to publish a truncated version. May slipped by. Even more exasperated than usual, Knopf informed Cash in early June that he was putting the book on the fall list and would publish what he had. He hated to do this, but Cash's silence and failure to write had forced his hand. More-

38. Interviews with Harriet Doar, September 17, October 28, 1985.
39. Alfred A. Knopf to W. J. Cash, January 4, 1940, in Morrison Papers.
40. Cash to Knopf, January 22, 1940, *ibid.*

over, he and his copy editor agreed that only the author could cut from this manuscript, and they earnestly hoped that Cash would do it.[41]

"I suppose I do seem a heel," Cash replied punctually. He had been telling the truth back in January. The last chapter had been within a section or two of being finished. But his anxiety over Nazi aggression and the threat of war had sidetracked him. "Worse, I was left hanging in the air as to how to wind up that book and increasingly convinced that some of the things I had said belonged in a different perspective." Everything combined to leave him in "a fog of anger and defeatism." Now, however, he knew that the job must be done. He would send the Knopfs, "in a few days," a complete and revised manuscript, including the final chapter.

Days went by. Weeks passed—six weeks in all.[42]

And then, without warning or fanfare, the mighty task was done. On July 27, 1940, Cash bundled up the final, concluding pages and posted them to New York City. He had also made the necessary cuts, most of which were minor, involving little more than a word here and there and excising or adding a few sentences and specifics. The bulky eight-hundred-page manuscript arrived safe and sound.

"God be praised," Alfred Knopf exclaimed. It was a miracle. "We can hardly believe that it is really at long last completed. And it is good." Knopf hoped for a November publication.[43]

Eight hundred pages, 160,000 words—each wrung from Cash's imagination, each a terrible strain on Cash's pysche, each "written in blood," as Cash, echoing Nietzsche, had said must be true of any writer. His cover letter was one last attempt, a completely honest, accurate explanation, one suspects, of why it had taken so long. "I have never been able to approach the task of continuing it without extreme depression and dislike. . . . The history of that book is strange stuff," Cash admitted.[44]

41. Knopf to Cash, June 12, 1940, *ibid.*
42. Cash to Knopf, June 19, 1940, *ibid.*
43. Knopf to Cash, August 1, 1940, *ibid.*
44. Cash to Knopf, July 27, 1940, *ibid.*

9 / Rendezvous with Fate

Surely, now that the book was done, W. J. Cash could be happy, maybe even know true contentment. The long, dark night of uncertainty was over. The book would soon be published. He even dared to think that it was good and would, just maybe, sell enough copies to free him to do what he had always wanted to do, write that novel. All along he had known that even old friends like Cam Shipp had doubted whether he would ever finish it. He could hardly blame them. That thought, that fear, had dogged his steps for years. But he had finished it. And standing by to share his joy and triumph was Mary, who doted on him, never doubted him, and had believed him when he said he would be free to marry her once the albatross was lifted from his shoulders.

Cash and Mary celebrated Christmas Eve, 1940, at the home of the Frank McCleneghens, a Charlotte couple whom Mary had known for years. She had introduced Cash to them several months earlier, and the four of them liked each other from the start. They shared liberal political and social ideas, a high regard for good conversation, a distaste for organized religion, and a fondness for drinking. As they drank and trimmed the tree, the affable talk came around to just when Cash and Mary were going to get married. The book was finished; they were in love; they wanted to get married. Why not now, Frank McCleneghen suggested. Within a few hours, said Frank, who was an attorney, they could all be in York, South Carolina, legendary goal of eloping teenagers, where the local justice of the peace could be roused at any hour of the day or night. The idea was fine by him, Cash said, but he had no ring; Frank offered his fraternity ring. Mary did not much like being married in York, but by around midnight the four tipsy revelers were on the road in the McCleneghens' automobile. W. J. Cash and Mary Bagley Ross Northrop were married early on Christmas morning.[1]

Was Cash's decision a spur-of-the-moment thing, induced by drink and that "worn-out" feeling he could not shake? They had all been drinking that night, and everyone was "pretty well oiled," Mary McCleneghen remembered years later, though she was sure no one was "really drunk" and Mary had not talked Cash into getting married. The question is of some importance because Cash's family, being strict Baptists, did not approve of Mary on several grounds, not the least of which was that she was a divorcee. Baptists considered marriage sacred and divorce a sin; weddings were to be properly planned and performed in a proper church. The Cashes, who never completely accepted Mary, could not believe that their boy, left to his own devices, would have wanted anything but a church wedding. His family admitted that he occasionally drank a beer, but no more because he had a very low tolerance for liquor. For years, rumors would float around in the Baptist community of Shelby and Boiling Springs that Cash had been tricked into getting married by a woman who was not the proper sort. Other friends and acquaintances, less convinced that Cash cared much about religion or formality, were also surprised by the evening's events. Editor Dodd, who saw Cash daily for years, was startled to learn that Cash had someone to marry. An old friend from Boiling Springs always said matter-of-factly, "Cash wasn't the marrying kind."[2]

But married he was as 1941 dawned, and they waited for publication of his book, scheduled for early February. Close friends in Charlotte such as the McCleneghens and Pete McKnight thought he was happy, at least as happy as Jack Cash, moody and withdrawn, was likely to get. The couple could not afford a honeymoon, nor could Cash be away from the paper on such short notice. But he had a loving wife to come home to, to talk to, to stand by his side, to share his joy. Their devotion to each other was strong and true; she delighted in preparing his meals and looking after his needs. He bragged about her cooking and

1. Interview with Mary McCleneghen, September 18, 1984; interview with Harriet Doar, October 28, 1985.
2. Interview with Lindsey Dail, October 28, 1985.

wanted to spend all of his free hours with her. The first couple of weeks were rocky. Cash suffered several bouts of the flu, and they were living in his cramped, two-room bachelor apartment. But when in early January Mary's mother left for Chapel Hill, where she had taken a position as a housemother at the university, the newlyweds moved into her place and settled down. According to Mary, Cash's sexual anxieties proved to be groundless, and they knew true marital happiness.[3]

Cash was a local celebrity. On publication day, February 10, Efird's Bookstore had an autograph party for him. Cash smoked nervously and smiled sheepishly, but he enjoyed the limelight, sitting and neatly inscribing copies of *The Mind of the South* as Mary handed them to him. The *News*, aware of Cash's nervousness, dispatched a young staffer to be on hand to lend moral support and take care of any unexpected needs. Bemused, Cash turned to the young man and jokingly called him "Hebe," an allusion to the mythological Greek cupbearer of the gods. Sensing that he had caught Cash in one of his genuinely happy moods, the young man replied playfully, "Now Mr. Cash, don't you think it's a little late in the day for you to become anti-Semitic." Tickled at the pun, Cash grinned a vigorous assent and lit another cigarette. But that night fears about what critics and readers might say tormented his sleep. At one point he awoke to hug Mary and tell her how frightened he was.[4]

To make sure he did not miss a single review, he subscribed to a clipping service. It did not help much to remind him that several reviewers had already applauded the book. Shipp, who had recently gone to Hollywood to write screenplays, raved about Cash's book in the Charlotte *News*, announcing that his buddy had produced a "forceful, marvelously informed and brilliantly written book." Shipp signed off to his readers and old friend saying, "Mr. Cash, I thank you." That same day, February 9, the Durham *Morning Herald* and the Raleigh *News and Observer* expressed pleasure with the book's scope and beautiful style. The critic at the Greensboro *Daily News*, a newspaper Cash deeply admired, announced that "here is a book destined to take a leading place in American life and letters, for it combines importance with courage and scholarship and tops them off with brilliant writing." Fine, fine, said Cash, but these were expressions of

3. Mary Cash Maury, "Recollections," MS in Joseph L. Morrison Papers, Southern Historical Collection, University of North Carolina, Chapel Hill.
4. *Ibid.*; telephone interview with Marion Hargrove, October 10, 1984.

local pride. But even Cash chuckled out loud when he spied Uncle John Dickson's admiring review in the Charlotte *Observer* (to which Dickson had moved the year before). "Mr. Cash has drawn such an accurate picture of the mind of the South that the Southern man feels a little naked in reading the book. Why, Cash is writing about him and his neighbors."[5]

To Cash's surprise and pleasure, praise came in from all over the South. Henry Nash Smith, who would one day in *Virgin Land* brilliantly chart the image of the West in the American mind, carefully and at length praised Cash's undertaking in the Dallas *Morning News*. Like some other academics, Smith complained mildly that, in neglecting specific ideas and thinkers to concentrate on "social forces," Cash was not a southern V. L. Parrington and grumbled that Cash might have used the tools of social science. But other than that, Smith sensed that Cash had triumphed over his materials. The Houston *Post* called Cash's book "a magnificent study" by someone who obviously loved the South. In Maryland, Cash's friend R. P. Harriss penned a mighty (and lengthy) approval in the Baltimore *Evening Sun*, saying that the book was "so persuasive, so charming, it makes the polished writing of Van Wyck Brooks seem pedestrian, almost stodgy, by comparison." In Birmingham John Temple Graves reproached Cash mildly for repeating the "falsehood" that his father had been in any way responsible for the Atlanta race riots of 1906 but saluted Cash's "objectivity" and "extraordinary" accomplishment. And so it went across the South, from the Jackson (Mississippi) *Clarion Ledger* to the Douglas (Georgia) *Enterprise*, though the Richmond *Times* was much more restrained, finding Cash too much of a "liberal" and too much of the *American Mercury* school. The only genuinely sour note in the chorus of praise from the southern press came from the Nashville *Banner*, where Richmond Beatty, one of the Agrarians, held sway.[6] Cash heard about the review but did not see it until April.

The southern press reaction was mainly positive, somewhat surprisingly given what Cash had said, but no one, not even Harriss or Shipp or Henry Nash Smith, sensed how important the book would become. The book columnist for the Augusta (Georgia) *Chronicle* recognized it

5. Greensboro *Daily News*, February 16, 1941; Charlotte *Observer*, February 16, 1941.

6. Dallas *Morning News*, February 9, 1941; Houston *Post*, March 9, 1941; Baltimore *Evening Sun*, March 14, 1941; Birmingham *Age Herald*, March 20, 1941; Richmond *Times*, February 16, 1941; Nashville *Banner*, February 26, 1941.

as an "important and interesting analysis" but thought that compared to Van Wyck Brooks's recent literary-social history *The Flowering of New England* it should have been called "The Deflowering of Dixie." Cash's conclusions made "pretty good sense," but the critic, astutely recognizing the autobiographical foundations for much of the book, would have liked more proof—something beyond "Mr. Cash's own primary experience."[7]

Cash and Mary were delighted and relieved. "What pleases me most," Mary wrote to Cash's parents after telling them that *Time* magazine had given the book an admiring review, "is that the Southern reviewers are whooping it up almost to a man. I had expected a lot of opposition there. If it had fallen flat, heaven only knows what effect it might have had on Wilbur's self-confidence." The book was a bestseller in Atlanta, a proud Mary exulted; "maybe the contagion will spread." Wilbur's only complaint thus far was that *Time* and many national publications were running the picture of him in his hat, the one that made him look like a gangster. "He sent it to the Knopfs," Mary reminded Cash's parents, "so I don't think he should complain."[8]

The national reviews were even better. "Anything written about the South henceforth must start where he leaves off," *Time* concluded. The critic for the *New York Times Book Review* praised Cash's scholarship, saying that in all the recent books on the South no one had attempted the scope or succeeded as brilliantly, in prose or argument, in analyzing the southern mind "in such a philosophical and illuminating manner." The *Atlantic*'s Wilson Follett said in a brief review (which Alfred Knopf liked and sent to Cash), "this is that one American book in ten thousand that makes us, for the sake of the national health, wish it could be made universal compulsory reading." John Selby, the Associated Press's syndicated reviewer, liked the book and argued in a separate column that it deserved to be ranked above Jawaharlal Nehru's autobiography and Roger Martin du Gard's new novel in any competition for the month's best book.[9]

7. Augusta (Ga.) *Chronicle*, March 5, 1941.

8. Mary Cash to Mr. and Mrs. Cash, February 20, 1941, in Morrison Papers.

9. *Time*, February 24, 1941, p. 98; Charles Lee Snyder, in *New York Times Book Review*, February 23, 1941, p. 4; *Atlantic*, CLXVII (April, 1941), 7; clipping, Charles H. Elkins Family Scrapbook, in the possession of Charles H. Elkins, Jr., Winston-Salem, North Carolina. One reviewer, James Orrick, concluded: "In the matter of style he [Cash] often carries individualism to the point of quaintness, and rhetoric to the point of Carlylese. But these are minor blemishes on a thoughtful and knowledgeable book" (*Nation*, CLII, [April 5, 1941], 414–15).

There was also a positive southern response from the national press. Gerald W. Johnson applauded in the *New Republic*, saying Cash had surpassed even Rupert Vance's outstanding *Human Geography of the South* and Howard Odum's monumental *Southern Regions of the United States*. Cash is a "frankly partisan" southerner, Johnson wrote, but his book is "unromantic, unsentimental, cool, clearheaded." Cash probably never saw Tennessee's George Fort Milton's review in the *Yale Review* (Summer, 1941), which saluted his treatment of the Ku Klux Klan, the Scopes trial, and the South's labor problems and antilabor attitudes.[10]

The most perceptive, probing analysis came from David L. Cohn, a son of the Deep South, a native Mississippian, a book man who wrote regularly for the erudite *Saturday Review of Literature*, Cash's favorite magazine. Cohn discussed Cash's major points admiringly and critically, arguing cogently but sympathetically that Cash had, in his marvelous zeal to get at the region's "mind," overstated the case for southern uniqueness, particularly its racial views and antiunion attitudes. Cohn, a close friend of William Alexander Percy, whose mind was as stoic and patrician as Cash's was romantic and critical, saw that *The Mind of the South*, "for all the author's heroic attempts at objectivity, is often a strangely embittered book. It is obvious that he is, in the Nietzschean phrase, a great despiser because he is a great adorer. And being such, he lashes out in language which reveals not only his admiration of the South but his own essential Southerness; he is no stranger to that Southern violence which he deplores." It took a southerner to take the measure of another southerner.[11]

If he saw it, Cash appreciated Cohn's review—like most authors Cash despised bland summaries that limped to a "this-is-a-useful-book" conclusion. But Cash was temperamental, emotional, and deeply sensitive. On reading Virginius Dabney's generally appreciative review in the *New York Herald Tribune*, Cash flew into a rage when his eye lighted on Dabney's judgment that "the book's rather tedious pace is stepped up in the last couple of hundred pages."[12] Furious, Cash dashed off an angry letter to Dabney, but Mary shamed him out of mailing it. The next day, Sunday, always a tough day for him to get through without liquor, Cash called a local bootlegger, got drunk,

---

10. *New Republic*, May 12, 1941, p. 673; *Yale Review*, XXX (Summer, 1941), 831–33.
11. *Saturday Review of Literature*, XXIII (February 22, 1941), 7, 16–17.
12. *New York Herald Tribune Book Review*, February 9, 1941.

wrote Dabney another mean letter suggesting that Dabney was jealous, and mailed it before telling Mary. He returned, said Mary, the conquering hero, saying, "You didn't talk me out of that one!" Several days later, a repentant Cash wrote Dabney an apology, which Dabney graciously accepted and told Cash that he had indeed liked his book.[13]

Cash's lamentable drunken outburst occurred on the heels of his book's appearance while praise was raining down on him. He was now somebody. North Carolina's literati were sure he was a shoo-in to win the Mayflower Cup and other prizes. He now had every reason to believe that now he might be awarded a Guggenheim Fellowship. Once he won that, he could write the novel he had been dreaming about. It was far too early to venture a guess about sales, and it was farfetched to think such a serious book would be a best-seller, but a Knopf salesman had passed through town and told Wilbur and Mary that it ought to sell up North. "They buy $3.75 books up there," Mary told Cash's parents in early February, when she explained that he had almost won the North Carolina State Press Association's award for the best editorial even though his contribution (on a sea battle) was not on a local subject. They would settle for Honorable Mention, but they could have used the hundred-dollar prize money.[14]

Alfred Knopf stopped off in Charlotte on February 20 to spend a day with his author and his new bride. As Knopf's guests, they dined at the Hotel Charlotte, where they talked about books, Cash's book, and what he might write next. Pete McKnight and a photographer from the *News* showed up to do an exclusive interview that would feature the town's new star. "Mr. Knopf is very fond of the *News'* associate editor," McKnight told his readers, and "believes he has a great literary future ahead."

"Do you think Cash can write a novel, Mr. Knopf?" McKnight asked.

"It's not up to me to say whether Cash can or can not write a novel," Knopf replied cagily, probably doubting that Cash would ever finish any other book. "It's up to Cash. He knows himself better than anyone else. And the best way for him to find out whether he can write novels or not is to try. If he can, swell. Nothing will be better news for us."[15]

13. Mary Cash Maury, "Suicide of W. J. Cash," in Morrison Papers; Virginius Dabney, *Across the Years: Memories of a Virginian* (New York, 1978), 161–62.

14. Mary Cash to Mr. and Mrs. Cash, January 21, 1941, *ibid.*

15. Charlotte *News*, February 21, 1941.

Knopf was clearly more interested in talking up Cash's book, "a great book in every respect." He had just come from Nashville, Knopf explained, where he had tried to convince Richmond Beatty and Donald Davidson, two of Vanderbilt University's Agrarians, that he and Cash really were good friends of theirs. But they were not buying a word of it. Beatty told Knopf the book was "monstrous" and he intended to demolish it in a forthcoming review. Davidson, in the *Southern Review*, a literary quarterly, also intended to savage the book, which in time he did. Beatty and the others had read the excerpt in the *Saturday Review of Literature* in which Cash portrayed the Agrarians as backward-looking sentimentalists. That section and everything else in the book infuriated them. Actually, by the time he wrote the book, Cash had toned down some of his criticisms considerably; had the Vanderbilt crowd known what he really thought of them they would have been even angrier. They are "mainly a gang of poseurs," Cash was given to saying in private. Allen Tate, the brightest of the bunch, was the worst. Cash had met him once in Charlotte and found him "an insufferable ass."[16]

"W. J. Cash better get out his shootin' irons next time he goes to Nashville," McKnight chortled in the *News* to Cash's great amusement. "For the Southern Agrarians who center their activities there are 'laying for him.'"[17]

Knopf beamed, too. Controversy never hurt sales. He looked forward to seeing Beatty's review and promised to send Cash a copy as soon as possible. As it happened, Cash's clipping service somehow missed Beatty's review in the Nashville *Banner* and Knopf did not mail a copy to Cash until April. Davidson's diatribe appeared in the summer, and Cash probably never saw it.[18]

"Mr. Cash is a geographic Southerner," Richmond Beatty began his snide, mean, petty review, "but there are all sorts of Southerners; the descriptive terms for some of them unprintable." Beatty fumed about Cash's central contention that the southern mind was best understood as a split pysche, "a sort of social schizophrenia." Apparently it took an enemy to see that Freud was the genius (an evil genius, according

16. W. J. Cash to R. P. Harriss, March 10, 1941, in Morrison Papers. Cash exempted Herbert Agar and John Donald Wade from his strictures.

17. Charlotte *News*, February 21, 1941.

18. Alfred A. Knopf to W. J. Cash, April 3, 1941, in Morrison Papers; Donald Davidson, "Mr. Cash and the Proto-Dorian South," *Southern Review*, VII (1941), 4–5, 20. On learning of Cash's death in July, Davidson tried unsuccessfully to stop publication of his review.

to Beatty) standing beyond many of Cash's major points. What sort of southerner would write such a book? Beatty snarled. One, obviously, who had never played football and was unmarried—news of Cash's new matrimonial status had not reached Nashville. Beatty knew exactly what Tennesseans would make of his sly homophobic slurs. Beatty also knew that his readers could decode the anti-Semitism of his contention that Cash relied on "authorities" with "interesting" names like Melville Herskovits. "It is an ambitious book, seething with contradictions and muddled-headedness, and composed, I suspect, with a shrewd eye for the lucrative northeastern market."[19]

Infuriated at having been accused of pandering to the Yankees, Cash retaliated in May. Reviewing William Alexander Percy's *Lanterns on the Levee*, also published by Knopf in 1941, Cash referred to "the most ill-natured book review" he had ever read, written, he said, by "a young man who grades English A at Vanderbilt University, and who belongs to the Agrarian group which loudly professes to be made up of Southern aristocrats." The claim that southerners had to pander was "idiotic," as every schoolboy knew, and "if Mr. Knopf and the other Yankee publishers had conspired to make a donkey of the fellow," Knopf could not have picked a better time to publish Percy's lament "hard on the heels of the review." Percy, said Cash, was an "authentic southern aristocrat, as distinguished from pretenders to the title."[20]

Aside from his understandably hurt feelings, Cash knew by spring that Beatty's notion of a "lucrative" northern market was, sadly, equally idiotic in his own case. Sales were slow. Only fifteen hundred copies sold during the first two months, and Cash had to settle for such comments from Knopf as "I'm afraid there is little likelihood of a runaway, but at least we have nothing to feel ashamed about." *Nothing to feel ashamed about*—each word was a bucket of ice thrown on a temperamental writer, newly married and eager to break free from his little world.[21]

In late March Cash wrote plaintively asking whether Knopf could send him $100. He hated to ask, but he was broke. His marriage had taken every cent he had. A proud man, he did not tell Knopf that he was still sending his parents part of his weekly salary of $50. But he

19. Nashville *Banner*, February 26, 1941.
20. Charlotte *News*, May 10, 1941.
21. Alfred A. Knopf to W. J. Cash, March 6, 1941, in Morrison Papers.

admitted that he had filed his income tax returns with the promise that he would be late in sending his taxes. He would understand, Cash said with his hat in his hand, if Knopf refused, but "at the moment I am simply stony broke."[22]

Knopf obliged with the money. The "book is plodding along," he explained in late March, and had earned about $600 for its author. After subtracting his advance of $450 and the "correction charges" against Cash, the firm had no problem with sending him the $100 against future sales.[23]

By early May sales were steady but "disappointingly slow." Knopf had spent over $1,200 promoting the book, but sales totaled only twenty-three hundred copies. By late May, after another two hundred sales, the book had earned only another $100 in royalties. Cash was bitterly disappointed. Like many authors, he was an innocent at heart who had allowed himself to dream that he could write a serious book and make money. Now he would have to make do with "the thought that it at least has had an excellent critical reception and is building me a reputation which I hope will be useful to both of us later on." He remained hopeful, he told Knopf, that he could build on his new reputation and write a novel that would free him from the drudgery of newspaper work.[24]

Knopf, too, was disappointed in the sluggish sales. (It was not a commercial disaster for the publisher; the first printing of twenty-five hundred copies had sold out and warranted a second edition. But the seasoned Knopf knew that if book sales are going to be substantial, they usually begin as soon as the book is published.) None of this, aside from his disappointment and decision to print a second edition, did he need to tell Cash. Knopf tried to put on the best face possible. "I think the difficulty is that the very nature of its subject matter simply doesn't interest enough people," Knopf wrote consolingly in late May in words that implied that he knew that the book had had its sales. "But you will find that in the long run even a sale of twenty-five hundred copies combined with the sort of press you had should give you a step up."[25]

22. Cash to Knopf, March 17, 1941, *ibid.*
23. Knopf to Cash, March 20, 1941, *ibid.*
24. Knopf to Cash, May 5, 1941; Cash to Knopf, May 20, 1941, *ibid.*
25. Knopf to Cash, May 26, 1941, *ibid.*

Disappointing sales aside, Cash had plenty of other reasons to feel good about himself. Admiring letters streamed in from readers, from old college classmates, from fellow journalists, including several formerly with the Charlotte *News*, and from would-be writers who yearned to tackle the South. Southern academics, from Austin, Texas, to Greensboro, North Carolina, to the president of Coker College in Hartsville, South Carolina, told him fulsomely how much his book had meant to them.[26] And could he possibly come to Memphis, Tennessee, he was beseeched in March, to be the main speaker at the local annual Southern Literary Festival? There was no honorarium, but the organizers would dig into their pockets and help with his expenses.[27] The *Yale Review* hoped he had time to write about Richard Wright's scathing new book *12 Million Black Voices*.[28] A social worker toiling in West Virginia had stayed up all night engrossed in his book. "All the critical analysis is there," she wrote, "but it is cloaked in the affectionate tolerance of every day living." The managers of the *Southern Literary Messenger* in Richmond, Virginia, hoped he could favor them with a radio interview. Ellen Glasgow sent congratulations from Maine, saying here was "a book for those who like to think."[29]

When Carson McCullers, already a best-seller at the tender age of twenty-four with *The Heart Is a Lonely Hunter*, came to Charlotte in March to visit Marian Sims, nothing would do but that Mr. and Mrs. Cash, Charlotte's newest celebrity couple, take lunch at the Hotel Charlotte with McCullers and be photographed conversing graciously with the Georgia visitor. A local radio station, an affiliate of CBS, pestered Cash to do a commentary on the heroic Yugoslav resistance to Hitler's invasion. Cash agreed, but as the hour for his appearance approached, he fidgeted, paced the floor, and then slipped out, found a bootlegger, and got drunk. Somehow, he mumbled his way through the broadcast.[30]

Still, it was very gratifying being somebody. "A great many people, famous and not famous," Cash told his friend R. P. Harriss, have writ-

26. Edward Matthews to W. J. Cash, February 19, 1941; D. M. KcKeithan to Cash, March 1, 1941; W. C. Jackson to Cash, February 28, 1941; G. Sylvester Green to Cash, February 14, 1941, all in Elkins Family Scrapbook.

27. Robert P. Falk to Cash, March 14, 1941, *ibid.*

28. Helen McAfee to Cash, December 24, 1940, *ibid.*

29. Marian P. Hart to Cash, March 8, 1941; F. Meredith Dietz to Cash, March 5, 1941; Ellen Glasgow to Cash, February 22, 1941, all *ibid.*

30. Charlotte *News*, March 22, 1941; Maury, "Recollections," in Morrison Papers.

ten. "And to my absolute amazement they have uniformly professed delight with it. I was absolutely wrong about the local reaction. The *News* has been greatly pleased with its reception, and if anybody in the town objects to it I haven't heard of him. On the contrary, I find myself somewhat embarrassed by the enthusiasm which comes my way." It was fun to be invited to meet an admiring English class at Queen's College in April, but when an awed coed asked him the main thing a writer needed to be successful, he gestured awkwardly and stammered, "You just have to have some ideas and *say* them!"[31]

But he took his new status seriously and practically wore himself out answering his mail in the evenings after returning home from his editorial duties at the newspaper. He now had, he told a friend, a much greater understanding of Charles Lindbergh's reaction to his public— "profoundly grateful" for the outpouring of admiration but wishing it were "possible to have it all without the eternal necessity of grinning and bowing & talking & writing extensively to total strangers." The Charlotte Bookshop honored him with a book and author session. Everything was going along fine; folks were buying his book; he sat inscribing each copy, seemingly enjoying himself. And then someone asked innocently whether he expected physical violence to erupt over the Negro question. "Certainly I do," Cash replied brusquely.[32]

In early March the new celebrity and his admiring wife treated themselves to a brief, belated honeymoon of sorts. The book was selling well in Atlanta, prompting Helen Parker, the energetic book buyer for Rich's Department Store, to invite Cash to town for a day of interviews and autographing. The newlyweds jumped at the opportunity to see Atlanta. Cash wrote Lillian Smith and Paula Snelling and took them up on their recent invitation to come visit them in Clayton, Georgia, should he ever be in the neighborhood. Smith and Snelling enjoyed entertaining writers or intellectuals or anyone with something interesting to say. These small "informal meetings" had had positive results, Snelling told Cash in January, and she and Smith hoped the Cashes could join them. The two women had admired Cash's writings for some time, as Snelling's review of his book indicated, and they appreciated the nice things he had said about the *North Georgia Review* in the excerpt from the book in the *Saturday Re-*

31. Cash to R. P. Harriss, March 10, 1941, in Morrison Papers.
32. Cash to Harriss, March 20, 1941, *ibid.*

view of Literature. "Last spring in conversation with Dr. Odum he referred to you more than once in terms of highest praise which may not be news to you," Snelling told Cash, "but perhaps it is not disagreeable to hear it again."[33]

Taking the bus to Clayton, Cash and Mary spent a leisurely Sunday, March 2, with Snelling and Smith at Smith's spacious home atop Old Screamer Mountain. It was one of those wonderful days writers truly enjoy: good food, animated talk about books and ideas, and leisurely strolls with kindred spirits. An added treat that day was the presence of Karl Menninger, the noted psychiatrist. "Dr. Menninger I thought a capital fellow," Cash commented afterward, and "all the rest of the company was interesting, you have obviously captured the perfect cook, and I am still muttering about that mountain and that house." There was much talk, of course, about *The Mind of the South.* As Cash, Smith, and company strolled along Old Screamer Mountain a wonderful serenity descended upon Cash. "This has been the happiest day of my life," he said to Lillian Smith at one point. But he felt, and he was sure Smith and Snelling would understand, "drained and emptied."[34]

"Both of you," Cash went on in his best southern manner, "talk as well as you write, and I don't need to tell you that I think you write brilliantly." Before he left, Smith had given him a chapter of a novel she was working on, which in time would emerge as the highly controversial *Strange Fruit,* a best-selling story of interracial love. Writing to Smith and Snelling, Cash said, "After reading that chapter from the novel I think Lillian Smith should finish that novel at all costs. It is moving stuff." Cash talked candidly about his anxiety over his own forthcoming novel and recent Guggenheim application.[35]

The next day in Atlanta, Cash started the morning with a radio talk with Helen Parker, followed by a newspaper interview which Cash made his way through despite an embarrassing "spasm of coughing and choking." There followed a formal lunch at which Ralph McGill of the Atlanta *Constitution* teased Cash about the "gangster" picture

33. Cash to Paula Snelling, January 29, 1941; Cash to Lillian Smith, February 26, 1941, both in Lillian Smith Papers, University of Florida, Gainesville; Paula Snelling to W. J. Cash, January 10, 1941, in Elkins Family Scrapbook.

34. W. J. Cash to Lillian Smith and Paula Snelling, March 10, 1941, in Smith Collection, University of Florida.

35. W. J. Cash to Smith and Snelling, March 10, 1941, *ibid.*; Joseph L. Morrison, *W. J. Cash, Southern Prophet: A Biography and a Reader* (New York, 1967), 114–18.

Knopf had released. Cash, ever touchy and never very comfortable in large groups, smiled gamely but was clearly unamused and said little and appeared listless. McGill, as Mary later learned, was struck by Cash's fatigue and general "wretchedness." Mary, too, was also seriously worried about her husband's fatigue, but she felt, at least in retrospect, that his withdrawn behavior reflected no more than his shyness and "normal lack of buoyance in the presence of a gathering of strangers." He was terrified, he had told Mary earlier, of another coughing attack "before all those people." She was to sit next to him and have his cough medicine ready. He got through the autographing session without embarrassing himself.[36]

That evening, as guests of Margaret Mitchell and her husband, Frank Marsh, at the exclusive Piedmont Driving Club, Cash and Mary relaxed and revived, downing several tumblers of scotch. "Country clubbers" and their private retreats normally gave Cash the willies, but not this time. Before meeting the famous author, Cash had worried excessively that she would be peeved that he had called Gone With the Wind "sentimental" and not praised her as he had Faulkner, Wolfe, and others. He had worried needlessly. Margaret Mitchell Marsh was the soul of charm and graciousness; she was genuinely and obviously delighted to meet him. They enjoyed several good laughs over the way everybody loved the myth of the Old South. "She had searched for years through attic trunks and library basements," she told the Cashes, and uncovered the existence of exactly one pretentious columned mansion in prewar Georgia to be the model for Tara, Gerald O'Hara's plantation house. "Wonderful," Cash exclaimed, as he thought about his version of Gerald O'Hara, his Old Irishman, employed to such great effect in his book and still very much in his mind for his projected novel.[37]

Mary recalled the evening as "delightful." "Those two Southern authorities began matching stories of what it was really like in the Old South, and, differently as their books had pictured it, no battles were joined, no issues had to be settled, neither took his stand for Dixieland—and the Scotch was good."[38]

36. Mary Cash Maury, "The Suicide of W. J. Cash," Red Clay Reader, IV (1967), 8. This is a much shorter, greatly revised version of the manuscript by the same name in the Morrison Papers. All references to the unpublished version will be identified as MS in Morrison Papers.
37. Maury, "Suicide," MS in Morrison Papers.
38. Maury, "Suicide," 8.

"I hear many fine things about 'The Mind of the South,'" Margaret Mitchell wrote in April, "and, what is best, I hear them from people who have discriminating minds of their own. As my scholarly father remarked last night, 'that book is a Southern milestone.'" She hoped Cash's projected novel would come easily. "One writer can't wish another writer better luck than that!" Indeed not, Cash replied gratefully—and with apologies that he had not written sooner to say how much he and Mary enjoyed themselves in Georgia. "The drinks practically saved our lives." He had been "swamped" with work. In addition to his newspaper job, he had attempted to do some magazine pieces and keep up with the seemingly unending task of answering letters.[39]

Cash still felt guilty (and wanted to apologize) about that "sentimental" crack. "Thinking it over, I have an idea that what inspired that carelessly thrown-off judgement was the feeling that your 'good' characters were shadowy. On reflection, I think the feeling may have proceeded less from themselves than from the fact they were set beside that flamboyant wench, Scarlett. There were good women all over the place in the South, of course. But Scarlett is a female to go along with Becky Sharp, wholly vivid and convincing. Beside her everybody else in the book, including even Butler, seems almost an abstraction."[40]

He hoped his remarks did not offend her. In the event they did, he was enclosing Beatty's review of his book—now, there was an example of someone "obviously out to do me dirt." The review proved that "lit'ry criticism in the highly genteel Agrarian circles starts with the ascription of canine ancestry and goes up." Mitchell replied sympathetically: "There is one burden writers must learn to bear with equanimity (if possible!), and that is having book critics review books we never wrote and would never write."[41]

Following their return from Atlanta, the skies brightened beautifully for Cash. The Guggenheim Foundation awarded him a grant of two thousand dollars for a year of uninterrupted work, beginning May 1, 1941. He had proposed to go to Mexico and write a novel. The conditions were flexible: he was simply to devote himself to creative

39. Margaret Mitchell Marsh to W. J. Cash, April 16, 1941, in Elkins Family Scrapbook; Cash to Marsh, April 23, 1941, in Morrison Papers.
40. Cash to Marsh, April 23, 1941, in Morrison Papers.
41. Marsh to Cash, April 28, 1941, in Elkins Family Scrapbook.

writing. His ideas for the novel were clear in his mind, he thought, and he planned to devote the first four months completely to the novel. "The material is already pretty well in hand," Cash told Knopf, "and in that period I think I can settle the question of my ability to do that kind of thing." To his friend Harriss, Cash vowed: "I plan stubbornly to do the novel. I have always wanted to do that, & still think I can do a better job of it than of anything else." If he failed, he would switch to a nonfiction project and probably come back to the United States.[42]

Cash's thinking about what he might do as a novelist had fluctuated over the years. In 1936 he had considered setting his novel in the Old South, but by late 1940 he toyed briefly with the idea of doing a Civil War novel that would include most of the battles of the war.[43] On second thought he realized that was too ambitious and decided to chart the rise of a wealthy cotton mill family in the piedmont. This would allow him to establish his "capacity as a novelist," he told Knopf. Cash was still thinking big, with a Faulknerian cast of characters in mind: his novel of the piedmont would be a historical saga, a family romance that explored the world of patriarchs, fathers and sons.[44]

The fragmentary sources Cash left behind suggest that, for all his passion to break free from the manuscript that had haunted him for a decade, he unconsciously intended to write more history. His Civil War opus would have to run to several volumes, "each of which would reach its climax in one or another of the climaxes of the Civil War—say, Sumter—Gettysburg—Vicksburg—Richmond—and Virginia." The research would be "very extensive." The cotton mill novel would chronicle the region's great industrial growth "and all the changes involved therein, the whole story of the South, indeed, from 1880 onward."[45]

Did Cash have the artist's sensibility to story and character, the novelist's willingness and skill to let a story evolve through the actions of the characters? Cash was an intellectual, an explainer, an analyzer. He was instinctively fascinated with ideas. He came alive in conversation only when someone advanced an interesting idea, but even his

42. Henry Allen Moe to W. J. Cash, March 12, May 7, 1941, *ibid.*; Cash to Alfred A. Knopf, March 17, May 5, 1941, to R. P. Harriss, March 20, 1941, all in Morrison Papers.

43. Application for John Simon Guggenheim Memorial Fellowship, October, 1936, in Morrison Papers.

44. W. J. Cash to Alfred A. Knopf, September 8, 1940, *ibid.*

45. *Ibid.*

friends admitted that he was a notoriously poor storyteller. His mind ran, almost effortlessly, to the abstraction, the conclusion, rather than the thousand and one particulars of a story. He was a grand generalizer. That was his strength, his genius. It had served him brilliantly as a historian. But could he have written a novel? "Only if he had rearranged his mind," said a sympathetic friend.[46]

Perhaps there were demons of creativity swirling in Cash's mind and psyche, just waiting to be released. He was only forty-one in 1941. Who knows what he might have done? But one thing is certain: Cash was still obsessed with the South and what it meant to be southern.

But even with a novel in mind, a Guggenheim in hand, and a year free for writing, there were signs of stress, and depression dogged his steps in the spring of 1941. Bertie, his kid sister, arrived in Charlotte to have an exploratory operation and Cash, always highly emotional, particularly about family matters, buckled under the strain. He went out and "got roundly drunk, and the next day was a fit subject for the hospital myself." Bertie was all right, but Cash forgot to mail his income tax returns on time and would have to pay a penalty. He confided to R. P. Harriss that his book was selling "slowly, but continuously" and was well into a second edition. "If it were not for the war I think it might eventually pile up a good sale, but with the case as it is I do not count on that." Macmillan's southern representative had looked him up to say that their "top man" in New York had read the book and "is greatly taken with it, is convinced I can do a good novel, and wants a shot at it if Knopf should waive the option. So altogether, I am more than satisfied." Perhaps he was satisfied. But he was also anxiety-ridden and unable to shake the feeling of being completely worn out. "I am not yet feeling that anything is really worth a damn," he confessed to Harriss.[47]

From Chapel Hill, Walter Spearman offered congratulations on the Guggenheim and said that he had stayed up half the night reading Cash's book. "I think it's one of the finest, most intelligent, most keenly analytical books that has ever come out the South." He had reviewed it glowingly for the university's weekly radio program devoted to books and the arts. He wanted Cash to come to Chapel Hill and address the university's annual Scholastic Press Institute in early May. No honorarium was available, but he could arrange to pay for

46. Interviews with Harriet Doar, September 17, 1984, October 28, 1985.
47. W. J. Cash to R. P. Harriss, March 20, 1941, in Morrison Papers.

some expenses and the trip would give Mary a chance to visit her mother one last time before they left for Mexico for the year.[48] From Texas came even better news. Homer P. Rainey, president of the University of Texas, was so impressed with Cash's book that he wanted him to give the commencement address in June. "I have been talking to the people of the State a great deal along the lines of your thesis and have been trying to encourage here a type of thinking about our problems similar to that which the group at the University of North Carolina under Dr. Odum's leadership has done." There would be an honorarium of two hundred dollars and expenses.[49]

Cash and Mary were elated. The extra money would allow them to wend their way comfortably to Mexico City, via New Orleans and Dallas. He told Mary to make sure and tell his parents when she wrote to them next—he left that task to her—that "the graduating class alone numbers 1200. Add the rest of the student body, about 10,000 students, the faculty, the mamas and papas and the visiting dignitaries, and you get a vast mob." She would need a new dress, even though they could not afford one, and Wilbur would have to have a new suit because they would be meeting all sorts of interesting, prominent Texans, perhaps even the governor, "Old Pass-the-Biscuits Pappy O'Daniel," Mary bragged for her husband. "Wilbur doesn't seem to be bothered, which is nice, considering that practically all the prominent people in Texas will sit there listening to him."[50]

In truth, Wilbur's parents were bewildered and deeply unhappy about the proposed trip. Why did he want to go to Mexico City? It was too far away. They would not see him for a year. What was wrong with Chapel Hill? It was dangerous in Mexico City; Wilbur himself had said so. There were Nazis there; Wilbur had said that, too. Mama had heard that Mexico was a "wild country," where they had riots and earthquakes. And did Wilbur really think it was wise to quit his job? Good jobs were hard to come by, his father reminded him, and lots of folks would gladly trade places with him as a "newspaper editor." They hated to be a financial burden to him—he was still sending home forty dollars a month, and he had not yet sent the money for May. Times were bad. And if they were bound and determined to go to Mexico City for a whole year, did he really have to go off first to Chapel Hill

48. Walter Spearman to W. J. Cash, April 8, 1941, in Elkins Family Scrapbook.
49. Homer P. Rainey to W. J. Cash, April 24, 1941, *ibid.*
50. Mary Cash to Mr. and Mrs. Cash, April 29, 1941, in Morrison Papers.

when he could come spend a couple of extra days "at home"? He had already patiently explained that Mary wanted to see her mother one last time. They understood that, they said, but did he understand how lonely they were?[51]

If they were trying to make their eldest, emotionally fragile son feel guilty, they succeeded, at least partially. Cash relieved Mary of her letter-writing responsibilities to explain to his father that he was genuinely sorry his parents were lonely and anxious about the trip. He knew it was a risky venture, and he had thought about turning the grant down and staying put. He genuinely hated to "leave you feeling as you do." But he had to go, he said in a plaintive tone that reveals the inner turmoil he felt in standing up to his parents, particularly his father, whom he had always feared, said one close friend.

I owe it to myself, to you and mama, to Mary, and the whole family to go ahead and try to have as good a career as I can, and to have been a Guggenheim Fellow gives you a long shove ahead—to say nothing of giving me a year free for writing and seeking what I can do toward achieving complete independence. I failed at that once before, but it was the terror of my economic condition that mainly paralyzed me. This time I'll have fair security for the year. And more than that, I now have reputation enough to make it easier for me to get a job if I need and want one. To ask for a job as one who is unknown, broke and down and out, who hasn't had a job for several years, and to ask for one as a Guggenheim Fellow with a solid record as an editorial writer and as the author of a book which has made a great reputation—these are different things. And I don't think you need to worry on that score. There wasn't any prospect of advancement here and not much of more money than the shabby salary I have been paid. So I thought it best to make the decision and go ahead.[52]

Mexico City it would be. To Mary 'he confided that his parents would have been just as upset had he chosen Oklahoma or anywhere else. In defying his parents, he was taking on a massive load of guilt. But so great was his resolve to get away and try his hand at a novel and so great was his conviction that he could not write it without getting as far away as possible that he stood up to his parents. Of course, Cash would have preferred Europe, but the war was on. Mary later said she was not keen on Mexico City, fearful that the lack of materials on the South would be a real detriment, but Cash wanted to go and she

---

51. Maury, "Suicide," MS in Morrison Papers; Cash to his parents, May, 1941, *ibid.*
52. Maury, "Suicide," 10; W. J. Cash to Father, [May, 1941], in Morrison Papers; interview with Harriet Doar, September 17, 1984.

wanted to see it with him. Mexico was what he wanted, and he was firm about that, she insisted years later, obviously having overheard his family's slander that she was behind the decision to go to Mexico, that Wilbur had agreed to go only to pacify her—a contention fueled in family circles by the widely repeated rumor that Cash and Mary had quarreled violently the night before they left.[53]

Mexico had certain advantages. With the exchange rate at five pesos to the dollar, they would be able to live comfortably on his stipend. They bantered with each other about the Nazis, Mary recalled, but they felt a slight chill when an unsolicited brochure from an innkeeper in Guadalajara arrived before there had been any public announcement that they were going to Mexico.[54]

After making the trip to Chapel Hill, where Cash addressed starry-eyed high schoolers, Cash and Mary returned to spend their last Sunday with Cash's parents and endure a round of family photographs. Cash resigned from the News and had to listen to Dowd tell him he was making a terrible mistake. But Dowd was always dour. He had even helped spike a recommendation from the newspaper nominating Cash for a year as a Nieman Fellow at Harvard. Cash and Mary's last few days in town were a whirl of activities. Cash worked on his Texas address, Mary made final plans for the trip, and the two said their good-byes. They traveled by train to New Orleans, where they splurged by staying at the St. Charles and lunching at Antoine's. But midway through the rich cuisine Cash started to feel sick and feared that he would not be able to keep any food on his stomach. "He was really ill in that damp heat," Mary recalled, "and the ceiling fans could do little."[55]

On the train to Dallas, where they were to transfer to Austin, Cash suddenly and without warning had a frightening temper tantrum over something he read in the newspaper. He completely lost control of himself in a "violent fit of anger, stamping a newspaper on the floor and biting his hands." What made it so odd, Mary remembered, was that when she later asked him what had set him off, he could not remember. Mary was puzzled and frightened.[56]

On their arrival in Austin, Mary was understandably nervous about

53. Interview with Henry Cash, August 9, 1984; Maury, "Suicide," MS in Morrison Papers.
54. Maury, "Suicide," MS in Morrison Papers.
55. Ibid.; Morrison, W. J. Cash, 121–22.
56. Maury, "Suicide," MS in Morrison Papers.

the commencement formalities, especially how he would speak. "At times he experienced a sort of closure of the throat and became guttural and hard to understand, and I was afraid it would happen on the rostrum." He told her not to worry, that he had been a teacher, after all, and was prepared to address a large group. To Mary he seemed "tired and depressed but not nervous." Fortunately, they were put up at a hotel with air-conditioning, and Cash felt much better. He got through the commencement ceremonies without any difficulty, though he decided to ignore his prepared remarks and generalized, along the lines of his book, about the southern mind. Someone in the crowd made a tape-recording and Cash's voice, though not strong or assertive, does not waver or suggest any great anxiety.[57]

After much handshaking and to-doing with the college authorities, Cash and Mary traveled by train to San Antonio, where they stopped for a day of sightseeing. But they were too fatigued to do much beyond visiting the Alamo and shopping in a store where Cash bought a small portable typewriter. The rest of the train trip along the spine of Mexico took two days and nights. The poor accommodations and the heat made the trip "exhausting" and seemingly interminable. Cash began cursing the new typewriter because its keyboard was too small for his pudgy fingers. They arrived in Mexico City hot, tired, and with ragged nerves. They found temporary accommodations before being directed to a tiny apartment—Cash called it a "midget apartment"—in a relatively new, clean neighborhood on the edge of the city. The apartment came with a maid, an emaciated Mexican girl, whose spectral appearance prompted Cash to nickname her the Holy Spirit.[58]

Other than that, nothing went right for the two provincials far from home. The altitude made them dizzy; the food made them nauseous; diarrhea attacked both of them. Neither felt like doing much sightseeing. Cash tried to work. He pecked out a straightforward piece of journalism about the city on his damnable portable, piercing the air with periodic oaths and obscenities and gnawing nervously at his hand. Serious writing seemed out of the question for the moment. Clearly, Cash was depressed and disturbed. Mary fretted about him but assumed that he would recover in time. Strangely, he could not learn one word of Spanish.[59]

57. Tape recording, *ibid.*
58. W. J. Cash to his father, June 14, 1941; Maury, "Suicide," MS in Morrison Papers.
59. Maury, "Suicide," MS in Morrison Papers.

The report he managed to hack out would have passed muster at the *News* (had Cash sent it there), but he had no luck syndicating it. His physical and psychological condition was so unstable that it is the one and only piece of writing he did in Mexico. Joseph Morrison points to it and one brief letter to his father as evidence that Cash was not depressed and completely unable to work. But the bit of reporting was the sort of thing that would normally have taken him no more than a morning to write. Moreover, he wrote to his father soon after they arrived on June 10. If Cash wrote anything else, it has not survived, nor did Mary ever mention any other work. Cash was more than depressed; something was drastically wrong with him.[60]

Mary's account of their actions is completely silent for the period from June 10, when he wrote his parents, until June 30. What was Cash doing? What was he thinking about? Had he tried to begin his novel, only to find that his lifelong dream had become a nightmare? Was he so sick from the altitude and diarrhea that he could write nothing, not even a single postcard home or to friends? Apparently no one received any communication from either of them. Was he drinking? Mary said he was not because his digestive problems made it impossible for him to tolerate alcohol.[61]

On June 30 the terror began. That evening Cash asked Mary whether she heard voices in the foyer outside their apartment door. On other occasions, stray bits of innocent conversation had wafted in from the foyer, but on this evening she listened intently and heard nothing. He implored her to listen even more attentively. He could hear people talking. They were plotting against him, and they were in the small foyer that opened onto the entrance hall, which led to the street. Fear mottled Cash's face. He began to whisper the words he was hearing. "They were Nazis and they planned to kill us—or was it only to kill him?" Listen, Mary, he commanded. She stood absolutely silent and listened as hard as she could—but she heard nothing. Then Cash began madly shoving furniture against the locked door.

Mary reasoned with him and tried to calm him down with sweet words. "You know you were tired when you got here and you've been

---

60. W. J. Cash to parents, June 10, 1941, in Elkins Family Scrapbook. Cash's letter contains only one socially relevant comment: "The Indians are the Negroes of Mexico, but they have it even harder than our Negroes, and they are more prepossessing."

61. Interview with Harriet Doar, September 17, 1984. Since Mary Cash Maury's account of Cash's last days in Mexico City, "Suicide," MS in Morrison Papers, is the only one extant, her narrative is the only source for the next few paragraphs.

sick ever since." Why would anybody want to kill them? Transfixed for a second, he stood listening silently for a moment, then started whispering about the killers outside.

Their apartment was on the ground floor, but the windows were high, Mary reminded him. Intruders would need a ladder. But he was not listening to her. Didn't she hear those voices? He ran to the windows, closing and locking them by darting back and forth so that "only his arm would be visible for a short moment as a target from the street."

Cash then grabbed their sharp carving knife and began frantically waving it about. Mary was terrified. She feared that he might kill himself, or her, or anyone who came through the door. She did not know what to do. He was "completely irrational." There was no telephone in the apartment. If she screamed for help and people came in, she feared Cash might stab them with the knife. Finally, at her wits' end, Mary began laughing heartily and calling him "The Terrible Turk," "Attila the Hun," and "Wild Bill Hickok." Finally, her cajoling worked. He calmed down when she promised to read to him from Ecclesiastes. He fell asleep listening to her reading from the Bible.

The next morning he was himself again. "He remembered the whole appalling thing," he said, and apologized. It was tourist sickness, they agreed. He consented, at Mary's urging, to see a doctor. While Cash picked at his breakfast, a fearful Mary went upstairs to ask an American couple for the name of an American psychiatrist she had heard was in the city. Mary telephoned the physician and made an appointment. But when she returned, Cash had vanished. For some inexplicable reason, Mary remembered, she did not feel apprehension, only surprise that he had not left a note. Mainly, she wondered how he would get along because he could speak no Spanish. Perhaps he had gone for a walk to clear his mind.

He returned a few hours later, but he was clearly out of his head again. She was not to fear, he explained excitedly. He had gone to a bank, rented a safety deposit box, and put their money and passports in it. Now the Nazis could not steal their key possessions. When Mary tried to tell him that he had agreed just a few hours earlier that he needed help, he ignored her. Finally, "grudgingly," he consented to see the doctor.

When they arrived at the doctor's office, Cash was visibly disturbed. When the psychiatrist attempted to administer what Mary assumed was a sedative, Cash "vehemently refused treatment of any kind, jerked away from the hypodermic needle like a child." Mary consoled him, but he consented to the injection with grave suspicion. Rather than a sedative, the doctor gave him an injection of vitamin B1. As they walked out, Cash muttered that he had been poisoned.

Once back at the apartment, Cash announced in an agitated voice that they could not stay—"the killers were getting too close." They left immediately and hailed a taxi. To her chagrin, Cash demanded that she crouch on the floor so that her red hat would not make them an easy target for the Nazis. They looked at four hotels before settling on the Geneve. With her mind racing for some solution, Mary could not figure out how to tip off the reservation clerks "without bringing on a scene of violence" that could be potentially dangerous for everyone. Once in their room, Cash ran to the corner and cowered in abject fear. Mary pleaded with him to allow her to telephone Ben Meyer, the journalist they had met several days earlier at the Associated Press offices. No, Cash cried out, the man at the other end of the line might be a Nazi pretending to be someone else.

Then Mary, truly terrified, made a decision she would question the rest of her life. She told Cash to lock himself in the room while she went in person to get Meyer. Her pleading worked. She left, found Meyer and a fellow newsman, and returned with them.

Cash was gone.

Mary lost control. Meyer called the police, warning that Cash could be dangerous. Policemen, detectives, and others came to the room. A general alarm went out. Meyer called hotels, starting with the elegant La Reforma, a favorite of tourists, where Cash had earlier gone for a haircut that had pleased him. No, no one named Cash or anyone fitting his description had checked in. The police dragnet yielded nothing. Later, around 10:00 P.M., Meyer called La Reforma again. Yes, a man named Cash had taken a room.

Mary, Meyer, police, newsmen, and some unidentifed people sped to the hotel. They rushed to Cash's room. The knock on the door brought only silence. The hotel manager, informed of the crisis, handed Mary the keys.

Mary went in. Wilbur Joseph Cash was hanging lifeless from the bathroom door.

Mary's screams brought the crowd crashing into the room. They gaped at the dead man hanging from his necktie. He had been dead, the autopsy determined, for several hours. It was July 1, 1941.

Stunned but unable to weep, Mary telephoned Pete McKnight to get in touch with Cash's parents and other appropriate people. She was then taken to police headquarters and questioned all night. Early in the morning a car and driver from the American embassy arrived to rescue Mary. The southern world of kin, manners, and history had gone to work: the United States ambassador to Mexico was old Josephus Daniels, from North Carolina, former owner-editor of the Raleigh *News and Observer*, father of Jonathan Daniels, who had been one of Cash's sponsors for the Guggenheim, and a distant relative of Mary's. The ambassador persuaded Mary to stay at the embassy until the ordeal was over.

Because Cash had talked about Nazis—and there were known Nazis in Mexico City—the authorities had questioned Mary at length about that before discounting homicide and concluding that Cash had taken his own life. She was free to go. But how was Mary to leave the country with her passport and money locked in the bank box? To open it, she would have to be declared Cash's executrix by a United States court. Ambassador Daniels intervened and made the necessary arrangements.

Unable to face the dreadful ordeal of making the four-day train trip back to North Carolina in the middle of the summer with Cash's body in a baggage car, Mary had his body cremated. In Shelby, Cash's stunned parents, who had heard the shocking news of their boy's death from a friend who had heard it on the radio, sent frantic telegrams voicing their objections, which actually arrived before the cremation took place. But having made her decision, she went ahead as planned and never let the family know that the cremation had not already taken place. The Cashes bitterly resented Mary's decision to the end of their days and, being good Baptists, resolutely refused to believe that their Wilbur had taken his own life, thereby condemning his soul to eternal damnation. The Nazis, or someone equally nefarious, killed him, Cash's mother, father, and family believed to the end of their days.[62]

Mary managed to get an airplane flight back to Charlotte. She ar-

62. Maury, "Suicide," MS in Morrison Papers; interviews with Henry Cash, August 9, 1984, and Allen Cash, August 7, 1984.

rived in Shelby stoically carrying Cash's ashes. She acquiesced in the family's decision to make all the funeral and burial arrangements.

And so it happened that Wilbur Joseph Cash had a conventional Christian funeral at Shelby's First Baptist Church on Monday, July 7, 1941, with the pastor of the Boiling Springs Baptist Church officiating. The parson, sound in the faith and all too aware of some of the things Cash had said about the local deities, took the opportunity to offer an apology of sorts for the wayward son, intoning that "underneath it all Wilbur was really a very good boy." The condescending words angered many in the congregation, including Cash's family. A fuming Mary practically had to be restrained by her mother from setting the man of God straight right then and there, but good manners prevailed and the remains of Cash's body were peaceably laid to rest at the Sunset Cemetery.[63]

As family, kin, and friends milled around his grave, they remembered him fondly and, in hushed tones, kept asking themselves why. It did not matter whether one believed that Cash had hanged himself or had been killed by Nazis or someone else. The great unanswered question was, why? Why did it happen? Was Wilbur's death God's will? God works in mysterious ways, the church folks reminded themselves, His wonders to perform. But it just did not figure that Sleepy Cash would kill himself. Remember how his eyes used to squint when he smiled, and how his face got even rounder when he grinned, and how he always slouched and looked down at the ground. He was always thinking. He knew lots more than most people, that was for sure. His head was often in the clouds, but he had good manners and was always extra good to his folks. Yes, sir, the last words his mama heard him say before he went off down to Mexico City were, "My mother never thinks she'll see me again." And she was right, bless her soul. Now her boy was gone, cut down in the prime of life. How old was he? Hadn't he just turned forty-one back in May? He was a great writer, that was a fact; that book of his was deep and wide, like the River Jordan. Had anyone else ever written such a powerful book? He would have written more wonderful books if only he had lived. And he had everything to live for, folks around Shelby said.

Not everyone, even in Shelby, said that, however. Years later, an old friend who had never stopped thinking about Cash turned, when

---

63. Maury, "Suicide," MS in Morrison Papers; interview with Henry Cash, August 9, 1984.

asked why he thought Cash had killed himself, looked away wistfully, and waved his hand, pointing at Shelby and all the past and present ghosts of Cleveland County, and said matter-of-factly, "He'd had enough of all this."[64]

Anything said about the cause of Cash's death is only speculation. Could he have been murdered? Who would have had a motive? There were Nazis in Mexico City, but Cash was of no concern to them; they probably had never heard of him. Cash and Mary knew few people in Mexico City, and none of them were enemies. He had very little money and few things of any value on him when he disappeared in the middle of the day, so murder following robbery can be ruled out. Nor is there any valid reason to think that Cash could not have killed himself as he did. It is entirely possible that he hanged himself with his necktie. And the rumor that his feet were near or touching the floor— even if true—does not prove that he could not have done it himself.

But why did he kill himself? Was it because he was distressed about what he had said about the South or because his book offended people? Such views have been bandied about, even advanced by noted scholars who usually link Cash's name with that of Clarence Cason, who killed himself in 1935 days before the publication of his bitterly critical book, *90° in the Shade*. Cason, a professor at the University of Alabama, was distraught about what his colleagues and countrymen would say, as Cash reported in *The Mind of the South*. But Cash's brief, matter-of-fact account of Cason's book and suicide gives no indication that Cash perceived any similarities between himself and Cason. When his book appeared, Cash was understandably nervous about what readers and critics would say, but the chorus of praise melted his anxieties quickly. At no time does he seem to have been noticeably upset or depressed by what he had said about the South. Cash, truly, had everything to live for.[65]

64. Interview with Lindsey Dail, October 28, 1985.
65. W. J. Cash, *The Mind of the South* (1941; rpr. New York, 1969), 334. Regarding suicide among southern intellectuals and writers, the distinguished scholar V. O. Key, Jr., generalized: "A depressingly high rate of self-destruction prevails among those who ponder about the South and put down their reflections in books. A fatal frustration seems to come from the struggle to find a way through the unfathomable maze formed by tradition, caste, race, poverty" (*Southern Politics in State and Nation* [New York, 1949], 664). Obviously misinformed about the reception Cash's book received, historian Dewey Grantham, Jr., later wrote, "Indeed, the violent criticism and personal abuse Cash encountered almost certainly contributed to his tragic suicide" ("Mr. Cash Writes a Book," *Progressive*, XXV [1961], 440–42).

There is no denying that Cash was depressed at the time of his death. During his last months, he was mentally fatigued and emotionally drained. He felt empty and exhausted. Even though his mind assured him that he was a successful writer with a worthwhile literary goal, nothing seemed worth doing, and he felt miserable much of the time. His moodiness, his feelings of emptiness, and his inability to will himself to psychic health were indications that Cash was suffering a monumental letdown. Given his history of emotional fragility, the enormity of the task he had set for himself, and the time and emotion he had invested in completing The Mind of the South, the feelings he experienced were inevitable. His inability to learn a single word of Spanish or to use his new typewriter were very likely signs of mental and emotional fatigue complicated by a sense of isolation in a foreign country, the anxieties of a new marriage, and feelings of guilt about leaving his family. As on previous occasions, he was lapsing into neurasthenia—depression.

But it is highly unlikely that depression caused him to kill himself. For one thing, he was a lifelong depressive. He probably had never known a day when he had not felt moments of fretfulness or emotional lassitude. Second, all his previous bouts of depression had been characterized by exhaustion and an inability to function, intellectually or physically. Typically, his emotional despondency had caused him to collapse into debilitating passivity. His depression at the end, however acute, was not likely to bring on the aggressive, violent behavior he exhibited during the last twenty-four hours of his life.

Other explanations must be found. Cash had a long, complicated history of hyperthyroidism, an endocrine disorder. An overactive thyroid gland increases the body's metabolism and can cause a deficiency of thiamine, vitamin B1. The symptoms of hyperthyroidism and thiamine deficiency—fatigue, lack of interest in one's work, depression, nervous irritability, fear, and anger—plagued Cash. Treatment was primitive in those days—usually injections of thiamine—and many physicians responded, as did Cash's urologist, to the emotional symptoms. To judge from the scanty records, Cash had a physical disorder that was treated as an emotional problem. Hyperthyroidism, however, can dissipate, as perhaps it did in Cash's case, and physicians at Johns Hopkins University in 1932 apparently found no evidence of it. Even so, he continued throughout the decade to exhibit the symptoms and may very well have been suffering from an endocrine imbalance, as his urologist thought and as the physician in Mexico City may have believed when he decided to give Cash an injection of vitamin B1.[66]

Or perhaps the doctor diagnosed Cash as an alcoholic and therefore in immediate need of thiamine. Regular consumption of alcohol can cause a thiamine deficiency by preventing the body from metabolizing food and vitamins. Cash had been drinking for years and during the last year or so had begun to consume hard liquor, much of it bootleg and therefore of an undetermined amount of alcohol. It appears certain that his drinking complicated his endocrine problem and further imbalanced his system.

Cash's earlier tantrums about Hitler and the Nazis may have been brought on by physiological as well as emotional distress and been foreshadowings of more severe disturbance. He arrived in Mexico City exhausted, probably from a combination of physical and emotional factors—the long train ride, the food, the stress of having left home. Soon after he arrived in Mexico City, he had an adverse reaction to the food and water. Neither he nor Mary was able to stabilize their digestive systems. Both developed severe diarrhea. Chronic diarrhea can dehydrate and upset the body's delicate but crucial electrolyte balance, and furthermore, according to Mary, Cash was suddenly unable to tolerate alcohol. Because he was accustomed to drinking heavily, this inadvertent abstinence put his body and mind at risk. He was unable to consume enough liquor to prevent alcohol withdrawal (delirium tremens). At the end, Cash very likely was in a state of psychotic delirium. He had auditory hallucinations and became hypervigilant to the point of uncontrollable paranoia. A person suffering from diarrhea and delirium tremens can become berserk—frightened, raging, raving, hallucinating—and suicidal.[67]

No one will ever know what really happened to Cash's body and mind that brought him to hang himself with his necktie. It is sad to speculate about the mental torture he endured in those last lonely hours. He killed himself, but it is hard to believe that he "decided" on death, that he was "guilty" of suicide, the unpardonable sin to his mother and father. At the end, he was alone, tormented, out of his head, frightened—to death.

66. Interview with Hendrik DeKruif, M.D., October 24, 1989; interview with Barry Fisher, M.D., November 17, 1989; Barry Fisher to author, December 4, 1989.
67. Barry Fisher to author, December 4, 1989.

10 / The Mind of the South *in History*

Death deprived W. J. Cash of knowing that he had penned a classic in historical literature, one that would help shape the southern mind for decades. In the half-century since its publication, *The Mind of the South* has never been out of print. The book has been required reading and not only for students of history. Its readers represent the broad spectrum of American intellectual life: novelists and literary critics, sociologists and civil rights advocates, journalists and churchmen, attorneys, schoolteachers, labor leaders. Readers of almost every contention find notions in Cash to set forth in their works. If Cash remains appropriately bothersome to sentimentalists and apologists, he has also had tough-minded, highly perceptive critics. Such a response is sensible and to be expected, for the book is not only a record but a confession, objective and idiosyncratic, daringly imaginative, brilliantly written, and cogently argued. Much of its message flows from sorrow and all of it from a profound sense of tragedy. In sum, *The Mind of the South* is a book "written in blood."[1]

Part of the explanation for the staying power of *The Mind of the South* is Cash's artistic, highly memorable, quotable style. His felicity of expression is a subtle blend of classy journalism and skillful juxtaposing of colloquialisms and erudite language, all enveloped in a driving nar-

1. For a searching, critical assessment of W. J. Cash and his book, see, C. Vann Woodward, "The Elusive Mind of the South," in *American Counterpoint: Slavery and Racism in the North-South Dialogue* (New York, 1971), 261–83. See also Michael O'Brien, "W. J. Cash, Hegel, and the South," *Journal of Southern History*, XLIV (1978), 379–98; Michael O'Brien, *Rethinking the South: Essays in Intellectual History* (Baltimore, 1988), 179–89; Edwin M. Yoder, Jr., "W. J. Cash After a Quarter Century," in Willie Morris, ed., *The South Today: 100 Years After Appomattox*

rative. Cash made splendid use of rhetoric, symbols, irony, and paradox. The various elements of his style give the book the quality of an
unfolding story, rich in drama, told by someone who cares, and cares
deeply. From the first pages on one senses the personal warmth of a
native son's love of his land and his people and his passionate identi-
fication with them. The book exudes an enduring charm in shining
prose. And yet the author, though a "loyal" son, has folded his arms
and cast a critical eye at everything he sees. As a result, a haunting
tension permeates the book. That tension gives birth to an urgency to
know the past, "to wrest from it what it still offered or be done with it
once and for all." [2]

Cash, the relaxed newspaperman, speaks to his readers as if they
were old friends. "I go too fast," he says, or "I must pause," or "I am
advised," or "but perhaps I labor the case." Gently, he asks, "Does the
reader perhaps suspect the account . . . I give here?" Cleverly, he anticipates skepticism: "You suspect me of picturesque extravagance?
Then hear the Presbyterian J. H. Thornwell declaiming." Cash knew
how to meld language, form, and content in a manner that seems per-
fectly natural, giving his words the pleasing ring of sincerity and honesty. In *The Mind of the South*, author and subject are one. In its very
best moments, and there are many, author, reader, and subject are one. [3]

When it suits his purpose, Cash is folksy. Virginia's first gentlemen,
hallowed aristocrats in silk and plumage, are "your fat and moneyed
squire." The South's cherished Celtic racial stock, the Scotch-Irish,
have been "dogged out of Pennsylvania and Maryland." The reader
observes the "ragged, throat-slitting Highlanders" and hears "the
war-whoop of the Cherokee." Colloquialisms like "hell of a fellow,"
"cracker," and "white trash" sound the southern voice. "My Irish-

---

(New York, 1965), 89–99; Bertram Wyatt-Brown, *Yankee Saints and Southern Sinners* (Baton
Rouge, 1985), 131–54; Fred Hobson, *Tell About the South: The Southern Rage to Explain* (Baton
Rouge, 1983), 244–73; Richard H. King, *A Southern Renaissance: The Cultural Awakening of the
American South* (New York, 1980), 146–72. Joel Williamson has complained that after 1941, "if
one needed to say something, almost anything, about the Southern ethos, one simply cited Cash
and moved confidently and comfortably on" (*The Crucible of Race: Black-White Relations in the
American South Since Emancipation* [New York, 1984], 3). Contributors to the recently published,
massive *Encyclopedia of Southern Culture*, ed. Charles Reagan Wilson and William Ferris (Chapel
Hill, 1989), cite Cash almost as often as William Faulkner and Thomas Jefferson.

2. W. J. Cash, *The Mind of the South* (1941; New York, rpr. 1969), 440; King, *Southern Renaissance*, 147.

3. Cash, *Mind of the South*, 18, 23, 29, 80, 83, 180; Michael P. Dean, "W. J. Cash's *The
Mind of the South*: Southern History, Southern Style," *Southern Studies*, XX (1981), 297–302.

man" becomes his self-made, prototypical frontiersman-planter, while his "man at the center" symbolizes the simple, impulsive, common white southerner. Mix in "Cloud-Cuckoo Land" (silently borrowed from Aristophanes via James Branch Cabell), "savage ideal," and "proto-Dorian convention" and there it is, the Cashian style. It still shows traces of Mencken to be sure, but only traces, and even fainter but indelible traces of Conrad and the late Victorian masters.[4]

Audacious? Yes, one may scoff at Cash's "Menckenian buffoonery." But Cash means to grasp the reader's lapels. Boldly, Cash contends that cracker culture was so encompassing, so unyielding that it could stunt anyone, even a John C. Calhoun or a Jefferson Davis. "Catch Calhoun or Jeff Davis or Abe Lincoln (whose blood stemmed from the Carolina foothill country, remember) young enough, nurse him on 'bust-head,' feed him hog and pone, give him twenty years of lolling— expose him to all the conditions to which the cracker was exposed— and you have it exactly." And there you have, exactly, an example of Cash's relaxed elbow at work.[5]

Cash reinforced his arguments by drawing freely on his own experience: "I have myself known university-bred men who confessed proudly to having helped roast a Negro." Such rhetorical asides allow what otherwise might be dismissed with hoots of skepticism: "There were men like old Ward, the ironmaker (I cite an authentic case), who told his workers that he was sorry that he had to cut their wages." Having observed the antievolution movement "at close range, I have no doubt at all that it had the active support and sympathy of the overwhelming majority of the Southern people." So, too, did Cash's observations as a newspaperman breathe freshness into his discussion of prostitution, bootleg whiskey ("bust-head"), shockingly high homicide rates, urban ghettos, mill village squalor, college students, academic changes in the twentieth century, and the problems of the writer in the contemporary South.[6]

Like Faulkner, Cash blurred the line between past and present, allowing readers to feel the past by putting them into it. To create the sensation of being in history while at the same time looking at it, that is, to invoke folk memory and imagination, Cash luxuriated in convoluted phraseology:

4. King, *Southern Renaissance*, 148; James Branch Cabell, *Beyond Life* (New York, 1919), 34.
5. Woodward, *American Counterpoint*, 265; Cash, *Mind*, 4, 9, 10, 26–27.
6. Cash, *Mind of the South*, 311, 346, 367.

If you were a planter, and recalled that you had played about a cabin as a boy, that as a youth you had hunted the possum with that slouching fellow passing there, or danced the reel with the girl who had grown unbelievably into the poke-bonneted sun-faded woman yonder (had maybe kissed on that moon-burning, unutterable, lost night when you rode away to New Orleans with Andy Jackson), why, the chances were that, for all your forgetfulness when your ambition was involved, for all your pride in your Negroes, and your doctrinaire contempt for incompetence, there was still at the bottom of you a considerable community of feeling with these people.[7]

Cash shifts the persona of the narrator from critical historian to the once-proud planter: "Under our planter eyes. Men we have known all our days, laughed with, hunted with, and, in many a case, fought side by side with. Human. White. With white women and white children. . . . Give them special advantages? We shall do nothing of the kind. . . . We shall curse them roundly for no-count trifling incompetents who richly deserve to starve—always in our peculiar manner, which draws the sting of what we say. But look after them we must and will." Has anyone, asks one of Cash's admirers, "so skillfully rendered a feeling for the ideal of *noblesse oblige* under duress"?[8]

Writing almost three decades after his initial complimentary if cautious review, C. Vann Woodward winced at Cash's "extravagant" style and the notion that the New South is an unbroken extension of the Old. Take a closer look at the symbols of this New South, said Cash, those factories and urban skyscrapers—why, the South "had little more use for them than a hog has for a morning coat." They were more puffs of the ancient curse of bragging and boasting. "Softly," Cash asked, "do you not hear behind that the gallop of Jeb Stuart's cavalrymen?" No, Woodward fumed, "not one ghostly echo of a gallop. And neither did Jack Cash. He only thought he did when he was bemused." But others disagree. "Thus at his best," writes Richard King, "and that was quite often in *The Mind of the South*, Cash fuses the Southern capacity for rhetorical extravagance with the less typical capacity for satire and irony. The result is a masterpiece of discursive prose, stylistically one of the most sophisticated works in American historiography."[9]

---

7. *Ibid.*, 37.
8. *Ibid.*, 169–70; King, *Southern Renaissance*, 148, 149.
9. Cash, *Mind of the South*, 224–25; Woodward, *American Counterpoint*, 282, 684; King, *Southern Renaissance*, 149. For a harsh comment on Cash's style and ideas see Louis D. Rubin, Jr., "The Mind of the South," *Sewanee Review*, LXII (1954), 683–95.

Fortified by Freud and formed by his own experiences, Cash was persuaded that the southern mind was "a fairly definite mental pattern . . . a complex of established relationships and habits of thought." As such, it was a psyche, or temperament, a folk mind, with deeply embedded fantasies and fears, many of them sexual and all of them enmeshed in the individual and collective ego. "'Strictly, the Southerner had no mind; he had temperament,'" said Cash quoting Henry Adams. A simple soul at bottom, the southerner "felt" but did not "think"—as Cash would show on every page. This vision of mind as "temperament" is the perception of a modernist intellectual who believes that the values, ideas, and feelings, the irrationality of the masses—and of the master class as well—are the stuff of history. Cash never for a moment considered following the lead of a Perry Miller, whose imposing work *The New England Mind* carefully delineates the refined and often esoteric thoughts of the learned clergy but ignores the man on the street. A writer, an intellectual, and, most of all, a nonacademic, Cash adopted an artist's approach, admittedly impressionistic and flamboyant, which would not exclude ordinary people and render him aloof from what historians today salute as *mentalities*. Cash's goal was that of the true artist: to put down on paper what Henry James once called "the lost stuff of consciousness." [10]

Thus it is beside the point to criticize Cash for writing a book about the southern mind while denying that one existed and quibbling, as Woodward has, to suggest that Cash should have chosen a title such as "'The Temperament of the South,' 'The Feelings of the South,' or more literally, 'The Mindlessness of the South.'" Cash was no pedagogue, nervously writing "intellectual history" with an envious eye on a professor's chair. He was a writer. He had something to say and a passion to say it. Cash spoke in his own voice, hoping to tell the truth and "fetch the reader." [11]

"The South was another land," different from the rest of the nation, Cash announced in his "Preview to Understanding." If diversity marked the surface, unity lay underneath: there was one South, one southern mind. It sprang from the same sources as the Yankee mind,

10. Woodward, *American Counterpoint*, 265; Cash, *Mind of the South*, 102; Henry James, "The Beast in the Jungle," in *The Altar of the Dead and Other Stories*, Vol. XVII of *The Novels and Tales of Henry James* (New York, 1907–1909), 117; Williamson, *Crucible of Race*, 4–5.

11. Woodward, *American Counterpoint*, 265.

but its Celtic heritage and "peculiar history" turned it into a distinctive, remarkably homogeneous mind. Cash added that the South, down to his day, had remained fundamentally unchanged. All the exuberant, self-congratulatory talk about a New South, industrialized in the Yankee mold and striding forth triumphantly into the modern world, was myth pure and simple—that hog in "morning coat." Nothing inherent had changed. The South was still the South. "The South, one might say, is a tree with many age rings, with its limbs and trunk bent and twisted by all the winds of the years, but with its tap root in the Old South."[12]

Cash began his story with the Great South, the South of 1820 onward, when the plantation began its triumphant march beyond the Appalachians. He nodded back at the colonial era and skipped gingerly over the revolutionary generation of George Washington, Thomas Jefferson—mentioned but three times—and James Madison. Brashly, Cash ignored the Jeffersonian tradition which New South liberals had consistently identified as the "true South." Speaking for generations of southerners in 1931, Virginius Dabney had exalted Jeffersonism in his widely read book *Liberalism in the South*, a work Cash knew well and admired. But Cash, thumbing his nose at convention, was far from convinced that Jefferson's influence had been especially that pronounced beyond academic and intellectual circles.[13]

By page 12, Cash was gazing happily at the triumph of King Cotton. He paused briefly along the way to lay a rude hand of rejection on the lingering but discredited Cavalier Myth, saying that Virginia's First Families were a self-made elite just a step or two from the rough-and-tumble frontier. They sprang not from English blue bloods but from the same common clay as the cracker. Cash doubted whether more than four or five thousand "cotton magnates" ("cotton snobs," Daniel R. Hundley, one of Cash's sources, had sneered back in 1860) constituted the southern ruling class by the outbreak of the Civil War. He doubted if the South ever had more than five hundred "proper aristocrats." Thus Cash's Great South was dominated by a relatively small number of aggressive, self-made men, late of the frontier.[14]

12. Cash, *Mind of the South*, vii, x.

13. Woodward, *American Counterpoint*, 265; King, *Southern Renaissance*, 150; Virginius Dabney, *Liberalism in the South* (Chapel Hill, 1932).

14. Cash, *Mind of the South*, 14, 31; William E. Dodd, Cash's main source, had said "three or four thousand" (*The Cotton Kingdom* [New York, 1921], 24). Daniel R. Hundley, *Social Relations in Our Southern States*, ed. with intro. by William J. Cooper, Jr. (1860; rpr. Baton Rouge, 1979).

Cash was at one with his generation's infatuation with Frederick Jackson Turner's frontier thesis, an idea much in vogue among the Chapel Hill sociologists. But for all of Cash's appreciation of their work, particularly Howard W. Odum's, the eclectic Cash was never a mere borrower. Unlike Odum, Cash felt little ambivalence about the effect of the frontier on southern culture. He had a sneaking admiration for frontier types like Andrew Jackson and Abraham Lincoln but contended that the frontier rewarded "cunning," "hoggery and callousness," and "brutal unscrupulousness and downright scoundrelism." The result was a hollow aristocracy painfully aware of its lack of refinement and true culture. And Cash, far more of a Freudian than Odum or any of the reigning regionalists, charged that the planters' awareness of their deficiencies went deep into their souls, into their "subconsciousness." Hence their loud bragging and boasting, their tendency to unreality, and their various "defense mechanisms" created to protect their "egos" against Yankee slurs.[15]

Throughout, Cash relied unobtrusively on a core of Freudian ideas and an economic argument with overtones of Marx and Charles Beard. The planters, said Cash, constituted a "ruling class." Society was divided into "Big Men and Little Men," with the big men clearly and disproportionately in control of the political, social, and economic life of the South. Viewed objectively, Cash was saying, the Old South was a society built on class and ruled, for the most part, along class lines. And yet the simple southerner of whatever class never saw it that way. He beheld his world "with essentially naive, direct and personal eyes." Hence "the Southerner's primary approach to his world was not through the idea of class," and there was no corresponding class consciousness. The Old South was unsettled, still a frontier in the making, and therefore naively oblivious to class lines in much of its day-to-day life. "Planters very commonly intermarried with yeomen, and alliances between planters and people who were pretty definitely reckoned poor whites were not unheard of." The thought of belonging to a class was not even in the planter's "subconsciousness." So deep went the illusions that even the poor whites lacked "genuine class feeling."[16]

15. Cash, Mind of the South, 19, 62–64; Daniel Joseph Singal, The War Within: From Victorian to Modernist Thought in the South, 1919–1945 (Chapel Hill, 1982), 137–39, 312; Howard W. Odum, An American Epoch: Southern Portraiture in the National Picture (New York, 1930), 34–38.

16. Cash, Mind of the South, 35–37, 41–42. A decade later, in a successful textbook Francis

To get to the bottom of this paradox, the lack of class consciousness in a class-ridden society, Cash fused his modernist assumptions and his reading in classical history to coin the intriguing phrase *proto-Dorian convention* to describe the intense racial consciousness and bonding between masters and poor whites that obscured class divisions—the "real interests" of the white masses. "Add up his blindness to his real interests," Cash says pointedly about the common white's untroubled view of his situation, "his lack of class feeling and of social and economic forces, and you arrive, with the precision of a formula in mathematics, at the solid South." The sticking point between Cash and many historians today is whether whites should have felt any class consciousness. Cash believed the common whites were exploited and dominated by a rigid class system, but "come what may, he would always be a white man. And before that vast and capacious distinction, all others were foreshortened, dwarfed, and all but obliterated." The common man's desires and fantasies, sexual and otherwise—to say nothing of basic racial prejudice—coalesced, forming the proto-Dorian bond. To explain exactly how this could be, Cash relied on his Freudianism to arrive at one of his most stunning conclusions: that the common white exuberantly followed the planters and their descendants during slavery and Reconstruction days because he so "identified his ego with the thing called the South as to become, so to say, a perambulating South in little, and hence found in the prescriptions of his captains great expansion for his ego—associated the authority yielded the master class, not with any diminution of his individuality, but with its fullest development and expression."[17]

Here spoke a self-taught intellectual with liberal social values who

---

Butler Simkins helped popularize Cash's arguments about the relative absence of class consciousness in language strikingly similar to Cash's: "A characteristically American lack of class consciousness," Simkins wrote, "was fostered by actual or assumed kinship between planter and yeoman, by intermarriage between the two classes, by the tendency of the grand gentleman to lay a familiar hand on the shoulders of poor neighbors at political meetings, and by the inviting of farmer neighbors and cousins to the festive board of big houses" (*The South Old and New: A History, 1820–1947* [New York, 1947], 57). "There was always substantial mobility into and out of the slaveholding class," James Oakes has written. "If marriage patterns are any indication, it appears that white Southerners paid little attention to class distinctions in choosing mates" (*The Ruling Race: A History of American Slaveholders* [New York, 1983], 67).

17. Cash, *Mind of the South*, 115. Simkins wrote, again echoing Cash: "The exploitative attitude which both rich and poor whites developed toward the slave created a solidarity of interests which was readily rationalized into a solidarity of class. A contempt for the black man made all white men brothers in a sense and elevated the common white man to a membership in a superior caste" (*The South Old and New*, 58).

had drunk deeply at the well of modernism and thus believed that the common whites' unconscious and simple myths (together with their simple but fantastic religion) served as their social vision and denied them any rational awareness of their relationship to the "ruling class." To Cash, it surely was not rational for dirt farmers in North Carolina or gap-toothed, illiterate Delta rednecks to identify with their masters and to identify the tiny ruling class as the South. But common southerners' egos, their desire to think highly of themselves, no matter what the odds, dominated and obliterated class consciousness—not only in everyday mundane matters of manners and morals but in the ultimate question of the cause one would die for when the South seceded.[18]

In thus reconciling—in his own mind, too, one guesses—the relationship of class, class consciousness, race, and ego, Cash confronted what might be termed the irony of southern history: why did poor whites not only endure life in a slavocracy but celebrate it, and then, when the bugles blared in 1861, gallantly and exuberantly march off to die for a social system that oppressed them? Cash's answer anticipates the conclusions of many modern historians, who, unlike Cash, stress the "democratic" nature of southern life. The white masses, said Cash, never felt oppressed. They believed that they were living in a political and economic democracy. Universal manhood suffrage for whites was virtually the rule in every southern state before 1850, modern historians have shown. What is more, whites passionately believed a version of the American myth: that the door of opportunity was wide open. Anyone with gumption could succeed by accumulating enough money to buy land and slaves. Never mind that less than a third of the whites owned any slaves and that a small minority of planters owned most of the slaves—ownership of slaves was as widespread as was ownership of wealth in the North. And though the relative number of slaveholders was actually decreasing by 1860, the absolute number was increasing, testifying daily to the myth of opportunity and success. Thus white southerners, whoever they were, tended to regard their society with respect and admiration. "The antebellum South," Carl Degler has written, "is quite understandable as a society in which the overwhelming majority of white southerners accepted slavery and the values that surrounded it, because that kind of society served their interests as well as those of the slaveholders." Cash's quib-

18. Cash, *Mind of the South*, 55–102.

ble with that assertion would be that the "true interests" of the majority were hardly being served.[19]

But the common white man, said Cash, identified with his masters and thus happily regarded himself as "the South in little." The southerner's comforting notion that he lived in a society every bit as open and democratic as the Yankee's was mortgaged, of course, to the white South's racist resolve to keep the black underclass oppressed. Such an arrangement, Degler continues in words that further echo Cash, "brought not only economic advantages, but social and psychological status as well." In perceiving how the proto-Dorian convention flourished in spite of class realities and recurring conflicts, says Woodward, and in showing how "class hegemony prevailed in the South," Cash had a "genuine insight into class relationships in the South. . . . This insight was Cash's main contribution and he deserves full credit for it." Yet Cash has not received anywhere near full credit from historians, particularly those who see the hand of class inexorably controlling people's lives.[20]

Cash's "one South," one unified mind, has touched off serious disagreement. He has been charged with ignoring the waves of antislavery sentiment that touched southern shores, starting in the revolutionary era and continuing until the late 1840s and a long list of home-grown abolitionists—from James G. Birney to the Grimke sisters of South Carolina. Each and all stand outside Cash's monolith. Furthermore, various historians assert, the Old South was politically divided throughout the 1830s and 1840s. Until the beginning of the secessionist crisis in the early 1850s, Whigs battled the reigning Democrats for the loyalty of southern voters. Democrats dominated the 1850s and 1860s, but Whiggery remained very much alive in Unionist sentiment and would reemerge during Reconstruction. There was also a "great body" of Unionist dissenters who "furnished some 200,000 troops to the Union Army" and "native Republicans, whites as well as blacks," who appeared after 1865.[21]

19. Carl Degler, *Place over Time: The Continuity of Southern Distinctiveness* (Baton Rouge, 1977), 79, 81; Oakes, *Ruling Race*, 38–68; William J. Cooper, Jr., *The South and the Politics of Slavery, 1828–1856* (Baton Rouge, 1978), 23–42, 69.

20. Degler, *Place over Time*, 82; Woodward, *American Counterpoint*, 273; Steven Hahn, *The Roots of Southern Populism: Yeoman Farmers and the Transformation of the Georgia Upcountry, 1850–1890* (New York, 1983), 116–33.

21. Woodward, *American Counterpoint*, 273–74; David M. Potter, *The Impending Crisis, 1848–1861* (New York, 1976), 485–513; Cooper, *The South and the Politics of Slavery*, 45–48,

To do justice to Cash these contentions must be analyzed. To begin with, the vast majority of indigenous abolitionists either kept silent in the 1830s or left the South. Second, Unionist sentiment is easily exaggerated or misread—some Unionists opposed secession because they were convinced that staying loyal to the Union was the best way to preserve slavery. There were patches of Unionist sentiment in the Deep South, but the overwhelming majority of southerners who joined the Union army came from the border states. And even there and elsewhere, as Cash knew, Unionism was a very frail reed in the storm of secession. In Virginia, North Carolina, and Tennessee, where Unionism was strongest on the eve of the war, it all but evaporated in the twinkling of an eye in the secessionist crisis.[22]

At the time Cash wrote, it was common for white historians to slip into racist-sounding generalizations and give blacks or their culture the barest of mention. Such in large measure was the case in *The Mind of the South*. Individual blacks such as W. E. B. DuBois and Booker T. Washington are merely mentioned, though DuBois' influence is subtly at work in Cash's thinking. Worse than his omission of blacks, Cash's language occasionally betrays a lingering tolerance for some racial shibboleths. The Negro is a "romantic," Cash says, a "hedonist," rolling lovely words in his mouth, heaping "them in redundant profusion one upon another until meaning vanishes and there is nothing left . . . but the play of primitive rhythm upon the secret springs of emotion." The Negro, Cash announced in Menckenian manner, "is a creature of grandiloquent imagination, of facile emotion, above everything else under heaven, of enjoyment." And Cash's asides about the sensuality of slave women have a racist ring, even when one remembers that he was attempting to catch up white attitudes: "For she was natural, and could give herself up to passion in a way impossible to wives inhibited by Puritanical training."[23]

Yet none of his generalizations ever, even for a moment, reflected a mean-spirited racism. Nor were his comments about blacks any more pointed or slanderous than his generalizations about whites. Cash

183–224, 266–67, 269–321; William J. Cooper, Jr., *Liberty and Slavery: Southern Politics to 1860* (New York, 1983), 192–212.

22. Daniel W. Crofts, *Reluctant Confederates: Upper South Unionists in the Secession Crisis* (Chapel Hill, 1989), 308–61; Degler, *Place over Time*, 38, 39, 104, 96, 97.

23. Cash, *Mind of the South*, 51–53, 321–22, 333, 51, 87; Woodward, *American Counterpoint*, 267–77; King, *Southern Renaissance*, 163.

never assumed or implied that blacks were somehow responsible for the abuse whites meted out to them, an assumption that frequently slipped into the writings of even the most benign New South liberals. He gave no credence to the widespread view that blacks were inherently inferior, naturally brutal, or trapped in their "savage" African background. Such notions were bandied about in scholarly works at the time and often used to justify the existence of slavery, which was said to have "civilized" or "uplifted" an inferior race. To have accepted such notions, Cash would have had to assume, as the New South generation had almost as an article of faith, that the white South, no matter what its sins, was basically decent and wholesome. Cash never succumbed to any apology for slavery because he was not convinced of the superiority of any one race, certainly not white southerners.

Nor should one overlook Cash's leap beyond racism. Most commentators on the Old South in Cash's day had pulled their chins wondering why slaves had not rebelled or why greater numbers had not tried to escape. Cash would have been the first to spy the racism—to say nothing of lack of knowledge of the slaveholder's power and the slave's defenselessness—that frequently lurks in that question. Cash did not ask those questions because he never for a moment projected on to oppressed slaves a heroic, rational, courageous self-image. Cash turned the tables and asked, by indirection, what could explain why whites, who were not in physical bondage, did not rebel.[24]

Moreover, Cash was uncompromisingly critical of slavery. It was "inescapably brutal and ugly" and "rested on force." Slaves were denied any freedom or human rights. "The lash lurked always in the background. Its open crackle could often be heard where field hands were quartered. Into the gentlest houses drifted now and then the sound of dragging chains and shackles, the bay of hounds, the report of pistols on the trail of a runaway." Few historians before the 1950s and 1960s matched Cash's invective—"mutilation and the mark of the branding iron were pretty common." Nor have many writers equaled Cash in exposing the white South's self-deceptions and attempts to "prettify" slavery. Why, "to have heard them talk, indeed, you would have thought that the sole reason some of these planters held to slavery was love and duty to the black man, the earnest, de-

24. King, *Southern Renaissance*, 162–63.

voted will not only to get him into heaven but also to make him happy in this world."[25]

Then, too, Cash understood the subtle, symbiotic nature of slave culture in which two races interacted, each silently but constantly shaping and molding the other. "Negro entered into white man as profoundly as white man entered into Negro—subtly influencing every gesture, every word, every emotion and idea, every attitude." Having made the point, Cash moved on, but he was keenly aware, as few white southerners of his generation were, that black-white relations were far more complex than apologists for slavery or segregation understood when explaining how the Negro had to be "civilized." The apologists usually assumed that the superior white race influenced the weaker brown brother. But blacks, Cash was saying, had subtly influenced whites at every turn, as modern historians have shown when discussing the "Africanization of the South."

Cash wrote a searing indictment of racism. He may be faulted for failing "to make the plausible move to the observation that the Negro, because he existed in two worlds, was far from the simple and uncomplex figure he was assumed to be." Perhaps had Cash explored the writings of black intellectuals, he might have modified some of his generalizations. But was Cash suggesting that blacks had no mind, or at least no mind worth considering? Cash assumed—rightly or wrongly—that there was in fact *one* mind of the South, a tenacious folk mind, a collective mind that ensnared and shaped blacks as much as whites. Such a view is not entirely farfetched. It was a black scholar who concluded that the black masses, "southerners always, have been directly influenced by many of the same geographical and cultural factors which W. J. Cash so excellently outlined in his *The Mind of the South*."[26]

Cash's treatment of blacks in the modern South was probing, sensitive, and sympathetic. Drawing on his newspaper days, he wrote caustically about black slums and the wretched, soul-destroying living conditions blacks were forced to endure, and perceptively about black

25. *Ibid.*, 163; Cash, *Mind of the South*, 85–86.
26. John W. Blassingame, *The Slave Community: Plantation Life in the Antebellum South* (1972; rev. ed. New York, 1979), 49–104, 249; King, *Southern Renaissance*, 162–63; Earl E. Thorpe, *The Mind of the Negro: An Intellectual History of Afro-Americans* (Baton Rouge, 1961), xi, xx. Thorpe is quoted in Arthur S. Link and Rembert W. Patrick, eds., *Writing Southern History: Essays in Historiography in Honor of Fletcher M. Green* (Baton Rouge, 1965), 150, 384.

soldiers returning in 1918 from the North or from Europe, where they had tasted "at least nominal and legal equality." Now they carried themselves "with a bolder lift to their heads, a firmer, more rolling step, and a new light in their eyes." He acknowledged and saluted black demands for education, the vote, and jobs. In spite of almost insurmountable obstacles, Cash argued sympathetically, some blacks were climbing the economic ladder. He wrote movingly about exploitation and racial oppression and cursed slums and ghettos as the cause of crime. But he used none of this to argue that white prejudice had diminished or that the debilitating effects on blacks of white prejudice had been exaggerated.[27]

Cash would have thought it highly presumptuous of him to "explain" the black mind. White southerners had been doing so ever since the first Africans stepped off the slave ships—and had mainly repeated and embroidered myths and stereotypes. Part of Cash's genius was that he never for a moment embraced the white South's cherished assumption that it "understood" the Negro, a fatuous notion that New South liberals had adopted with a pride that forever denied them any understanding of blacks. Even the most benign, well-meaning liberals of the preceding generation, such as Edgar Gardner Murphy and Woodrow Wilson, had congratulated themselves on their ability to understand the Negro.[28]

Cash would have none of this blinkered Victorianism. Instead, he emphasized that white southerners—and by extension himself—*did not know* the Negro. When Cash looked at the Negro face, a face forever glancing down to avoid the white man's gaze, and with eyes "lying half hidden most of the time," he saw not ignorance or inferiority. Nor did he see a grinning simpleton, content with his lot. Cash at no time treats the Negro anecdotally as did his friend Jonathan Daniels in *A Southerner Discovers the South* (1938). Nor was there a shred of that nostalgic longing for the "good old Negro" of slavery days that permeates William Alexander Percy's *Lanterns on the Levee* (1941). When Cash looked at the Negro, he saw a mask of mystery and rebuke—a rebuke to centuries of southern boasts and illusions. He understood, aided by W. E. B. DuBois, that blacks hid their true feelings behind a veil. But what was behind that mask, asked

27. King, *Southern Renaissance*, 163; Cash, *Mind of the South*, 319.
28. Hobson, *Tell About the South*, 264; Bruce Clayton, *The Savage Ideal: Intolerance and Intellectual Leadership in the South, 1890–1914* (Baltimore, 1972), 185–216.

Cash, was the question that bedeviled even the commonest whites. Outwardly whites boasted that they knew the Negro, but inwardly they shuddered: what was going on behind that grin? "What was back there, hidden? What whispering, stealthy, fateful thing might they be framing out there in the palpitant darkness?"[29]

Cash did not know. He thought he knew a good bit about the cries and whispers, hopes and fears, good and evil intentions of his own race that he had tried so desperately to understand, but he did not presume to know the Negro mind. Surveying the state of scholarship on the Negro since Reconstruction, George Tindall asked plaintively in 1965, as he could well ask today: "Is there no writer who can do for Southern Negroes what Howard Odum did for southern white folk in his *American Epoch* or Wilbur Joseph Cash in his *The Mind of the South?*"[30]

Fortified by Freud and a keen introspective intelligence, Cash sensed that most of the labels and negative things racist whites said about blacks were "projections" of a master race not entirely convinced in its psyche of its superiority. Projections, Cash knew, are ways an individual or a group attributes to others what it secretly fears (or believes) to be true about itself. Racist projections were the white South's "defense mechanisms," said Cash, designed, unconsciously for the most part, to bolster its "ego" and to shield itself from a candid self-examination or honest look at the Negro. Behind the projections, the self-denial, Cash perceived, stood a lingering guilt, a natural product of a class too close to its frontier origins to feel truly secure as an aristocracy and a class that, for all its racism and haughtiness, shared the nation's assumptions about democracy and natural rights.

Contrary to some charges against Cash, he did call attention to the numerous abolitionist societies that had sprung up in the South, but he underlined their collapse after William Lloyd Garrison unleashed his withering attack on the South. The Garrisonian condemnation caused local abolitionists to fold their tents and created "a society be-

29. King, *Southern Renaissance*, 163; Cash, *Mind of the South*, 326, 327; Hobson, *Tell About the South*, 264; Jonathan Daniels, *A Southerner Discovers the South* (New York, 1938), 120–32, 250–61. For a discussion of subtle but important changes occurring in Daniels' thinking, see Charles S. Eagles, *Jonathan Daniels and Race Relations: The Evolution of a Southern Liberal* (Knoxville, 1982), 47–82.

30. George B. Tindall, "Southern Negroes Since Reconstruction: Dissolving the Static Image," in Link and Patrick, eds., *Writing Southern History*, 359.

set by the specters of defeat, of shame, of guilt—a society driven by the need to bolster its morale, to nerve its arm against waxing odds, to justify itself in its own eyes and in those of the world." In justifying itself, in scurrying to protect its "ego," the South sneered at the Yankee as "crass" and tried "to beget in his bourgeois soul a kind of secret and envious awe." In spite of this "nearly perfect defense mechanism," southerners "could not endow their subconsciousness" with assurance and banish their sense of guilt—a contention that continues to be debated by historians.[31]

Not surprisingly, a secular, deeply critical attitude toward religion permeates *The Mind of the South*. Cash was not oblivious to the ways evangelicalism helped spread the fever of democracy, and he understood how religion had intensified the planters' feelings of isolation from the liberal tradition. But his passion was to detail religion's role in blocking off new ideas and narrowing the southern mind. The Old South's mind was split and needed healing, said Cash. But religion made it worse by imposing a self-denying Puritanism on an emotional, hedonistic people. The result was "a sort of social schizophrenia" that reinforced the region's "naive capacity for unreality." Never fond of parsons, Cash lashed the clergy for blindly resisting modern ideas, foisting a tribal god on the people, and fomenting violence. "In the end, indeed," said Cash, surveying the last days of the Old South, "almost the only pleasures which might be practiced openly and without moral obloquy were those of orgiastic religion and those of violence."[32]

Yet Cash, who knew his Bible from "lid to lid," as his sister said, turned effortlessly to its cadence and imagery. Southern politics, he wrote, was "the temple wherein men entered to participate in the mysteries of the common brotherhood of white men, to partake of the holy sacrament of Southern loyalty and hate. And the shining sword of battle, the bread and wine—if I may be permitted to carry out the theological figure—through which men become one flesh with the Logos,

---

31. Cash, *Mind of the South*, 62, 64, 71, 86–87; Charles G. Sellers, "The Southerner as American," in Sellers, ed., *The Travail of Slavery* (New York, 1966), 40–71; Eugene D. Genovese, *The World the Slaveholders Made: Two Essays in Interpretation* (New York, 1969), 137, 145–46, 149, Kenneth Stampp, *The Southern Road to Appomattox*, Cotton Memorial Papers, No. 4 (El Paso: University of Texas at El Paso, 1969); William W. Freehling, *Prelude to Civil War: The Nullification Controversy in South Carolina, 1816–1836* (New York, 1965) 72–78, 86; Oakes, *Ruling Race*, 114, 97, 117; Cooper, *Liberty and Union*, 178–84.

32. Cash, *Mind of the South*, 58–60, 136–37.

was, of course, rhetoric, a rhetoric that every day became less and less a form of speech strictly and more and more a direct instrument of emotion, like music." So spoke the son of the Baptist piedmont.[33]

As with religion and blacks, Cash's analysis of women was confined to their participation in and reflection of the southern mind. Few women merit more than the briefest mention, and most of them are writers—Ellen Glasgow, Julia Peterkin, Margaret Mitchell, Lillian Smith—yet presciently and boldly he understood what has come to be called "the cult of true womanhood." As the angry, defensive white South pondered the Negro, said Cash, the symbolic value of the white woman soared. She was venerated in the southern psyche, mythologized as purity itself. She was the virtuous, lovely, feminine alternative to the rough, often violent world of competitive males. This process of creating what modern historians call gender roles and rules was at work in the North, but in the South, as Cash pointed out, the presence of the Negro gave the process a particular racial-sexist twist. Woman's sexual purity became a fetish. As "perpetuator of white superiority in legitimate line," she had to be "absolutely inaccessible" to black males. Thus mythologized, she became "the focal center of the fundamental pattern of proto-Dorian pride." She was the center of the racist psychological game, a deadly serious game that the South was playing out with itself and the North. As fair Athena, southern woman was proof of Dixie's Great Heart. Did the Yankee charge that the white South abused blacks, sexually and physically; that miscegenation was the rule, that the slave South was characterized by bestiality? "The Yankee must be answered by proclaiming from the housetops that Southern Virtue, so far from being inferior, was superior, not alone to the North's but to any on earth, and adducing Southern Womanhood in proof."[34]

So great was this "downright gyneolatry," Cash trumpeted, that "at the last, I verily believe, the ranks of the Confederacy went rolling into battle in the misty conviction that it was wholly for her that they fought." More dollops of extravagance? Obviously. And yet his words find a loud echo in Bertram Wyatt-Brown's magisterial *Southern*

33. *Ibid.*, 81–82.

34. *Ibid.*, 87, 89; Catherine Clinton, *The Plantation Mistress: Woman's World in the Old South* (New York, 1982), 222. Clinton writes: "The ante-bellum patriarchs simultaneously emasculated male slaves, dehumanized female slaves, and desexualized their own wives. The imposition of this difficult and twisted balance had become the indispensable counterpoint to a racial dynamic of sexuality that was of the white masters' own creation."

Honor, a book that reflects many of Cash's themes and contentions. "Certainly the guns that blasted the walls of Fort Sumter," Wyatt-Brown concludes regarding the entrenched sexual codes, "did not destroy the ancient code as well. Instead they expressed the determination to keep it holy."[35]

Cash saw that the plantation established narrow, constricting, well-understood (if occasionally resented) gender and sexual roles for women. In words strongly reminiscent of recent feminist scholarship, Cash wrote: "In the isolation of the plantation world, the home was necessarily the center of everything; family ties acquired a strength and validity unknown in more closely settled communities; and, above all, there grew up an unusually intense affection and respect for the women of the family—for the wife and mother upon whose activities the comfort and well-being of everybody greatly depended." Cash also perceptively recognized that sexual taboos, particularly those aimed at preventing racial mixing, had not worked. Put on a pedestal, the plantation mistress became desexualized, even for white males, a point only recently fully appreciated by historians. The result was the great transgression: miscegenation. If even mentioned, it was to be roundly condemned. Usually it was denied, hotly. Yet illicit sexual liaisons between white males and black women occurred regularly in the antebellum South. White women knew what was going on, said Cash, but they had to look the other way, feigning blindness that "the maid in her kitchen was in reality half sister to her own daughter." White male transgressors were occasionally punished, but the large number of mulattoes by 1850 suggests clearly that white males were relatively free to have their way with slave women. Nor did miscegenation decline after the war, Cash argued—wrongly, it seems from the skimpy evidence available—when efforts were made everywhere to stop it or, failing that, to deny it even more vigorously. Richard King writes that by placing miscegenation in the context of veneration of women and the rape complex, "what Faulkner did for incest, Cash did for miscegenation: he gave it wider social and cultural implications."[36]

35. Cash, *Mind of the South,* 89; Bertram Wyatt-Brown, *Southern Honor: Ethics and Behavior in the Old South* (New York, 1982), 324.

36. Cash, *Mind of the South,* 88, 131; Wyatt-Brown, *Southern Honor,* 165–66, 287–89, 305–24; Anne Firor Scott, *The Southern Lady: From Pedestal to Politics, 1830–1930* (Chicago, 1970), 3–44; Clinton, *Plantation Mistress,* 36–58; Joel Williamson, *New People: Miscegenation and Mulattoes in the United States* (New York, 1980), 17, 25–42, 88–91; King, *Southern Renaissance,* 165–66.

Cash's notion that there was one southern mind precluded any real sensitivity to or appreciation of the daily lives and responsibilities of women. Moreover, when women entered his thoughts he instinctively, unconsciously, thought of their sexual relationship to men—or, more accurately, men's sexual desires for women. In this, he was very much a man of his time. There were no historical and few literary works available to him (and he read Ellen Glasgow's and Julia Peterkin's novels as a male intellectual, looking for ideas about history, meaning white male history) that would have led him to consider critically the wide range of human experiences that are today more properly understood as restricting gender rules and relationships. There is an irony here that Cash would have enjoyed acknowledging: he understood that the South had plumbed its deepest and only half-understood psychic needs in making woman a totem and any talk of her sexuality a taboo. But his own participation in a male perspective of sexuality escaped his notice—as it would escape the notice of most male historians of the South until the 1980s.

Revealingly, Cash's view of rape—which to his generation always meant a black man's rape of a white woman—focused on the white southern male: his (not the victim's) sexual fears and fantasies. Cash ignored the Negro in this connection because he knew, as two generations of writers had pointed out, that rape was rarely the real cause of lynchings and violence; probably no more than a third of the victims of lynchings were rapists. Then Cash hints, in something of an unconscious sexist aside, that some of the fear was merely a "projection" of the sexual fantasies of neurotic, even hysterical old maids and young girls, well understood today, Cash the modernist said knowingly, but hardly understood at all in those benighted days.[37]

But to Cash the deeper meaning of rape and violence was not in statistics but in psychology. At issue was the "rape complex," a set of interlocking myths and fantasies in the mind of the white southerner triggered by the ending of slavery. Since the white South had all along identified itself with white woman—the crucial link in the proto-Dorian bond—it followed that freeing the Negro was not merely or even mainly a political act. It was an attack on the white South and was, therefore, rape. Once they were freed, what was to stop blacks from desiring complete equality, meaning, of course, sex, the not-so-hidden

37. Cash, Mind of the South, 88–89, 117–18.

but always unspoken meaning in the southerner's obsessive warnings against "social equality." Cash is more than suggesting that the rape complex pointed to a male-dominated culture that, ironically and unknowingly, thought of itself as feminine—which, from the perspective of the times, meant an inferior, weak culture always in danger of being thrown on its back and ravished.[38]

This highly controversial sexual interpretation—replete with sexual imagery—dominated Cash's view of Reconstruction. "Not Ireland nor Poland," he writes vividly, "not Finland nor Bohemia, not one of the countries which prove the truth that there is no more sure way to make a nation than the brutal oppression of an honorably defeated and disarmed people—not one of these, for all the massacres, the pillage, and the rapes to which they have so often been subjected, was ever so pointedly taken in the very core of its being as was the South." The cunning Yankee Republicans—the odious "tariff gang" who plundered the South—and the Radicals, those zealots with blood in their eyes and foolish notions about the rights of the freedman, were brutal rapists in the unconsciousness of postbellum white southerners—and to Cash. Thus did Cash, so daring and emancipated on many issues, use a radical, daring sexual argument to reaffirm the prevailing myths.[39]

Cash never speaks of "Negro domination" or anything else so crudely simple or racist. But once again his vivid style betrays a lingering tolerance for racist imagery. Listen to him describe the reactions of the master class during Reconstruction: "The most superior men, with the exception of an occasional Robert E. Lee or Benjamin H. Hill, seeing their late slave strutting about full of grotesque assertions, cheap whisky, and lying dreams, feeling his elbow in their ribs, hearing his guffaw in high places, came increasingly to feel toward him very much as any cracker felt; fell increasingly under the sway of the same hunger to have their hands on him, to ease the intolerable agony of anger and fear and shaken pride in his screams." Cash's generation of intellectuals felt deeply ambivalent toward the South—certainly Cash did—and by laying into the Yankee for the botched job of Reconstruction they could make up for all their criticisms and "give some public assurance of their *bona fides* as Southerners." Perhaps Cash had

---

38. *Ibid.*, 117–18, 125; Walter F. White, *Rope and Faggot: A Biography of Judge Lynch* (New York, 1929); Arthur F. Raper, *The Tragedy of Lynching* (Chapel Hill, 1939); Williamson, *Crucible of Race*, 117–20.

39. Cash, *Mind of the South*, 108.

fallen for the New South's "balanced" view that judged the South guilty of secession and the North guilty of Reconstruction. To his credit, however, Cash never for a moment used the myths of Reconstruction to justify any of the white South's bestiality toward the Negro.[40]

Cash's lengthy analysis of the rage and patriotism generated by Reconstruction buttressed his argument that the South had been, for a second time, turned into a frontier. The white southerners' extreme resistance intensified basic assumptions and patterns of life—the worst, for the most part—to fashion the modern-day South. Radicals drove Rebels deeper into themselves. Racial attitudes hardened. Whites rededicated themselves to mastery. The proto-Dorian convention sank even deeper roots, further obscuring the common whites' awareness of their oppression. In turning inward, the South became violently intolerant, particularly about the Negro or any other sensitive issue. Ancient totems and taboos were reinforced and southerners took the "easy step to interpreting every criticism of the South on whatever score as disloyalty—to making such criticism so dangerous that none but a madman would risk it." Out of this caldron of intolerance sprang the "savage ideal"—"whereunder dissent and variety are completely suppressed and men become, in all their attitudes, professions and actions, virtual replicas of one another." Myth leaped from paradox. As the Old South receded further into the past, the legend of its grace and charm, its settled beauty, grew luxuriously. Sleepy hamlets awoke to pen odes to the Confederate dead and enshrine their memory in statues. All were part and parcel of the ancient tendency to romanticize and escape into unreality.[41]

However much Cash slandered the Yankee for Reconstruction, he evened the score with a vengeance by portraying the post-1877 South as a rough, violent world, whose savage ideal put him in mind of Hitler's Germany and Stalin's Russia. The increase of sadistic violence in the post-Reconstruction and modern South prompted such comparisons. The lynching rope, held in check by the master class and usually reserved for white miscreants during slavery, was in the postbellum South increasingly used to brutalize the Negro. True to what he had learned as a newspaperman, Cash dismissed the standard

40. Ibid., 116–17, 108; King, Southern Renaissance, 165–66; Clayton, Savage Ideal, 185–206.

41. Cash, Mind of the South, 93–94, 121, 138, 124–27.

and comforting view that lynchings were the work of the irrational masses who could be cured of their sickness by education. Having had firsthand knowledge of some lynchers and having been around educated men and women who held racist views, Cash looked for deeper meanings in lynchings. The frequency of lynchings by the 1890s, the high-water mark in the practice of such cruelty, and the white South's obsession with the black rapist, prompted Cash to contend that lynchings were public acts of racial solidarity and patriotic expressions of a sick society. Lynchings were perceived as acts of chivalry with definite "ritualistic value in respect to the entire Southern sentiment." By looking beneath the surface of public history with its well-defined and widely understood roles, Cash predated recent anthropologists and historians who study public events and places for their deeper meaning, both for the individual and for the community.[42]

In his unflinching documentation of racism, particularly the violent lynchings that disgraced the South before World War I, Cash applied what he had learned as a newspaperman and consistently blamed the descendants of the planters and the community's "men of the better sort," as the New South liberals called them. Such men, the conventional wisdom wished to believe, would never be guilty of gross or brutal prejudice. When discussing the coming of the mills and factories and the South's love of moneymaking, Cash argued that the better sort came to see that lynchings (which were often well-attended, planned public frolics) bred a general unruliness in the white masses and threatened to sweep blacks into "mass hysteria" and shake them out of their "submissiveness." And then, as though he had become aware that he had, à la New South liberalism, come close to attributing benign rationality to the better sort, Cash backed off to find the "real" source of the decline of lynchings in progress and its ultimate symbol, the machine, the embodiment of order and rationality, the opposite of the irrational lynching mob.[43]

Once again, Cash argued, race triumphed over class, resulting in a "suppression of class feeling that went beyond anything that even the

---

42. *Ibid.*, 121, 125; Williamson, *Crucible of Race*, 117. For an example of the way a sophisticated historian examines the Ku Klux Klan, see Charles L. Flynn, Jr., *White Land, Black Labor: Caste and Class in Late Nineteenth-Century Georgia* (Baton Rouge, 1983), 44–46. Flynn builds on the perceptive work of Natalie Zemon Davis, *Society and Culture in Early Modern France: Eight Essays by Natalie Zemon Davis* (Stanford, 1975), and E. P. Thompson, "'Rough Music': Le Charivari Anglais," *Annales: Economies; Societies; Civilisations*, XXVII (1972), 285–312.

43. Cash, *Mind of the South*, 313.

Old South had known." In vanquishing the hated Republicans the master class tightened its grip on the Democratic party, stripped the masses of effective action, made politics its "private property," and sank "deeper into the naive and complacent assumption of their interest as the public interest." Thus was completed the ruling class's divorce from "the proper business of politics—that is, the resolution of the inevitable conflict in interest between the classes, and the securing of a reasonable degree of social equity." The process brought about the "wholesale expropriation of the cracker and the small farmer, and extinction of appreciable numbers of larger farmers" and the emergence of the tenant and cropper—a "mighty and always multiplying horde of the landless." [44]

Like many historians who have written after him, Cash found the roots of the Populist revolt of the 1890s in the economic and political inequities spawned in the overthrow of Reconstruction. As the masses, black and white, slipped deeper into tenancy and sharecropping and as the depression of the 1890s worsened agricultural distress, rural discontent erupted in the Populist challenge to the Democratic party, which in some sections preferred the more honest label of Bourbon or Conservative. But as always, Cash advanced his own controversial interpretation. In keeping with his arguments about unity and continuity and the triumph of racism over class consciousness, Cash concluded: "However mighty were the forces tending to project these common whites into class awareness and revolt, the forces tending to hold them back were mightier yet." Cash doubted whether many farmers ever had much genuine class feeling. Thus he readily accepted the prevailing scholarly view that Populism was "essentially only a part of the national agrarian movement; it represented an outburst of farmer interest against the great cities of the East rather than a class movement within the South itself." Distressed southern farmers were simple people who fumed at Wall Street with no clear notion of what was wrong. "No," Cash says, as though sensing the thoughts of future historians, "we cannot take the movement here as proceeding from, or as testifying to the appearance of, an overt and realized class awareness in the South." [45]

44. Ibid., 112, 133, 132.
45. Ibid., 166, 162 165; C. Vann Woodward, *Origins of the New South, 1877–1913* (Baton Rouge, 1951), 14–15, 175–263.

Yet in assessing the reigning party's fear of Populist successes, Cash more than implies that class antagonisms and the specter of class consciousness disturbed the complacency of the master class. "Who did not see again, that, despairing of their racial status and made frantic by the desperate contest for bread, these whites would eventually be swept fully into the bitterest class consciousness; that the slow impluse, which the master class was at least vaguely aware of from the beginning, would develop a power no barrier and no argument could hold back? Who could not see, in a word, that here was chaos? That if it was allowed to run its course, it was very likely to destroy the entire Southern fabric?" The danger was there but so was the proto-Dorian bond. As Cash saw (and historians would one day document), the frightened Democrats successfully vanquished their opponents by screaming white supremacy and invoking the verities of the ancient bond. Hearing (and fearing) his captains, the Populist renegade "flung himself back fully into the Democratic frame and made the walls of Dixie solid again." [46]

Yet Cash's treatment of Populism has brought few kudos from historians. His frequent flippancy suggests a lack of moral indignation and obscures his basic sympathy for the downtrodden farmers, and his conviction that the farmers were easily defeated by the proto-Dorian bond has distracted attention from his perceptive comments about class. Then, too, he completely ignored black participation in the Populist movement, its critique of capitalism, and the prominence and significance of Tom Watson. Like most of his generation, Cash concentrated on the pseudo-Populist Ben Tillman. Most southern historians and writers of the previous generation had been embarrassed by Populism and either passed over it in silence or scorned it as the politics of self-interest. [47]

Cash's contention that the dynamic racism inherent in the proto-Dorian bond vanquished Populism still breathes with freshness and vitality. Yet even historians willing to acknowledge the destructiveness of racism have been deeply troubled by the unyielding determinism lurking in Cash's argument. Surely there were alternatives to the racist

46. Cash, *Mind of the South*; 176–77, 174.
47. King, *Southern Renaissance*, 167. Little had been done on the Populists when Cash wrote, and he seems to have missed C. Vann Woodward, *Tom Watson: Agrarian Rebel* (Chapel Hill, 1938). Edwin Mims ignored the Populists completely in *The Advancing South* (New York,

response that flowered in the rise of Jim Crow. To many minds, the South was never completely locked into any Cashian prison of unity, and southern history might have turned out differently if only the Liberals, or Conservatives, or Populist Radicals had not been vanquished. But they were vanquished. The racists won—that was proved by Cash and C. Vann Woodward (who has argued that alternatives existed). Viewed from Cash's perspective, any notion of the viability of "forgotten alternatives" betrays a well-meaning, optimistic, even sentimental and therefore deluded view of southern history, a view built on the sand of faith, not the granite of fact and realism.[48]

But Cash was not immune to sentimentality. He swallowed whole the popular refrain that the plight of the "downgoing white" produced pangs of conscience in the "landed gentry," giving rise to a new, dynamic noblesse oblige. The Old South's cap'ns had become captains of industry, but they were barons with a heart and a conscience. In the name of progress, they built schools and factories to save the whites from poverty and the shame of falling as low as the Negroes. Such was the view rolling from the propaganda mills of the textile industry and from the pulpit, lectern, and editorial office. In taking on the challenge of progress, of rebuilding the South in the Yankee mold of factories and moneymaking—"crass commercialism" had been the derisive cry of southern gentility—the region was once again made into a frontier, only this time by its own people.[49]

1926), and the northern scholar Paul Buck, in his influential *The Road to Reunion, 1865–1900* (New York, 1937), which Cash read and reviewed, sent Populism packing in a sentence, blaming the farmers for resurrecting the racial issue and bringing back "some of the turbulence of Reconstruction again" (296). Bertram Wyatt-Brown has noted that though Cash's dismissal of the Populists touched off no debate, Richard Hofstadter's attack on them as a bunch of deluded, narrow-minded, backward-looking rustic nativists "unleashed a fearsome pack of dissertation writers in dissent." (Wyatt-Brown, *Yankee Saints and Southern Sinners,* 139; see also Richard Hofstadter, *The Age of Reform* [New York, 1955], 36–45; Jonathan M. Wiener, *Social Origins of the New South: Alabama, 1860–1885* [Baton Rouge, 1978], 33, 84, 96). Charles L. Flynn, Jr., found "a great deal of class oppression in the New South," but, like Cash (whom he never cites) Flynn seeks to unravel class from race. Racism, Flynn concludes, was stronger and could be manipulated to control white labor as well as black, but it was aimed at blacks. (*White Land, Black Labor,* 31, 148).

48. C. Vann Woodward, *The Strange Career of Jim Crow* (1955; 3rd rev. ed. New York, 1974), 31–60. Joel Williamson has argued that "radical" racists overwhelmed Liberals and Conservatives in the 1890s and 1900s and established a climate of opinion that completely sapped liberalism's strength. In time, Williamson continues, conservatism triumphed (after a fashion), but timid Conservatives were unable to resurrect any real interest in truly protecting the Negro. (*Crucible of Race,* 5–8, 111–39, 459–522).

49. Cash, *Mind of the South,,* 211–20, 223–26.

It is astounding that Cash could believe any of this about either the builders of the mills or the politicians who openly and proudly tied their advocacy of public schools for whites to their campaign to disfranchise and segregate blacks. Cash sneered at the racism of Arkansas' Jeff Davis, Mississippi's James K. Vardaman, or South Carolina's Cole Blease, "the capstone of it all," and underscored their cynical calculation that some advocacy of schools for blacks would ensure the Yankees' compliance in the great campaign for Jim Crow. Yet so great was Cash's desire to be charitable that he skipped over the blatant racism of Charles Brantley Aycock, North Carolina's "education governor." He apparently never perceived that the Aycocks exploited racism and used the promise of schools for whites as a cynical way of selling disfranchisement to illiterate whites who feared they too might be disfranchised by the new literacy tests.[50]

Cash was even more uncritical in accepting the conventional wisdom about the social altruism of the grasping founders of the textile industry, many of whom reaped enormous profits from their trumpeted paternalism. And in bestowing blessings on the founders' paternalism, Cash was far closer to the assumptions of the New South liberals than he dreamed. Perhaps Cash was honoring his own family's modest role in the founding of the mills. He based his views on the writings of Gerald W. Johnson and on Broadus Mitchell's widely praised book *The Rise of Cotton Mills in the South* (1921), the standard work when Cash wrote.[51]

In a seeming about-face, Cash balanced his account of progress and paternalism with a vengeance. He lashed out at the numbing conditions of life for the mill hands: low wages, long hours, child labor— "baby labor," really, Cash says, pointing out that many entered the mills with their families at the tender ages of six or seven. He drew heavily upon his own observations and upon the writings of the child labor reformers of his day, who were reviled by the mill managers and their followers. Cash drew a vicious picture of the so-called model mill villages as pigsties and the "proletarian rooming houses" as "swarming warrens, with four or five persons herded into each room." In his descrip-

---

50. *Ibid.*, 175–80, 253; Woodward, *Origins of the New South*, 325–34.
51. Cash, *Mind of the South*, 180–81. Given the stature of Broadus Mitchell's book and his considerable reputation as a writer of detachment and, on occasion, cynicism, it was unfair of Woodward to deride Cash for relying on Mitchell's "celebrated monograph" (*American Counterpoint*, 278).

tion of the wretched mill workers, Cash was positively Dickensian: "A dead white skin, a sunken chest, and stooping shoulders. . . . Chinless faces, microcephalic foreheads, rabbit teeth, goggling dead-fish eyes, rickety limbs, and stunted bodies abounded." The women, old long before their time, "were characteristically stringy-haired and limp of breast at twenty, and shrunken hags at thirty or forty." The mill hands, plagued by tuberculosis, insanity, epilepsy, and pellagra, knew fleeting whispers of class consciousness, said Cash. But progress, meaning money in the pockets of mountaineers and simple country folk who seldom had ten dollars to their name, combined with the mill hands' simple needs and the shouts of their Dorian captains, triumphed and bestowed a sense of belonging, an ego-boosting sense of being white in a white man's country. "As in the old days, there was nearly always some more or less exalted person to invite him into the closet for a drink. And as of old, there was the inevitable great lawyer, towering, leonine, long of coat and mane, the breathing epitome of the Confederacy, to drop a familiar hand upon his shoulder and warm his heart with confidential chat about the Proto-Dorian bond of the Democratic Party."[52]

In the liberal fashion of the 1930s, Cash assumed that he was helping the workers by criticizing the mill owners—their tightfistedness, their rabid antiunion mentality, and their false paternalism—and denouncing the sordid conditions in the mill villages. But ironically, by portraying the workers as stunted, oppressed, and pitiable, Cash indirectly helped stereotype the mill hands and inadvertently denied them any individuality and hence any true worth in history. (Nietzsche says somewhere that those we pity we cannot respect.) Cash and his well-meaning generation set the parameters of research by their attitudes and their questions about paternalism, the docility of workers, and the travail of unionism in the South.[53]

Progress, said Cash, even as it extended down through the 1920s and 1930s, not only had left the essential South intact, it had driven violence, the savage ideal, the proto-Dorian convention, the veneration of women, religiosity, and such deeper into the southerner's soul.

---

52. Cash, Mind of the South, 203–204, 218, 229; Harriet Herring, Welfare Work in Mill Villages: The Story of Extra-Mill Activities in North Carolina (Chapel Hill, 1929).

53. Only with the appearance in the 1980s of a new southern social history that took common people and folk culture seriously were new questions asked. See Jacquelyn Dowd Hall et al., Like a Family: The Making of a Southern Cotton Mill World (Chapel Hill, 1987), xvi.

The South was still the South. It had cities and factories, slums and skyscrapers, a handful of first-rate universities, Yankee hustle, and Rotary—which, Cash had to remind himself constantly, "was not invented in the South." But underneath, the southerner was the same simple, emotional, racist, religious, individualistic, bragging, boasting, violent Celt he had always been.[54]

Cash's reputation continues to hinge largely on the validity of his notion of continuity. Some see the South's history of slavery, secession, war, Reconstruction, and the New South—to say nothing of the more recent Sunbelt South—as reflecting discontinuity. To that list, C. Vann Woodward would add Populism and the twisting, turning "strange career of Jim Crow," with its "Second Reconstruction" of the 1940s through the 1960s, when courageous native blacks played the leading roles. But another view demands equal time. Continuity is at the center of Faulkner's imagination and creations, neither of which historians could ignore in their attempts to understand the South. And one strand of scholarly evidence suggests that the modern-day South is still very much a distinctive culture, different, as Cash said, from the rest of the nation. After painstaking investigations of southern attitudes, beliefs, and patterns of popular culture, John Shelton Reed has concluded that "the South remains," in Cash's words, "'not quite a nation within a nation, but the next best thing to it.'" Such are the contentions advanced by fifteen southerners in *Why the South Will Survive* (1981). Like Reed, they chart the "persistence" of southern "distinctiveness"—reincarnations, in effect, of Cash's twin theses of unity and continuity.[55]

But the jury is still out. And it will remain out as long as scholars and writers puzzle their minds about the South. And no one has argued more eloquently, and yes, "extravagantly" in the courtroom of history than W. J. Cash.

54. Cash, *Mind of the South*, 226.
55. Woodward, *American Counterpoint*, 275; John Shelton Reed, *The Enduring South: Subcultural Persistence in Mass Society* (Chapel Hill, 1974), 9–16, 83–104; Reed, *One South: An Ethnic Approach to Regional Culture* (Baton Rouge, 1982), 3, 188; Fifteen Southerners, *Why the South Will Survive: Fifteen Southerners Look at Their Region a Half Century After "I'll Take My Stand"* (Athens, Ga., 1981), with an Afterword by Andrew Lytle. Woodward, in one of his most celebrated essays, "The Search for Southern Identity," found distinctiveness in the region's uniquely un-American history of poverty, defeat, persistent sense of guilt, and consuming sense of place, which made up a large part of the "burden" of southern history (*The Burden of Southern History* [1960, rev. ed. Baton Rouge, 1968], 18–23).

Nearly half a century after Wilbur Joseph Cash launched *The Mind of the South*, the man and the book, being one, continue to inspire, irritate, challenge, provoke, and, above all, unsettle. Whether it is right or wrong about unity or continuity, race or class, mind or temperament, or any of a half dozen other topics, Cash's book has been a stick of dynamite, one of those explosions of art posing as history that keep the waters of the mind from freezing. How many other historians, fifty years after their deaths, provoke any comment at all? Was Cash right? Was Cash wrong? Our answers frequently tell us as much about our own minds, hopes, and fears, as Cash's disturbing book. Did his audacity, his daring willingness to say exactly what was on his mind, slip into historical impiety? If so, it is an intriguing irony that the book remains hauntingly unforgettable. It is one those books that makes us crane our necks to see through time, not because we want to, or can, but because, after reading Cash, we must try. We may not want to hear about the intractability of violence and racism and the cant and myths that blinded our ancestors. But Cash's voice—authentic, passionate, audacious—intrudes into our consciousness reminding us that the past is never quite past, never quite dead. That much we know if only because it consumed Cash's life, tortured his conscience, and brought forth a wrenching cry, *The Mind of the South*.

It was, above all, a cry from the heart. The South devoured him, consumed his mind and heart. That thing called the South, which may exist only in the mind, fastened itself on Cash's psyche about the time country folks started calling him "Sleepy," long before he could know what had happened to him or what fate (his people would have said God) had in store for him. The South was his great love, but it was a tempestuous, tormented love. His South was a possessive lover, who would not—cannot, it seems—tolerate being neglected. The troubled, sensitive Jack Cash hardly knew a moment's peace from the second he discovered that the South was his love.

That his lover was flawed, fundamentally flawed at the center, made it next to impossible for Cash to finish his book. His was no dispassionate academic mind able, perhaps eager, to analyze, coolly and with impersonal objectivity, how people's lives had been shaped, perhaps made wretched by class or race, perhaps snatched from them by the lyncher's rope or a diet of fatback. Cash could not be detached. Neither his own psyche, irrevocably shaped by the South, nor his subject allowed that detachment. That was his great inheritance and his great

curse. In concluding that southern history was unbroken and dominated by a self-imposed savage ideal that was unyielding and stultify-
ing, Cash was implying that southern history was a prison to which all
the jailer's keys had been thrown away by the inmates. But no one was
ever to admit that or even hint at it. The first and great command-
ment was to act as though everything was perfectly normal. That
Cash saw.

The assumption that southerners were trapped in history was the
tragic theme that informed Cash's mind and book. He was surely not a
man who lacked any "feeling for the seriousness of human strivings,
for the tragic theme in history," as Woodward charged. The distinguished professor, also a son of the South, could not have been more
wrong about the underpaid, chain-smoking, shy, nervous newspaperman. The deep river of tragedy that flows quietly but relentlessly
through the great writers of the Southern Renaissance—from Faulkner
to Robert Penn Warren and even Thomas Wolfe—runs equally silently, equally relentlessly, throughout Cash's pages as he shows how
deeply enmeshed southerners were in history. To be thus entrapped, to
be cut off from following any "alternatives," forgotten or otherwise,
was Cash's own "burden of southern history." It was his burden, as it
was Faulkner's, to be obsessed with that history, to stride into its
darkness, to expose its darkest secrets, to seek and caress what little
beauty it had to offer.

That the South Cash portrayed distressed him even while it obsessed him is obvious. It was profoundly disturbing for him to follow
his conscience and criticize his people, those who were bone of his
bone, flesh of his flesh—his cousins, his family, his mother and father.
That was the anxiety standing behind his comment to Knopf that he
could never approach his task without "extreme depression and dislike." It was far more than the despair most serious writers feel about
facing their task. It was a deep despair born of what he saw. All that
waste, all that blindness, all that violence, all that racism, all that
pain—this Cash faced. The South's tragedy was his tragedy.

For those who yearn to believe that southern history might have
been different if only some "forgotten" or all-too-well-known alternative had been followed, Cash's portrayal of the South is too bleak,
too depressing, too uncompromising. But perhaps it is they—and not
the despairing, disturbed Jack Cash—who lack genuine appreciation
for the "tragic theme in history." Perhaps that is the reason so many

have embraced Thomas Jefferson as the "true southerner," or gazed fondly on Robert E. Lee as the southern saint, or believed that Tom Watson, if only (oh, if only) he and the Populists had not been so thoroughly vanquished, might have made history take a different turn. Perhaps ideas about alternatives are so much myth, another version, perhaps, of New South optimism, outfitted in fancier clothes and more elegantly stated than the older myth but myth nonetheless. In the end, Cash's tragic sense is another sign of his bravery, his courage to look squarely at southern history, unflinchingly, to see the racism, the ugliness, the rope, the suffocating sentimentality, the narrowness, the ranting demagogues, the wickedness he found infecting all classes, and say, *that* was true history, and like all true history, it had to be. Cash's temperament, his sense of honesty, compelled him to hold to a stark version of historical inevitability. That at bottom was his tragic vision.

His effort was heroic. He tried to write southern history on a grand scale and succeeded. No one has come close to matching him. No historian has had the courage or audacity or ability even to try what Cash did. He tried because he was, in his soul, an artist, a writer in the grand tradition of Gibbon, Tocqueville, Burckhardt, Macauley, and Huizinga. Because he was always in the thrall of being a novelist—and hence a "real writer"—Cash dreamed of doing for southern history what Conrad had done for the Englishman abroad or Faulkner for southern letters. Though his modesty forbade the merest mention of it, Cash fully intended to write a noble work, a masterpiece. Country boys from the piedmont, who have never roamed far from that patch of Dixie and who spend part of each day fighting off depression and those daily, subtle reminders that they were odd, perhaps even crazy, are not encouraged to think too highly of themselves and what they might accomplish as artists. Even so, Cash tried to do what every true artist, every writer, seeks to do, that is, to speak some great truth, to say what it is that makes a people distinctive, to know what it is that rules their lives, for good or ill. Cash burned to know why his people were different. That they were different, he had no doubt. But what made the South the South? That he would know even if it killed him. And if he failed in that noble task, a task far nobler, more demanding, more difficult, than all but a few ever try, he failed as all great artists finally fail. As Faulkner said of Thomas Wolfe, if W. J. Cash failed, he failed for all the right reasons.

No one who reads Wilbur Joseph Cash is ever quite the same again.

11 / To Do Justice to the Matter

In September, 1941, a sorrowful John William Cash wrote the Knopf Publishing Company a plaintive letter. He and Nannie were still grieving over the "mysterious" death of their boy. They read his letters over and over again and recalled how much he meant to them—how he sat in his room and wrote his book, and how they helped him all they could, and that the Knopfs had suggested that he write the book after reading his essays in Mencken's *American Mercury*. Now they were wondering "if there might be any possibility of getting his book before the committee in regard to the 'Pulitzer Prize.'" Could Mr. Knopf help in this matter? Their son had had a small insurance policy and had left a "small Estate of which his widow is entitled to half which she needs for her support." If *The Mind of the South* were to be considered for the award, and should it win, the prize money would be greatly appreciated. Surely, winning the Pulitzer Prize would help sales, John Cash said. John and Nannie were in their sixties and had known hard times for a decade. They would miss the financial help Wilbur had been providing. But their own economic needs, however important, were as nothing: "The vacant chair in our home and the aching void in our hearts is greater than any earthly possessions and is something that we can never overcome." Could the Knopfs help? Anything they could provide would be greatly appreciated, John Cash explained, because he wanted to put a monument at his son's grave. The father's aim was to honor his boy's achievement and thus "to do justice to the matter."[1]

1. John Cash to Mr. and Mrs. Alfred A. Knopf, September 8, 1941, in Joseph L. Morrison Papers, Southern Historical Collection, University of North Carolina, Chapel Hill.

Business considerations hardly allowed for justice to be done. Alfred Knopf replied patiently that he too greatly admired their son's book and he would be glad to nominate it for the prize, but they should not get their hopes up. Competition for such awards was fierce. Nor could he hold out much hope regarding future royalties. The book's sales had been modest from the start and had slowed to a trickle. Knopf was genuinely sorry to have to reply in this fashion but such were the facts.[2]

At some point, and unbeknownst, apparently, to Cash's family, Mary worked out a very modest financial settlement with the Knopfs by which the publishing house of A. A. Knopf retained exclusive rights to any and all future editions or royalties. She was entirely within her rights in doing so, and there is no reason to suspect that Knopf acted improperly or foresaw any future sales; he certainly could not have imagined the book's success as a paperback.

John and Nannie Cash, simple country folk, bravely accepted their fate and bought a modest flat stone to mark their son's grave in the Cash family plot in Sunset Cemetery. Utterly unwilling to believe, or even to consider, that their boy had killed himself, John and Nannie made sure that any who came to Shelby to pay homage to their son's grave could look down at his flat stone and read, "Behind the dark unknown standeth God within the shadow, keeping watch above his own."

In time, mother and father would rest alongside the native son. At the foot of Cash's grave Senator Clyde R. Hoey would one day be buried amid considerable ceremony befitting his long political career. Around the corner, in the Gardner family plot, a large statue would be erected to honor the gravesite of another of Shelby's leading citizens, O. Max Gardner, by turns governor and senator. And just slightly to the South, within a stone's throw of Cash's grave, friends of Thomas Dixon would erect a substantial monument to commemorate their hero's varied career.

Time and changing values have dimmed considerably the reputations of Shelby's solons and novelist, but W. J. Cash's name has grown in stature, higher than the tallest monument or maple tree in Sunset Cemetery. Perhaps time has done justice to the matter.

2. Alfred A. Knopf to John Cash, September, 1941, *ibid.*

Bibliographical Essay

PRIMARY SOURCES

Most of W. J. Cash's letters and published and unpublished materials relating to his life are in the Joseph L. Morrison Papers, Southern Historical Collection, Wilson Library, University of North Carolina at Chapel Hill. In the 1960s Morrison assembled the various Cash manuscripts and documents in preparation for the publication of *W. J. Cash, Southern Prophet: A Biography and Reader* (New York, 1967). Morrison corresponded with or interviewed members of Cash's family and many of his friends and acquaintances and worked closely with Cash's widow, Mary Cash Maury, who wrote several valuable though brief accounts of her life with Cash. One of these, "The Suicide of W. J. Cash," became the basis of Mary Cash Maury's published piece by the same title in the *Red Clay Reader*, IV (1967), 8–9. Upon his death, Morrison bequeathed all of his papers, including his notes on interviews and letters to him from Cash's friends and family, to the Southern Historical Collection. The Morrison Papers will also be the repository of notes of interviews with members of Cash's family and acquaintances and all the letters I have received from Cash's friends, many of whom, including Burke Davis, Harriet Doar, Reed Sarratt, Erma Drum, Lindsey Dail, Henry B. Cash, Allan H. Cash, and Mr. and Mrs. Charles H. Elkins, Sr., were helpful.

The collection contains photocopies of all of Cash's correspondence with Blanche and Alfred Knopf and all of their letters to Cash, including copies of the contract Cash signed in 1936 and the author's form he completed in 1940. The original letters between Cash and the Knopfs are in the Knopf Papers, Harry Ransom Humanities Research Center, the University of Texas at Austin. The Morrison collection includes copies of the applications for John Simon Guggenheim Memorial Fellowships Cash submitted in 1932, 1936, and 1940. A tape recording of W. J. Cash's Commencement Address at the

University of Texas in 1941 is in the Morrison Papers. All students of W. J. Cash owe Joseph L. Morrison a large debt of gratitude, particularly since Cash wrote very few letters, was careless about keeping letters he received, and never kept a diary or a journal or wrote a memoir or autobiography.

Fortunately, Mary Cash and his family saved a number of letters and clippings, mainly from the late 1930s and during 1940–1941. These are in the Charles H. Elkins Family Scrapbook in possession of Charles H. Elkins, Jr., Winston-Salem, North Carolina. Elkins, son of Cash's sister, Elizabeth (Bertie) Cash Elkins, also possesses the original manuscript of *The Mind of the South*, a copy of which is in the Morrison Papers. Cash's annotated copy of Adolf Hitler's *Mein Kampf* is the property of Mr. and Mrs. Allen Cash, Rock Hill, South Carolina.

There are a few letters from W. J. Cash in the Henry L. Mencken Papers, New York Public Library, New York City, as well as copies of Mencken's letters to Cash. These letters, though not lengthy or numerous, are an important supplement to Cash's eight articles in the *American Mercury* from 1929 to 1935. The Lillian Smith Papers at the University of Florida Libraries, Gainesville, contain a handful of letters from Cash. There are two letters from Cash in the Thurman D. Kitchen Papers, Reynolds Library, Wake Forest University, Winston-Salem, North Carolina, and one lengthy letter from Cash in the Howard W. Odum Papers, Southern Historical Collection, Wilson Library, University of North Carolina, Chapel Hill. There is a brief note from Cash in the Edwin Mims Papers, the Jean and Alexander Heard Library, Vanderbilt University, Nashville, Tennessee.

The Public Library of Charlotte and Mecklenburg County, North Carolina, has a collection of photocopies of W. J. Cash's editorials, signed columns, book reviews, and literary columns from the Charlotte *News*. The collection of pieces, numbering around two hundred, was far from complete when I began researching the Charlotte *News* for the years 1935, when Cash began working for the newspaper, until 1941, when he left. I found scores of new pieces by Cash that were of immense help in understanding the range of Cash's life and thought. All of my photocopies of hitherto unknown pieces by Cash from the Charlotte *News* will be deposited in the Public Library of Charlotte and Mecklenburg County along with a listing of all known newspaper pieces by W. J. Cash.

For a fuller understanding of the world W. J. Cash lived in, the following magazines and newspapers were invaluable: *Wake Forest Student*, 1920–1923; *Old Gold and Black* (Wake Forest, North Carolina), 1920–1923; Gaffney (S.C.) *Ledger*, 1900–1913; *Cleveland* (Shelby, N.C.) *Star*, 1900–1935; Shelby (N.C.) *Star*, 1935–1941; *Cleveland Press* (Shelby, N.C.), October, 1928–January, 1929; Charlotte *News*, 1928, 1935–1941; and Charlotte *Observer*, 1923, 1928, 1941.

SECONDARY SOURCES

All students of W. J. Cash's life should start with Joseph L. Morrison, *W. J. Cash, Southern Prophet: A Biography and a Reader* (New York, 1967), a concise, sprightly, always sympathetic and charming overview. Morrison foreshadowed his main themes in "The Obsessive 'Mind' of W. J. Cash," *Studies in Journalism and Communications* (School of Journalism, University of North Carolina at Chapel Hill, Series Editor Norval Neil Luxon, Study Number 4, May, 1965), 1–12. Morrison discovered a file of the *Cleveland Press* only after he had completed his book, and he narrated Cash's brief career as a newspaper editor in 1928 in "Found: The Missing Editorship of W. J. Cash," *North Carolina Historical Review*, XLVII (1970), 40–50. In "The Summing Up," *South Atlantic Quarterly*, LXX (1971), 477–86, Morrison argued the case for Cash's astuteness and accuracy of interpretation in *The Mind of the South*.

C. Vann Woodward has been the most cogent critic of *The Mind of the South*. He reviewed it favorably (with reservations) in the *Journal of Southern History*, VIII (1941), 400–402, but thirty years later gave it a thoughtful, highly critical reading in "The Elusive Mind of the South," in *American Counterpoint: Slavery and Racism in the North-South Dialogue* (New York, 1971), 161–83. Woodward criticizes Cash's style as so much "Menckenian buffoonery," faults Cash for writing an impressionistic, highly personal history (rather than the precise intellectual history academics aspire to write), charges that Cash's twin arguments of unity and continuity are woefully wrong, and concludes that Cash lacked a feeling for the tragic theme of history. Michael O'Brien has echoed some of Woodward's criticisms and added some of his own in "A Private Passion: W. J. Cash," in *Rethinking the South: Essays in Intellectual History* (Baltimore, 1988), 179–89. O'Brien is somewhat ambivalent toward Cash and underscores the romantic strain in his thinking but argues that he misunderstood romanticism. In an earlier version of this essay, O'Brien explored the dialectical impulse operating in *The Mind of the South*, though he admits that there is no evidence that Cash ever read Hegel or any great dialectician. See Michael O'Brien, "W. J. Cash, Hegel, and the South," *Journal of Southern History*, XLIV (1978), 379–98. More fervid in his criticisms of Cash's style and ideas is Louis D. Rubin, Jr., "The Mind of the South," *Sewanee Review*, LXII (1954), 683–95. In *The World the Slaveholders Made: Two Essays in Interpretation* (New York, 1969), 137–50, Eugene Genovese dismissed Cash's notion that white southerners were plagued by a sense of guilt over slavery.

But Cash has had more admirers than detractors. From the 1940s on, many of Cash's arguments were used with great effect by historians as diverse as Francis Butler Simkins, *The South Old and New: A History, 1820–1947* (New

York, 1947); William R. Taylor, *Cavalier and Yankee: The Old South and American National Character* (New York, 1961); Bruce Clayton, *The Savage Ideal: Intolerance and Intellectual Leadership in the South, 1890–1914* (Baltimore, 1972); and Bertram Wyatt-Brown, *Southern Honor: Ethics and Behavior in the Old South* (New York, 1982). After conceding some of Woodward's criticisms, Wyatt-Brown has called attention to the continued usefulness of Cash's employment of a typological approach to culture in "W. J. Cash and Southern Culture," in *Yankee Saints and Southern Sinners* (Baton Rouge, 1985), 131–54. Cash's influence has spread far beyond the South. In *The Mind of South Africa* (New York, 1990), Allister Sparks writes, "Ever since reading W. J. Cash's *The Mind of the South* . . . I have wanted to write a book that might give the same kind of insights into South Africa that it gave me into the psyche of the American South" (xiii).

Several literary scholars have assessed Cash's mind perceptively, exploring the way his book illuminates patterns of thinking. In "Narcissus Grown Analytical: Cash's Southern Mind," in *A Southern Renaissance: The Cultural Awakening of the American South* (New York, 1980), 146–72, Richard King pays tribute to Cash's style and awareness of how southerners, enmeshed in what Freud called the "family romance," were fated to reenact the dramas of the past. Fred Hobson in "The Meaning of Aristocracy: Wilbur Cash and William Alexander Percy," in *Tell About the South: The Southern Rage to Explain* (Baton Rouge, 1983), 244–94, traces some of the antecedents of Cash's concepts as well as his early stylistic and intellectual indebtedness to H. L. Mencken, a point Hobson had spelled out in *Serpent in Eden: H. L. Mencken and the South* (Chapel Hill, 1974), 111–20. In Hobson's view, Cash's "rage to explain" the South was of such psychological depth and independence that his perceptions surpassed those of all of his predecessors in their attempts to explain the South.

Equally convinced of the perceptiveness of Cash's psychological perceptions, shaped by his existential reading of Freud, is Bruce Clayton, "A Southern Modernist: The Mind of W. J. Cash," in *The South Is Another Land: Essays on the Twentieth-Century South*, ed. Bruce Clayton and John A. Salmond (Westport, Conn. 1987), 171–86. In "W. J. Cash and the Creative Impulse," *Southern Review*, XXIV (1988), 777–90, Clayton explores the way Cash's psyche shaped his continuing fascination with creative literature. For a discussion of Cash's racial thought see Bruce Clayton, "The Proto-Dorian Convention: W. J. Cash and the Race Question," in *Race, Class, and Politics in Southern History: Essays in Honor of Robert F. Durden*, ed. Jeffrey J. Crow, Paul D. Escott, and Charles L. Flynn, Jr. (Baton Rouge, 1989), 260–88. For a journalist's appreciation of Cash see Edwin M. Yoder, "W. J. Cash After a Quarter Century," in *The South Today: 100 Years After Appomattox* (New

York, 1965), 89–99. Michael P. Dean, "W. J. Cash's *The Mind of the South*: Southern History, Southern Style," *Southern Studies*, XX (1981), 297–302, is a brief, admiring look at Cash's "southern" style. Joseph K. Davis, "The South as History and Metahistory: The Mind of W. J. Cash," *Spectrum*, II (1972), 11–24, underscores Cash's imaginative understanding of the role of myth and mythmaking in the southern past. For a perceptive comparison of Cash and William Alexander Percy, see William J. Cooper III, "Southerners Betwixt Times: A Comparative Interpretation of the Lives and Writings of Wilbur J. Cash and William Alexander Percy" (Senior thesis, Princeton University, 1987.)

Index